Third Edition
Solutions

Intermediate

Workbook

Tim Falla   **Paul A Davies**

OXFORD
UNIVERSITY PRESS

OXFORD
UNIVERSITY PRESS

Great Clarendon Street, Oxford, OX2 6DP, United Kingdom

Oxford University Press is a department of the University of Oxford.
It furthers the University's objective of excellence in research, scholarship,
and education by publishing worldwide. Oxford is a registered trade
mark of Oxford University Press in the UK and in certain other countries

© Oxford University Press 2016

The moral rights of the author have been asserted

First published in 2016

2020 2019 2018 2017 2016

10 9 8 7 6 5 4 3 2 1

ISBN: 978 0 19 450452 2

Printed in China

This book is printed on paper from certified and well-managed sources

ACKNOWLEDGEMENTS

Back cover photograph: Oxford University Press building/David Fisher

The authors and publisher are grateful to those who have given permission to reproduce the following extracts and adaptations of copyright material:

p.19 Adapted extracts from "Interview: Australian Rollerblading Open 2014 Female Champion Tiffany Street" by Jesse Kuch, www.rollerblading.com.au, 17 September 2014. Reproduced by permission of rollerblading.com.au and Tiffany Street.

p.23 Extracts from www.streetgames.org. Reproduced by permission of StreetGames.

p.67 Adapted extract from "Graduate with market-stall patter wins top job by holding a sign outside Tube station" by Mark Blunden, www.standard.co.uk, 17 July 2014. © The Evening Standard 2014. Reproduced by permission of ESI Media.

p.76 "Our Meetings" from *Collected Poems* by Andrew Waterman (Carcanet, 2000). Reproduced by kind permission of Andrew Waterman.

Sources:

p.35 "Sleepy Teens: High School Should Start Later in the Morning" by Mark Fischetti, http://blogs.scientificamerican.com, 26 August 2014.

p.45 "10 Of The Most Unusual Homes In The World" by Tom, www.boredpanda.com, 23 January 2013.

p.86 "FAQs" by Mobile Operators Association, www.mobilemastinfo.com, accessed June 2015.

p.115 "Bedtime 'has huge impact on sport'" by James Gallagher, www.bbc.co.uk, 30 January 2015.

p.120 "Wuppertal Suspension Railway", http://en.wikipedia.org, accessed 14 March 2015.

p.120 "Khlong Saen Saep boat service", http://en.wikipedia.org, accessed 5 January 2015.

p.120 "Monte (Funchal)", http://en.wikipedia.org, accessed 24 June 2014.

p.121 "British man becomes first person to visit all 201 countries... WITHOUT using a plane" by Matt Blake, www.dailymail.co.uk, 27 November 2012.

123RF pp.22 (golf field/Michal Bednarek), 34 (woman with mug/Patrick Chai), 35 (sleeping student/photodeti), 44 (modern house with pool/Franck Boston), 59 (girl playing video game/Daniel Garcia), 66 (broadcasting antenna/Alexandr Demeshko), 66 (map of Sierra Leone/Peter Hermes Furian), 95 (bouquet/Nataliia Peredniankina), 95 (teddy/Alex Hinds), 101 (Millennium Bridge/Anton Balazh), 114 (girls playing hockey/Nico Smit), 121 (express boat in Bangkok/combodesign); Alamy Images pp.19 (rollerblading contest/Cernan Elias), 22 (ice rink/David L. Moore), 36 (stroller striders/ZUMA Press, Inc.), 64 (Sarah Margaret Fuller/Interfoto), 79 (ship wall mural/Gregory Wrona), 80 (acrobats/Larry Lilac), 98 (bus tour guide/David L. Moore), 101 (aeroplane/Kevin Clark), 114 (school bus and cyclists/Colin Underhill), 118 (Banksy street art/PYMCA); Alamy Stock Photo pp.58 (teacher & boys/Blend Images), 58 (computer class/Frederick Kippe), 84 (man on phone/Goran Bogicevic); Capella PR p.23 (teens playing football/Capella PR/Streetgames); Getty Images pp.7 (Krubera Cave, Caucasus Mountains/Stephen Alvarez), 9 (world's oldest woman and family/Theo Westenberger), 13 (Kris Jenner/Amanda Edwards), 13 (Kim Kardashian/Amanda Edwards), 13 (Khloe Kardashian/Jon Kopaloff), 13 (Kourtney Kardashian/Aaron Davidson), 13 (Rob Kardashian/Denise Truscello), 33 (robot/Kiyoshi Ota/Bloomberg), 46 (cottages by the beach/Daniel Loiselle), 46 (White Park Bay, Northern Ireland/Brian Lawrence), 46 (cottage with Alps in background/Katarina Stefanovic), 46 (cottage on the

River Wylye in Wiltshire/John Downing), 58 (students using digital tablets with instructor on monitor/Ariel Skelley), 65 (Google New York headquarters/The Washington Post), 68 (picking apples/Matt Cardy), 68 (workers packing strawberries/Monty Rakusen), 75 (composer Mamoru Samuragochi/Jigi Press), 80 (Diversity/Ollie Millington/Redferns), 89 (plum blossom/Datacraft Co Ltd), 90 (woman on phone after car crash/Peter Samuels), 99 (space shuttle Endeavour/NASA), 101 (Robert Falcon Scott's party at the South Pole/Universal History Archive), 111 (piano lesson/gilaxia), 116 (boys playing video game/Paul Bradbury), 116 (girl using laptop/Brendan O'Sullivan), 118 (Carnaby Street/Waterman), 120 (crowded train/Jim Dyson), 121 (cable railway/AIZAR RALDES), 121 (flea market, Germany/Patrik Stollarz), 121 (toboggan/Peter Adams); Kobal Collection pp.12 (Big film still/20th Century Fox/Hamill, Brian), 81 (The Theory of Everything/Working Title/Universal/Daniel, Liam); Oxford University Press pp.5 (teens arguing/Chris King), 29 (teens in cafe/Chris King), 32 (cross-country skiing/Digital Vision), 52 (teen girl talking online/OJO Images), 73 (class/Monkey Business Images), 95 (box of chocolates/PHB.cz (Richard Semik)), 97 (boat on the beach in Thailand/Mateo_Pearson/Shutterstock), 107 (snorkelling/Martin Valigursky), 107 (friends on the beach/Image Source); Rex Features pp.45 (The Mist House, Tokyo, Japan. Architect: TNA, 2012/View Pictures), 56 (Google glasses/ddp USA), 57 (robots play football at a Robocup Tournament/Yu Li), 80 ('Le Corsaire' – dancers/Alastair Muir), 118 (Lord Kitchener Toby jug/Bournemouth News); Shutterstock pp.22 (gym/mashurov), 22 (bowling ball and pins/nikkytok), 22 (indoor climbing/Matusciac Alexandru), 22 (running tracks/katalinks), 29 (snackbar/Pavel L Pavel and Video), 36 (crossfit competition/Colman Lerner Gerardo), 43 (mountain bikers/Rocksweeper), 58 (virtual reality headsets/Stefano Tinti), 73 (shelter kitchen/Monkey Business Images), 77 (woman's face before and after re-touch/Valentina Razumova), 80 (United Nations Orchestra/Martin Good), 85 (couple discussing text message/Nas Cretives), 87 (touch screen phone/Georgejmclittle), 90 (collapse/Miriam Doerr), 111 (street musicians/Italianvideophotoagency), 112 (twin babies/Dirk Ott), 116 (woman reading tablet/Stuart Jenner), 117 (pile of gadgets/Pressmaster).

Illustrations by: Mark Draisey pp.11, 25, 96; Mark Ruffle pp.4, 18, 40, 74, 86; Laszlo Veres/Beehive Illustration Agency pp.8, 20, 30, 58, 102.

Unit		A Vocabulary	B Grammar	C Vocabulary	D Grammar				
I Introduction	p4	Holidays	Present tense contrast	Adjectives	Articles, *will* and *going to*				

Unit		A Vocabulary	B Grammar	C Listening	D Grammar	E Word Skills	F Reading	G Speaking	H Writing
1 Generations	p8	Ages and stages	Past tense contrast	Family tensions	*used to*	Phrasal verbs (1)	Family fortunes	Role-play	A message
Review 1	p16								
2 Leisure time	p18	Love it or hate it	Present perfect and past simple contrast	Eating out	Present perfect simple and continuous	Compound nouns and adjectives	Sport changes lives	Stimulus-based discussion	A blog post
Review 2	p26								
Exam Skills Trainer 1	p28	**Reading**: Multiple choice **Listening**: True / false **Use of English**: Banked cloze **Speaking**: Photo comparison and role-play **Writing**: A message							
3 The human body	p30	Parts of the body	Speculating and predicting	The body's limits	Future continuous and future perfect	Word families	Body clock	Photo description	An opinion essay
Review 3	p38								
4 Home	p40	Describing houses and homes	Comparison	Young and homeless	Imaginary situations	*do, make* and *take*	Alternative living	Photo comparison and discussion	An email
Review 4	p48								
Exam Skills Trainer 2	p50	**Reading**: Multiple choice **Listening**: Sentence completion (short answers) **Use of English**: Paired multiple-choice gapfill **Speaking**: Role-play **Writing**: An opinion essay							
5 Technology	p52	Computing	Quantifiers	Navigation nightmare	Modals in the past	Adjective + preposition	Intelligent footballers	Photo comparison	An internet forum post
Review 5	p60								
6 High flyers	p62	Describing character	Defining relative clauses	Margaret Fuller	Non-defining relative clauses	Phrasal verbs (2)	Out of work	Guided conversation	A for and against essay
Review 6	p70								
Exam Skills Trainer 3	p72	**Reading**: Multiple matching **Listening**: Multiple choice **Use of English**: Multiple-choice cloze **Speaking**: Photo comparison and discussion **Writing**: A for and against essay							
7 Artists	p74	Talking about the arts	The passive	Poetry in motion	*have something done*	Indefinite pronouns	Street art	Photo comparison and role-play	Article: a film review
Review 7	p82								
8 Messages	p84	On the phone	Reported speech	Global network	Reported questions	Verb patterns: reporting verbs	Storytelling	Photo description	A narrative
Review 8	p92								
Exam Skills Trainer 4	p94	**Reading**: True / false / not given **Listening**: Multiple matching **Use of English**: Open cloze **Speaking**: Photo comparison **Writing**: A review							
9 Journeys	p96	Travel and transport	Third conditional	Travel solutions	Participle clauses	Verb patterns	Miscalculations	Guided conversation	A formal letter
Review 9	p104								
Exam Skills Trainer 5	p106	**Reading**: Missing sentences **Listening**: True / false / not given **Use of English**: Word formation **Speaking**: Photo comparison and topic discussion **Writing**: A formal letter							
B2 Exam Skills Trainer 1	p108	**Reading**: Multiple choice **Listening**: True / false **Use of English**: Open cloze **Speaking**: Role-play **Writing**: An article							
B2 Exam Skills Trainer 2	p110	**Reading**: Multiple matching **Listening**: Multiple choice **Use of English**: Banked cloze **Speaking**: Photo comparison **Writing**: A letter to the editor							

Cumulative Review 1 p112 (Units I–1)	Cumulative Review 2 p114 (Units I–3)	Cumulative Review 3 p116 (Units I–5)	Cumulative Review 4 p118 (Units I–7)	Cumulative Review 5 p120 (Units I–9)

Writing Bank p122 **Functions Bank** p126 **Wordlist** p128 **Irregular verbs** p136

Introduction

Vocabulary

A Holidays

I can talk about what I did in the school holidays.

1 Label the pictures with the words below.

castle   harbour   monument   opera house   ruins
square   statue   zoo

1 _____   2 _____

3 _____   4 _____

5 _____   6 _____

7 _____   8 _____

2 Where can you do these things? Complete the words.

1 see animals from places like Africa in natural, open spaces:
   w_____ p_____
2 see unusual fish: a_____
3 buy fruit, vegetables, etc.: m_____
4 find a wide variety of shops: s_____ d_____
5 see beautiful countryside: n_____ p_____
6 see where kings and queens live or lived: p_____
7 see ships and boats: h_____
8 see a play: t_____
9 see a lot of beautiful, old buildings:
   o_____ t_____
10 see interesting, valuable, old objects: m_____
11 climb up high and get a good view: t_____
12 go on rides: t_____ p_____

3 Complete the postcard with the verbs below. Use the past simple.

not be   not buy   go   go   have
play   sunbathe   not want

AIR MAIL

Hi Rose,

We're having a great time in Italy. We spent the
first day on the beach. I ¹_____ kayaking.
Sam ²_____ to come with me – he
³_____ on the beach. Yesterday, the
weather ⁴_____ great, so we
⁵_____ to the shopping district in the
morning, but we ⁶_____ any souvenirs.
After lunch, we ⁷_____ cards and board
games. Last night, we ⁸_____ dinner in a
pizza restaurant. Back on Sunday. See you then!

Love,

Anna

Rose White
4 Old Road
Brighton
UK

4 Complete the dialogue with the verbs below. Use the past simple.

be   do   go   go   go away   have
hire   stay   stay   visit   visit

James   ¹_____ you _____ a good holiday?
Lucy   Yes, it ²_____ good. We ³_____ my
        cousin in Germany.
James   Cool. What ⁴_____ you _____ ?
Lucy   We ⁵_____ on the Baltic coast. We
        ⁶_____ bikes and we ⁷_____ on
        a boat trip. What about you? ⁸_____ you
        _____ ?
James   No, I ⁹_____ here. I ¹⁰_____ on
        a couple of excursions with my family, and
        I ¹¹_____ a theme park with Josh.

5 What did you do in the summer? Write three sentences. Use the past simple.

1 _____
  _____
2 _____
  _____
3 _____
  _____

Present tense contrast

I can use different tenses to talk about the present and future.

1 **Circle the correct tense.**

1 'What **do you do / are you doing** tonight?' 'I stay / I'm staying at home.'

2 Can you text me when you **get / 're getting** home?

3 The sun **rises / is rising** in the east and **sets / is setting** in the west.

4 Why **do you laugh / are you laughing**? It isn't funny!

5 My dad **leaves / is leaving** home every day at eight o'clock.

6 My sister **always borrows / is always borrowing** my clothes. It's really annoying!

7 What time **does your train arrive / is your train arriving**?

2 **Match sentences 1–7 in exercise 1 with the uses of tenses a–g below.**

Present simple

a for habits and routines ☐

b for a permanent situation or fact ☐

c for timetables and schedules ☐

d in future time clauses (starting with *when, as soon as, after, if,* etc.) ☐

Present continuous

e for something happening now or about now ☐

f for describing annoying behaviour (with *always*) ☐

g for future arrangements ☐

3 **Complete the dialogue with the present simple or present continuous form of the verbs in brackets.**

Martin Hurry up! The film ¹_____ (start) in ten minutes.

Hannah I ²_____ (look for) my phone. ³_____ you _____ (know) where it is?

Martin No. Why ⁴_____ you always _____ (lose) things? It's so annoying!

Hannah I usually ⁵_____ (keep) it on my bedside table, but it isn't there.

Martin ⁶_____ you _____ (remember) when you last used it?

Hannah No – that's the problem.

Martin You ⁷_____ (not need) your phone at the cinema. Look for it when we ⁸_____ (get back).

Hannah I won't have time when we get back. I ⁹_____ (go) straight out again ... It's OK. Here it is! It was in my pocket!

4 **Some of the sentences are incorrect. Rewrite them correctly. Tick the correct sentences.**

1 Mel is belonging to the drama club. ☐

_____

2 Do you prefer beach holidays or adventure holidays? ☐

_____

3 Call me as soon as you're arriving. ☐

_____

4 Jack is hating spaghetti. ☐

_____

5 Why are you always interrupting? ☐

_____

6 I'm not understanding this maths calculation. ☐

_____

5 **Complete the sentences with the verbs below. Use the same verb in each pair of sentences. Use the present simple and present continuous.**

have   look   think

1 a That food _____ delicious!

   b What _____ you _____ at?

2 a What _____ you _____ about?

   b Who _____ you _____ will win the match?

3 a 'Where's Tom?' 'He _____ a shower.'

   b Dogs _____ a good sense of smell.

6 **Complete the questions with the verbs in brackets. Use the present simple or present continuous. Then write true answers, in complete sentences.**

1 Where _____ you usually _____ on Saturday mornings? (go)

_____

_____

2 What _____ you usually _____ on Saturday mornings? (do)

_____

_____

3 What time _____ school _____ and _____ ? (start / finish)

_____

_____

4 What _____ your parents _____ now? (do)

_____

_____

Adjectives

I can form and use a variety of adjectives correctly.

1 Complete the definitions with the adjectives below.

anxious   ashamed   bored   confused   cross
delighted   disappointed   envious   proud
relieved   shocked   terrified   upset

1 _____ : angry
2 _____ : sad because something is worse than you hoped or expected
3 _____ : happy because something is better than you hoped or expected
4 _____ : not able to understand what is happening
5 _____ : worried
6 _____ : not interested in what is happening
7 _____ : very pleased
8 _____ : very frightened
9 _____ : feeling bad because you did something wrong
10 _____ : unhappy because you want something that belongs to somebody else
11 _____ : happy about something you have achieved
12 _____ : very surprised and upset
13 _____ : unhappy about something that happened

2 Read the speech bubbles. How is each speaker feeling? Choose the best adjective from exercise 1.

1
> Have you seen Molly's new coat? She's so lucky. I wish I had one like that.

_____

2
> It's OK, I've found my keys. They were in my bag. That's good!

_____

3
> Stop taking my pen. I need it. You're being really annoying!

_____

4
> How strange. I'm sure I got a text from him, but I can't see it on my phone.

_____

5
> I really needed more than 60% in my test, but I only got 55%. I worked hard too.

_____

6
> I feel really bad because I lied to my parents about where I was last night.

_____

3 Complete the sentences with personality adjectives from below. There are six extra adjectives.

brave   confident   flexible   hard-working
honest   kind   loyal   organised   outgoing
patient   punctual   reliable   sensitive   shy

1 She's _____ : nothing frightens her.
2 He's _____ : he has one job during the week and another at weekends.
3 She's really _____ : all the books in her bookcase are in alphabetical order.
4 He's very _____ : he's hardly ever late.
5 She's _____ : she always tells the truth.
6 He's _____ : he loves being with people and making new friends.
7 She's _____ : she's always careful not to upset anyone.
8 He's very _____ : he always supports his friends, whatever the situation.

4 In your opinion, what are the two most important personal qualities for these people? Choose two adjectives from exercise 3.

1 A teacher should be _____ and _____ .
2 A doctor should be _____ and _____ .
3 A TV presenter should be _____ and _____ .
4 A police officer should be _____ and _____ .

5 Circle the correct adjective.

1 When I took part in my first school play, I was **terrifying / terrified**, but it was an **exciting / excited** experience.
2 I enjoy gymnastics, but it's **tiring / tired**.
3 When my dad was ill last month, it was a **worrying / worried** time for all the family.
4 Have you heard the **shocking / shocked** news?
5 My brother was **disappointing / disappointed** about failing his driving test.

6 Complete the questions with a negative prefix. Then write true answers.

1 Are you patient or _____patient?

_____

2 Are you enthusiastic about your school work or _____enthusiastic?

_____

3 In general, are you organised or _____organised?

_____

4 Are you generally reliable or _____reliable about social arrangements?

_____

ID Grammar
Articles, *will* and *going to*
I can use articles and talk about plans and predictions.

1 Read the dialogue. Tick the correct answers.

Paddy What are you doing at ¹___ weekend?

Ellie I'm going caving. There's ²___ great place for it in the mountains near my uncle's house.

Paddy It's ³___ dangerous hobby, isn't it?

Ellie Not really. My uncle is ⁴___ rock climbing instructor. He says ⁵___ caving is safer than ⁶·___ climbing.

Paddy I'd love to learn how to climb.

Ellie My uncle could teach you, but he charges £25 ⁷___ hour.

Paddy I can't afford that. But I think there's ⁸___ indoor climbing wall in town. I could practise there.

1	☐ a	☐ the
2	☐ a	☐ no article
3	☐ a	☐ the
4	☐ a	☐ no article
5	☐ the	☐ no article
6	☐ the	☐ no article
7	☐ an	☐ no article
8	☐ an	☐ the

2 Complete the text with *a / an*, *the*, or no article (–).

This man is inside ¹a cave. He's ²_____ professional caver, but he's still feeling nervous. Why? Because ³_____ cave is much bigger than it looks. In fact, it's ⁴_____ deepest cave in the world. It's called ⁵_____ Krubera Cave, and it's near ⁶_____ Black Sea. It is ⁷_____ only cave on Earth that is more than 2 km deep. Caves like this are fascinating places for ⁸_____ explorers because there are always new parts to discover. In 2005, ⁹_____ Ukrainian caver called Alexander Klimchouk organised ¹⁰_____ expedition into the cave. ¹¹_____ expedition involved 56 people and went deeper than 2 km. In 2012, a Ukrainian diver called Gennady Samokhin went even deeper by diving down through the muddy water at ¹²_____ bottom.

3 Circle the ending that is more natural.

1 'There's somebody at the door.' 'OK,
  a I'm going to answer it.'
  b I'll answer it.'

2 'These boxes are too heavy. Look out –
  a I'm going to drop them!'
  b I'll drop them!'

3 'Would you like something to drink?' 'Yes,
  a I'm going to have a glass of water, please.'
  b I'll have a glass of water, please.'

4 'Show me your picture. I promise
  a I'm not going to laugh.'
  b I won't laugh.'

5 'What are your plans for the afternoon?'
  a 'I'll stay in and watch TV.'
  b 'I'm going to stay in and watc

6 'We're going to the Caribbean this year.
  a It will be my first visit.'
  b It's going to be my first visit.'

7 'I've forgotten my pencil case.' 'Don't worry,
  a I'll lend you a pen.'
  b I'm going to lend you a pen.'

8 'That's a fantastic pass!
  a They'll score a goal!'
  b They're going to score a goal!'

9 'I'm going to the cinema tonight.' 'Really?
  a What will you see?'
  b What are you going to see?'

4 Complete the dialogue with the correct form of *will* or *going to* and the verbs in brackets.

Jack I ¹_____ (go) ice skating on Saturday evening with Luke. Would you like to come?

Annie Yes, please. Where ²_____ (you / meet)? At the ice rink?

Jack No, at the bus stop near my house.

Annie I live really near to the ice rink, so I ³_____ (see) you there. What time?

Jack Six o'clock in the evening. I think it ⁴_____ (be) quite busy.

Annie Yes, definitely. It's more expensive on Saturday evenings, isn't it?

Jack Don't worry. I ⁵_____ (get) a ticket for you. I've got some vouchers, so it ⁶_____ (not cost) too much.

Annie Thanks! I ⁷_____ (see) you on Saturday, then.

Jack At six o'clock.

Annie I ⁸_____ (not be) late, I promise.

Generations

 A

Vocabulary

Ages and stages
I can talk about the different stages of people's lives.

1 Label the pictures with the life stages below.

centenarian   elderly   infant   in his / her teens
in his / her twenties   middle-aged   toddler   young child

1 She's a _____ .

2 He's _____ .

3 _____ .

4 _____ .

5 _____ .

6 _____ .

7 _____ .

8 _____ .

2 Complete the life events with the words below. Use all the words.

be   be   emigrate   fall   get   get   go   inherit
learn   move   split   start

1 _____ born
2 _____ a business
3 _____ in love
4 _____ (money, etc.)
5 _____ to drive
6 _____ up
7 _____ to university
8 _____ house
9 _____ your first job
10 _____ engaged
11 _____ brought up (by)
12 _____ from abroad

away   a change of career   divorced   down
a family   from work   a grandparent   home   a house or flat
married   school   school   up

13 get _____
14 leave _____
15 start _____
16 settle _____
17 leave _____
18 start _____
19 have _____
20 become _____
21 grow _____
22 pass _____
23 buy _____
24 get _____
25 retire _____

3 Write six true sentences about you or members of your family using different phrases from exercise 2.

My grandad retired when he was in his sixties.

1 _____
2 _____
3 _____
4 _____
5 _____
6 _____

4 🎧 **1.02** Listen to a teenage girl asking people in the street about the best age to do certain things in life. Complete the table.

Best age to leave home:	
1 Woman	
Best age to learn to drive:	
2 Girl	
Best age to start a family:	
3 Boy	
Best age to buy a house or flat:	
4 Girl	

Past tense contrast

I can talk about the past using a variety of past tenses.

1 Complete the table with the *-ing* form, past simple and past participle form of the verbs.

Base form	*-ing* form	Past simple	Past participle
1 marry			
2 fight			
3 die			
4 meet			
5 retire			
6 think			
7 stop			
8 ride			
9 fall			
10 learn			

2 Circle the correct answers.

1 My parents **bought / were buying** a house just after they got married.
2 John **had got engaged / was getting engaged** before he left university.
3 Liam inherited a lot of money and **was emigrating / emigrated** to Australia.
4 **Did Pam phone / Had Pam phoned** while you **watched / were watching** television?
5 I opened the door and **stepped / had stepped** outside. It **rained / was raining**.
6 I didn't know where you were because you **weren't phoning / didn't phone**.
7 I **had / 'd had** this watch for two years when the battery ran out.

3 Some of the verb forms and tenses in the sentences are incorrect. Rewrite them correctly. Tick the correct sentences.

1 Why **did you be** angry with Mary? ☐
_____
2 **Had you eaten** before you **went** out? ☐
_____
3 I **couldn't go** out until I **had did** my homework. ☐
_____
4 It **wasn't rain** when we **left** the house. ☐
_____
5 I **wasn't feeling** well this morning. ☐
_____
6 We **was eating** when you **phoned**. ☐
_____
7 Where **had** you lunch? ☐
_____

4 Write the negative and interrogative form of the sentences.

1 Jason had been to Italy.
Jason hadn't been to Italy.
Had Jason been to Italy?
2 Tom grew up in London.
_____
_____
3 Her parents split up last year.
_____
_____
4 Harry was living in Scotland.
_____
_____
5 Sally had eaten lunch.
_____
_____

5 Complete the sentences with the verbs below. Use the past simple, past continuous or past perfect.

go out   leave   not listen   lose   shine   snow

1 I couldn't pay for the pizzas because I _____ my money at home.
2 I put on my coat and _____ .
3 You didn't understand the question because you _____ .
4 When we woke up, everything was white because it _____ during the night.
5 I borrowed my brother's jacket because I _____ _____ mine.
6 It was a really cold day, but the sun _____ .

6 Complete the text with the verbs in brackets. Use the past simple, past continuous or past perfect.

When Sarah Knauss ¹_____ (die) on 30 December 1999, she ²_____ (live) in Pennsylvania, USA, where she ³_____ (spend) all her life. At the time of her death, only one person before her ⁴_____ (live) longer. Sarah ⁵_____ (have) one daughter, who ⁶_____ still _____ (live) when Sarah died.

Family tensions

I can identify the attitude and intention of a speaker.

Revision: Student's Book page 11

1 Read the sentences. What is each speaker's attitude? Circle the correct answers.

1 'Quick! Shut the door, before it's too late!'
   a aggressive   **b** calm
   c sarcastic   **d** urgent

2 'This town was wonderful when I was a boy.'
   a accusing   **b** miserable
   c nostalgic   **d** optimistic

3 'Poor you. I hope you feel better soon.'
   a bitter   **b** grateful
   c sympathetic   **d** urgent

4 'Don't worry. Everything will be fine, I'm sure.'
   a accusing   **b** calm
   c nostalgic   **d** pessimistic

5 'I expect I'll come last in the race. I usually do.'
   a arrogant   **b** enthusiastic
   c grateful   **d** pessimistic

6 'I can't forgive him for how he behaved.'
   a bitter   **b** complimentary
   c optimistic   **d** sarcastic

7 'Your hair looks fantastic!'
   a aggressive   **b** complimentary
   c grateful   **d** urgent

8 'You left my phone outside in the rain? That was a really clever thing to do!'
   a enthusiastic   **b** grateful
   c nostalgic   **d** sarcastic

Listening Strategy

Sometimes, the words alone do not fully express the speaker's intention. You need to pay attention to the tone of voice as well. For example, an urgent tone of voice suggests that the speaker is giving a warning.

2 🔊 **1.03** Read the Listening Strategy. Then listen and circle the tone of voice the speaker uses.

1 The next train leaves in half an hour.
   a calm   **b** urgent

2 That's made me feel a lot better.
   a grateful   **b** sarcastic

3 This is going to be rather painful.
   a aggressive   **b** sympathetic

4 We were too poor to even go on holiday.
   a bitter   **b** nostalgic

3 Try reading aloud each sentence from exercise 2 using the other tone of voice.

4 🔊 **1.04** Listen. Which adjective below best describes each speaker's tone of voice? There are three extra adjectives.

arrogant   enthusiastic   grateful   nostalgic
pessimistic   sympathetic   urgent

Speaker 1 _____
Speaker 2 _____
Speaker 3 _____
Speaker 4 _____

5 Match the intentions (1–5) with the tone of voice you are most likely to use.

1 persuading somebody: _____
   a enthusiastic   **b** grateful   **c** sarcastic

2 remembering something: _____
   a arrogant   **b** nostalgic   **c** sympathetic

3 thanking somebody: _____
   a accusing   **b** bitter   **c** grateful

4 praising somebody: _____
   a calm   **b** complimentary **c** optimistic

5 complaining about something: _____
   a enthusiastic   **b** miserable   **c** optimistic

6 🔊 **1.05** Listen to four monologues. Decide what tone of voice each speaker is using. Choose from the adjectives in exercise 5.

Speaker 1 _____
Speaker 2 _____
Speaker 3 _____
Speaker 4 _____

7 🔊 **1.05** Listen again. Match speakers 1–4 with sentences A–E. There is one extra sentence. Use your answers to exercises 5 and 6 to help you.

Speaker	1	2	3	4
Sentence (A–E)				

A The speaker is persuading people to buy something.
B The speaker is remembering a family tradition from when he / she was younger.
C The speaker is thanking his / her guests for coming to a special family meal.
D The speaker is praising a family member for preventing a family argument.
E The speaker is complaining about a bad experience at a family reunion.

Grammar

used to

I can talk about things that were different in the past.

1 Complete the sentences with the correct form of *used to*.

1 I know this town well. We _____ (visit) here a lot when I was younger.

2 You _____ (love) swimming. Why don't you like it now?

3 Your dad is fantastic at football. _____ he _____ (play) a lot?

4 Our town _____ (have) good sports facilities, but now there's a great new sports centre.

5 She sounds American. _____ she _____ (live) in the USA?

6 I _____ (argue) a lot with my dad, but we get on really well now.

7 He speaks Spanish really well because he _____ (go) to university in Madrid.

8 I _____ (be) interested in films, but I go to the cinema a lot now.

9 My mum _____ (make) dinner every night, but now my dad cooks at weekends.

10 My grandparents _____ (go) abroad at all, but these days, they often visit other countries.

2 Complete the sentences with the correct form of *used to*. Use the word in brackets and any other necessary word.

1 (sea) *We didn't use to live near the sea*, but we live near it now.

2 (glasses) _____ , but I wear them now.

3 (milk) _____ , but I don't drink it now.

4 (dogs) _____ , but I'm not afraid of them now.

5 (stamps) _____ , but he doesn't collect them now.

6 (teacher) _____ , but she isn't one now.

7 (Japanese) _____ , but she speaks it now.

3 Complete the sentence in five different ways with *used to* (affirmative or negative) and the verbs in brackets.

When I was eight years old, ...

1 (eat)
_____

2 (wear)
_____

3 (play)
_____

4 (like)
_____

5 (be afraid)
_____

4 Look at the pictures of Jackie twenty years ago. Complete the questions with the correct form of *used to* and the verbs below. Then write the answers.

go have ~~live~~ play sleep wear work

1 Did she use to live in London?
  No, she used to live in Paris.

2 _____ short hair?
_____

3 _____ in a shop?
_____

4 _____ football at weekends?
_____

5 _____ a tracksuit?
_____

6 _____ skiing in the winter?
_____

7 _____ in a hotel?
_____

5 Tick the correct phrase to complete the sentences.

1 She moved to Canada two years ago, but she ___ living in a cold country.
  a didn't use to ☐ b hasn't got used to ☐

2 I ___ angry a lot, but I'm much calmer now.
  a used to get ☐ b got used to ☐

3 They ___ like the same music, but they don't now.
  a used to ☐ b got used to ☐

4 I like your new glasses. ___ wearing them?
  a Did you use to ☐ b Have you got used to ☐

5 I hated this flat when we moved in, but I ___ it now.
  a used to ☐ b have got used to ☐

1 Complete the sentences with the correct form of the phrasal verbs below.

get up to   go in for   go through with   live up to
put up with   run out of   sign up for

1 We _____ money two days after we arrived!

2 He's so annoying. How do you _____ him?

3 Personally, I don't _____ dangerous sports.

4 She wasn't brave enough to _____ the plan.

5 At the hotel reception, you can _____ some really interesting excursions.

6 What did you _____ on holiday?

7 Part 2 of the trilogy could never _____ Part 1.

2 Complete the plot summary of the film *Big* with the correct form of the phrasal verbs below.

catch up with   fit in with   get away with   get on with
get up   go back   make up   walk out on

At a travelling carnival, twelve-year-old Josh Baskin is embarrassed when he is too small for one of the rides. He puts a coin in a fortune-telling machine, which tells him to make a wish – so Josh wishes he was big. When he ¹_____ the next morning, he notices that his wish has come true: he is an adult, although still a child inside. His mother thinks he is a burglar, so he has to leave home. He tries to ²_____ to the carnival, but it has left town.

On his own, Josh needs money, so he finds a job at a toy company. He doesn't really have the skills he needs for work, but he ³_____ it because he loves toys. In fact, he does well at work, but he finds it difficult to ⁴_____ the other adults there. The only person he really ⁵_____ is a female colleague called Susan Lawrence.

One day, Josh's friend Billy tells him that the carnival is back in town. Josh ⁶_____ Susan in the middle of an important meeting at work. When she ⁷_____ him, he is at the fortune-telling machine. Finally, she realises that he did not ⁸_____ the story about being a child. The two say goodbye before Josh puts another coin in the machine and becomes a child again.

3 Complete the sentences with one or two prepositions below.

away   back   for   for   in   in   on   to   up   up   up

1 **Look** _____ his address on the internet.

2 It was so dark inside the cave that he was afraid to go _____ .

3 I've always **looked** _____ my grandmother; she's a brave and intelligent person.

4 He's very reliable; he never **goes** _____ a promise.

5 I like sport, but I don't really **go** _____ martial arts.

6 The beach was fantastic. It **made** _____ the hotel, which wasn't great.

7 The police saw the burglar, but he still managed to **get** _____ .

> **VOCAB BOOST!**
>
> When you come across a new phrasal verb, write down examples to show whether it is separable or inseparable. For example, 'come across' is inseparable:
> *I came across a new verb today.*
> *I came across it today.*
>
> However, 'write down' is separable:
> *I wrote down two examples.*
> *I wrote them down.*

4 Rewrite the sentences replacing the underlined object with a pronoun (*him, her, it, them,* etc.).

1 She likes my friends and tries to get on with <u>my friends</u>.
She likes my friends and tries to _____

2 I don't know where the restaurant is. Let's look up <u>the location</u> on the internet.
I don't know where the restaurant is. Let's _____

3 They'd planned the robbery carefully, but didn't go through with <u>the plan</u>.
They'd planned the robbery carefully, but _____

4 We haven't eaten here before; we just came across <u>the restaurant</u> while we were walking around town.
We haven't eaten here before; we just came across _____

5 He's always so rude. I don't think I can put up with <u>his rudeness</u> much longer.
He's always so rude. I don't think I can put up with _____

6 I knew the answer, but I didn't have time to write down <u>the answer</u>.
I knew the answer, but I didn't have time _____

7 The flight was terrible, but the holiday made up for <u>the journey</u>.
The flight was terrible, but the holiday _____

Revision: Student's Book page 14

1 Complete the table.

	Noun	Adjective
1	adolescence	_____
2	_____	dependent
3	freedom	_____
4	_____	emotional
5	privacy	_____
6	_____	idealistic
7	impatience	_____
8	_____	concerned
9	safety	_____
10	_____	irritated
11	criticism	_____
12	_____	distrustful

2 Complete the sentences with the correct form of the nouns and adjectives in exercise 1.

1 My diary is _____ — I don't let anyone else read it.
2 Mark is always complaining that his parents don't give him enough _____ . He wants to do what he likes when he likes.
3 Kathy hates waiting for people. She's so _____ !
4 _____ can be a difficult stage in life.
5 You never believe what I say! Why are you so _____ ?
6 Strong _____ such as love and anger are sometimes difficult to deal with.

3 Read the text. Choose the best summary.

1 The Kardashians agreed to make a TV show, but they think it's had a bad effect on the family.
2 The Kardashians' show was successful, but the family are now too busy to make more shows.
3 The Kardashians' show has many viewers, but it doesn't appeal to everybody.

Reading Strategy
Read the missing sentences carefully. Then read the sentences in the text that come before and after each gap. Look for words that link with vocabulary in the missing sentences (e.g. synonyms, paraphrases, words with the opposite meaning, pronouns).

4 Read the Reading Strategy. Then match sentences A–F with gaps 1–4 in the text. There are two extra sentences.

A She has three girls – Kourtney, Kim and Khloé – and one son, Rob.
B Throughout the series, many family events have been shown.
C But who are they and why are they famous?
D Other reality TV shows are about singing, dancing, or cooking.
E A lot of Americans disapprove of the family's behaviour on TV and in the press.
F Kim married rap star Kanye West and has a daughter called North.

KEEPING IT IN THE FAMILY

The Kardashians are currently one of the USA's most well-known families. They are often in the news, and Americans follow their lives in the papers and celebrity magazines. ¹___ The Kardashians are reality TV stars, with their own family show called *Keeping up with the Kardashians*.

It all started in 2007 when the family was asked by an American channel to make a TV series about their lives. The show focused on mother Kris and her four children. ²___ Their father was lawyer Robert Kardashian, who died a few years earlier. The show became a success in its first season, mainly because of the three sisters and their extrovert personalities.

Since then, there have been eight more seasons and the show is still running. ³___ Two of the sisters got married on the show. Kim got married twice! And two of the sisters are now parents. Furthermore, the three sisters have used their fame to establish careers in the fashion industry. They have opened clothes shops and launched several clothing collections and perfumes. Kim has even launched a successful mobile phone game called *Kim Kardashian: Hollywood*.

Although the show has many fans, it also has many critics. ⁴___ They are irritated by the sisters' desire for fame and fortune, and think the show is meaningless. The Kardashians are only 'famous for being famous', but they don't mind because it has made them rich.

Role-play

I can role-play a conversation about an exchange programme.

1 Complete the second sentence so that it has a similar meaning to the first. Use the words in brackets and no more than three other words.

1 It would be a good idea to phone home when you arrive. (should)
You _____
home when you arrive.

2 I recommend that you take a gift for the family. (ought)
You _____
a gift for the family.

3 It wouldn't be a good idea to take too much money with you. (should)
I don't think _____
too much money with you.

4 In my opinion, phoning your parents every day would be a bad idea. (ought)
I don't think _____
phone your parents every day.

5 It would be a good idea for us to decorate the bedroom. (ought)
We _____
the bedroom.

6 It's a good idea for you to speak English as much as possible. (should)
I think _____
English as much as possible.

2 🎧 **1.06** Listen to a student and examiner doing the task below. Which of the four topics do they spend most time on? Which do they not discuss?

Recently, a student from England stayed with you and your family for a month. Speak to a friend from another country who is expecting an English student soon. Here are four topics that you need to discuss.

1 accommodation for the student
2 fitting in at your school
3 food and drink preferences
4 advice about making the student feel at home

Most time: topic ☐   Not discussed: topic ☐

3 Think of one or two ideas for the topic not discussed in exercise 2.
_____
_____
_____

4 🎧 **1.06** Complete the sentences with the correct form of the verbs below. Then listen again and check.

do do make miss share take

1 Did he _____ your room?
2 We need to _____ the room nice for her.

3 It _____ him a few days to feel comfortable there, though.
4 Did he have to _____ the homework?
5 He actually _____ well in some subjects.
6 Will she _____ her friends and family?

> **Speaking Strategy**
> Use your preparation time well. Read the task carefully. Then think of just one thing to say about each topic. If you have more time, think of more ideas.

5 Read the Speaking Strategy. Read the task and answer the questions below.

An exchange student from England stayed with you for three weeks last month. Speak to a student from another country who is expecting an exchange student next month. Here are four topics that you need to discuss.

1 preparing for the exchange student's visit
2 communicating with the visitor
3 entertaining the visitor
4 advice about keeping in touch after the visit

In which topic 1–4 are you most likely to discuss:

A going to the cinema? ☐
B swapping Skype addresses? ☐
C using a bilingual dictionary? ☐
D tidying your visitor's room? ☐

6 Now try to think of at least one more idea for each topic in the task.

1 How should you prepare for the visit?
_____
_____

2 What communication problems might you have and how could you solve them?
_____
_____

3 What kinds of entertainment could you offer at home? Where could you go out?
_____
_____

4 What are the best ways to keep in touch with somebody in another country?
_____
_____

7 Now do the speaking task from exercise 5. Use your notes from exercise 6.

A message

I can write a message in response to an advertisement.

Preparation

1 Complete the polite requests with the words below.

could   if   mind   possible   wonder

1 Would it be _____ for you to ... ?
2 _____ you please ... ?
3 Would you _____ telling me ... ?
4 Would you mind _____ ... ?
5 I _____ if ...

2 Rewrite the imperatives as polite requests. Include the word in brackets.

1 Tidy your room! (possibly)

_____

2 Give me your address! (mind)

_____

3 Phone me later! (wonder)

_____

4 Bring me some coffee! (possible)

_____

> ### Writing Strategy
> Make sure that you a) include all of the points in the task and b) develop each point, that is, add some extra information or detail. Try not to write just one sentence for each point.

3 Read the Writing Strategy. Then read the message. Match the extra information 1–5 with A–D in the message. There is one piece of information you do not need.

> Hi! My name is David and I live in Budapest, the capital of Hungary. [A] I'm sixteen years old, and I live with my parents and my younger brother. [B]
>
> I'm a huge fan of music and I love going to gigs. I also play guitar in a band. [C] I also enjoy going to the cinema and watching films at home.
>
> I've got a computer in my room and I often chat to my friends online. I wonder if you could send me your Skype address. [D]

1 We aren't very good because we don't practise enough! ☐
2 That is why I'm interested in finding a penfriend. ☐
3 Our flat is in the centre of the city, near the river. ☐
4 It would be fun to speak to you some time. ☐
5 His name is Miles and he's into computers. ☐

Writing Guide

> Hi! My name is Lucy. I'm fifteen years old and I live in Birmingham in the UK. I'm in interested in chatting (in English!) with teenagers from different countries using Skype. Please send me a message and tell me a little about yourself, your family and your hobbies. Also, please say why you are interested in chatting. I'm waiting to hear from you!
>
> Click here to reply to Lucy.

You have seen this advertisement on a website. Write a message in reply and provide the information Lucy asks for. Include a request for information in your message.

4 Read the advertisement and the task above. Then make brief notes under headings 1–4.

1 Information about yourself

_____
_____

2 Information about your family

_____
_____

3 Hobbies and interests

_____
_____

4 What information are you requesting?

_____
_____

5 Write your message. Use your notes from exercise 4 and include a phrase from exercise 1 for your polite request.

_____
_____
_____
_____
_____
_____
_____
_____
_____
_____

> ### CHECK YOUR WORK
> **Have you ...**
> ☐ included and developed each point in the task?
> ☐ checked your spelling and grammar?

Review Unit 1

Vocabulary

1 Rewrite the sentences with the words below.

a centenarian   an infant   in (your) teens   in (your) twenties
middle-aged   a toddler   a young child

1 My niece is only four months old.
_____

2 My little brother is six.
_____

3 My great-grandfather is over a hundred.
_____

4 My cousin Jack is fifteen.
_____

5 My mother is fifty next year.
_____

6 My nephew is two years old.
_____

7 My sister was twenty-three on her last birthday.
_____

Mark: ___ / 7

2 Complete each pair of life events with a suitable verb.

1 _____ born / brought up
2 _____ a flat / a house
3 _____ home / school
4 _____ married / engaged
5 _____ a business / a family
6 _____ a house / money

Mark: ___ / 6

3 Complete the sentences with the correct form of the verbs below.

emigrate   grow up   move   pass away   retire   settle down

1 My grandfather is in his seventies, but he has no plans to _____ from his job.
2 I missed my friends terribly when we _____ house.
3 They're thinking of leaving the UK. They'd like to _____to Australia.
4 My best friend_____ in France, so she's bilingual.
5 When I leave university, I want to go travelling before I _____ and have a family.
6 Tom's grandmother is ill in hospital. He'll be extremely upset if she_____.

Mark: ___ / 6

Word Skills

4 Replace the underlined words with the correct form of the phrasal verbs below.

catch up with   fit in with   get on with   go through with
live up to   put up with   run out of   sign up for   walk out on

1 Connor didn't <u>fulfil</u> his parents' expectations and failed to get a place at university.
_____

2 After her father <u>abandoned</u> his job, the family moved house.
_____

3 That child doesn't <u>behave like</u> the rest of the class because he prefers to play on his own.
_____

4 When Amy <u>agreed to do</u> a job as a waitress, she didn't think it would be such hard work.
_____

5 My brother is always making ambitious plans, but he never <u>completes</u> them.
_____

6 He'll never <u>succeed in reaching</u> the other runners because he's much slower than they are.
_____

7 I couldn't <u>tolerate</u> the heat any longer, so I went out and bought a fan.
_____

8 She couldn't finish the exam because she had <u>used all of the</u> time.
_____

9 My little brother and I don't <u>have a good relationship with</u> each other.
_____

Mark: ___ / 9

5 Complete the sentences with the correct form of the correct verb in brackets. Include a pronoun where necessary.

1 The room was full, so he needed to take a deep breath before he _____ . (go in / go in for)
2 The teacher didn't notice that we hadn't done the homework. We _____ . (get away / get away with)
3 The starter wasn't very tasty, but the main course _____ . It was delicious! (make up / make up for)
4 I didn't answer the phone because I _____ yet. (get up / get up to)
5 If you don't understand a word, _____ in the dictionary. (look up / look up to)
6 If you make a promise, you shouldn't _____ . (go back / go back on)

Mark: ___ / 6

Review Unit 1

Grammar

6 Complete the text with the correct past tense form of the verbs in brackets.

Fauja Singh used to take part in amateur races when he was younger, but he ¹_____ (not start) running marathons until he was in his eighties. He ²_____ (not run) a race since 1947 when he joined his local running club at the age of 84. The coach nearly ³_____ (send) him home on the first day because he ⁴_____ (wear) a suit.
Mr Singh's first race was the London Marathon, which he ⁵_____ (complete) in six hours and 54 minutes, a new record for the over-nineties. The previous record holder ⁶_____ (set) a time of seven hours and 52 minutes.
Today, at the age of 103, Mr Singh is still running marathons.

Mark: / 6

7 Complete the dialogues with the correct form of *used to* and the verbs in brackets.

1 **A** _____
(you / watch) a lot of cartoons when you were a child?
B No, I _____(not watch) much television.
I _____ (play)
outside with my friends when I could.

2 **A** My brother has got a new job in a shop.
B Really? What _____? (he / do)
A He _____ (work) in a factory, but
he _____ (not like) it very much.

3 **A** Where _____ (you and your
family / spend) the summer holidays?
B We _____ (not have) a family
holiday because my parents were working. But my
brother and I _____ (go)
and stay with my grandparents in the country.

Mark: / 9

8 Complete the sentences with *used to* or *get used to*.

1 My sister _____ cry a lot when she was
a baby.
2 Mike has just moved to the city from the country and he
can't _____ the noise.
3 I'll never _____ wearing contact lenses.
To be honest, I prefer my glasses.
4 We _____ live in a small flat, but we've
recently moved to a house.
5 I _____ see my best friend every day,
but now I'm too busy.
6 You'll have to _____ drinking tea if you
go and live in the UK.

Mark: / 6

Use of English

9 Circle the correct answers.

The film *Boyhood* follows the life of a boy called Mason as he is ¹___ up. Mason's parents are divorced, so he and his sister are ²___ up by their mother, Olivia. Olivia eventually marries her university professor, but the children don't like him because they ³___ used to his strict discipline. Finally, the couple ⁴___ , but Olivia soon marries again. By this time, Mason is in his teens and he soon ⁵___ in love himself. The film finishes when Mason ⁶___ university and meets a new group of friends, who he accompanies on a trip to the desert. The thing that makes *Boyhood* remarkable is the fact that the director ⁷___ nearly twelve years to make it. Once a year, he ⁸___ meet up with the actors to develop the next part of the film. He wanted to know what ⁹___ in their real lives in the previous months, especially in the case of the child actor who played Mason. As a result, the film succeeds in portraying what the boy ¹⁰___ during each stage of his childhood.

1	a	getting	b	growing	c looking
2	a	brought	b	made	c signed
3	a	aren't	b	didn't	c don't
4	a	pass away	b	settle down	c split up
5	a	falls	b	gets	c goes
6	a	goes	b	goes to	c goes to the
7	a	took	b	was taking	c had taken
8	a	got used to	b	was used to	c used to
9	a	happened	b	was happening	c had happened
10	a	thought	b	was thinking	c had thought

Mark: /10

Total: / 65

I can ...

Read the statements. Think about your progress and tick one of the boxes.

★ = I need more practice.   ★★★ = No problem!

★★ = I sometimes find this difficult.

	★	★★	★★★
I can talk about the different stages of people's lives.			
I can talk about the past using a variety of past tenses.			
I can identify the attitude and intention of a speaker.			
I can talk about things that were different in the past.			
I can use three-part phrasal verbs.			
I can understand a text about a famous family.			
I can role-play a conversation about an exchange programme.			
I can write a message in response to an advertisement.			

2 Leisure time

Vocabulary

A Love it or hate it

I can talk about likes and dislikes and

1 Label the sports and activities.

1 _____ 2 _____ 3 _____

4 _____ 5 _____ 6 _____

7 _____ 8 _____ 9 _____

10 _____ 11 _____ 12 _____

2 Complete the leisure activities with the verbs below.

bake   collect   hang out   make
read   read   text   use   watch

1 _____ cakes
2 _____ with friends
3 _____ books
4 _____ clothes
5 _____ magazines
6 _____ your friends
7 _____ videos online
8 _____ social media
9 _____ figures, cards, stamps, etc.

3 Complete the table with the sports and activities below. Then add the sports and activities from exercise 1.

basketball   BMXing   board games   cycling   drama
martial arts   a musical instrument   photography
rollerblading   running   shopping   skateboarding   volleyball

do +	
1 _____	4 _____
2 _____	5 _____
3 _____	6 _____
play +	
1 _____	5 _____
2 _____	6 _____
3 _____	7 _____
4 _____	8 _____
go +	
1 _____	7 _____
2 _____	8 _____
3 _____	9 _____
4 _____	10 _____
5 _____	11 _____
_____	

4 🎧 1.07 Listen to three people talking about their hobbies. Which two activities from exercises 1 and 3 do the speakers mention?

1 _____ and _____
2 _____ and _____

5 🎧 1.07 Listen again. Match the speakers (1 and 2) with the sentences (a–d).

This person:
a started a new hobby recently. ☐
b has bought some new equipment. ☐
c didn't use to like team sports. ☐
d finds it difficult to make time for his / her hobbies. ☐

6 Write about two sports and activities you enjoy doing. Say where and when you do them and why you enjoy them.

_____
_____
_____
_____
_____
_____

Present perfect and past simple contrast

I can use the past simple and present perfect tenses correctly.

1 Circle the correct answers.

1 Fran **went / has gone** ballroom dancing last night.
2 **Did you finish / Have you finished** vlogging yet?
3 I **had / have had** this camera for over a year.
4 I **read / have read** the whole magazine in an hour.
5 Sam isn't hungry because he **already ate / has already eaten**.
6 **Did you go / Have you been** cycling last weekend?

2 Correct the mistakes in the sentences.

1 I didn't go rollerblading before. Is it fun?
_____

2 I've fallen over while I was ice skating.
_____

3 Did Jasmine text you yet?
_____

4 Dan has gone bowling on his birthday.
_____

5 I didn't go camping since last summer.
_____

3 Complete the sentences with the verbs in brackets. Use the past simple in one sentence and the present perfect in the other.

1 a I _____ skateboarding lots of times. (go)
  b Katie _____ shopping yesterday. (go)
2 a When _____ you _____ that cake? (bake)
  b I _____ cakes since I was ten. (bake)
3 a Joe loves karate. He _____ it for ages. (do)
  b I _____ ballet for a year, but I gave it up. (do)
4 a *Northern Lights* is a great book. _____ you _____ it? (read)
  b I _____ four novels last month. (read)

4 USE OF ENGLISH Complete the second sentence so that it has a similar meaning to the first. Use the words in brackets and the past simple or present perfect. You will need to add other words.

1 I can still remember my tenth birthday party. (never)
  I *have never forgotten* my tenth birthday party.
2 Tomorrow, Jason will go horse riding for the first time. (never)
  Jason _____ horse riding before.
3 I haven't played table tennis for a year. (ago)
  I last _____ .
4 Tom has just texted me. (a moment ago)
  Tom _____ .
5 The last time I vlogged was a year ago. (for)
  I _____ a year.
6 Is this your first time at this gym? (ever)
  _____ before?
7 My brother has collected stamps since he was six. (collecting)
  My _____ when he was six.

5 Complete the interview with the past simple or present perfect form of the verbs in brackets.

Interviewer When ¹_____ you _____ (start) rollerblading?

Tiffany I first ²_____ (go) rollerblading when I was nine. I ³_____ (stop) for a few years, then I ⁴_____ (take) it up again when I was in my teens.

Interviewer How often do you practise?

Tiffany As often as I can. But it ⁵_____ (be) very wet recently, so I ⁶_____ (not be able) to get out on the streets much, which is very frustrating.

Interviewer Who are your favourite rollerbladers?

Tiffany I love watching Chris Haffey. I ⁷_____ (always / admire) him. In 2011, he ⁸_____ (break) the world record for the longest jump – 30 metres!

Interviewer ⁹_____ you _____ (have) much success in competitions?

Tiffany Yes, I ¹⁰_____ (win) quite a few competitions. I ¹¹_____ (come) first in the 2014 Street Rollerblading Open Championship.

Interviewer That's fantastic!

Eating out

I can identify the context of a dialogue.

1 **Complete the labels for the pictures with the words below. There are three extra words.**

curry   pie   pudding   ~~risotto~~   salad   sandwich
soup   stew   stir-fry

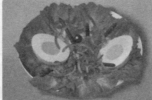

1 risotto

2 egg _____

3 prawn _____

4 cherry _____

5 vegetable _____

6 chicken _____

Think about dishes which are popular in your country. Write down:

two types of curry or stew.

_____, _____

two types of salad or sandwich.

_____, _____

two types of soup or pie.

_____, _____

Listening Strategy

In a listening task, you sometimes need to identify the context of a conversation. The context is implied, not stated, so you have to listen for clues. The information you need may be:

a when the conversation is taking place.

b where it is taking place.

c why the conversation is taking place.

d who is speaking.

---

3 🎧 **1.08** **Read the Listening Strategy. Then listen and circle the correct answer.**

a shortly **after** / **before** dinner

b **inside** / **outside** a restaurant

c They might have the wrong **day** / **restaurant**.

d a woman and her **father** / **son**

4 🎧 **1.09** **Listen to two short dialogues. Read the questions about context and circle the correct answers.**

Dialogue 1

1 Who is the woman talking to?

  a a waiter

  b the man she's having dinner with

  c a man at the next table

2 Why is the woman unhappy with her food?

  a It isn't what she ordered.

  b It doesn't look very tasty.

  c She can't eat it.

Dialogue 2

3 Where is the conversation taking place?

  a at home

  b in a restaurant

  c in the town centre

4 What time is it, approximately?

  a 7 p.m.

  b 9 p.m.

  c 11 p.m.

5 **Complete the useful phrases with the words below.**

bit   nothing   pretty   real   up   world

1 a _____ special

2 a _____ let-down

3 _____ special

4 _____ average

5 not _____ to standard

6 out of this _____

6 🎧 **1.10** **Listen to a dialogue between two friends. Check your answers to exercise 5.**

7 🎧 **1.10** **Listen again. For each question, write the correct speaker: Tom (T) or Zoë (Z).**

Which person …

1 is planning to book a restaurant? ☐

2 can't remember last year's meal? ☐

3 always checks online reviews for restaurants? ☐

4 recommended an Italian restaurant? ☐

5 is going to ask about a special diet? ☐

Present perfect simple and continuous

I can use the present perfect simple and continuous correctly.

1 Complete the text with the present perfect continuous form of the verbs below.

ask   attract   focus   get   not go
post   not update   visit   write

Purple POPCORN

Sam Delaney, a student at Imperial College London,
¹_____film reviews since he was
eleven years old. At first, he posted them on Facebook, but
for the past four years, he ²_____
them on his own website – Purple Popcorn. The website
³_____ the attention of the media
recently, since it emerged that several Hollywood producers
⁴_____ it to read his reviews.
'They've finally noticed me,' says Sam, proudly. 'They
⁵_____ if they can put lines from my
reviews on their own websites and adverts.'

Since September, Sam ⁶_____
his site very often. That's because he ⁷_____
to the cinema very much while he's preparing for exams.
'I ⁸_____ on my university work,' he
says. Even so, his website ⁹_____
a lot of hits thanks to a growing number of followers on Twitter.

2 Complete the sentences with the present perfect continuous form of the verbs in brackets and *for* or *since*.

1 She _____ (collect) badges _____
ten years. She's got thousands!

2 _____ (you / learn) Japanese _____
a long time?

3 I'm going home. I _____ (not feel)
well _____ this morning.

4 My sister_____ (drink) coffee
_____ most of the evening and now she can't sleep!

5 I don't know why he's being so impatient. He
_____ (not wait)_____long.

6 I should do well in my exams. I _____
(work) hard _____ the start of term.

3 Circle the correct answers.

1 You're two hours late! What ___ all afternoon?
   a have you done   b have you been doing
2 This farm ___ to our family for two centuries.
   a has belonged   b has been belonging
3 'I sent you an email.' 'Really? I ___ it.'
   a haven't received   b haven't been receiving
4 Is Tom OK? I ___ him three times this week, but he hasn't replied.
   a 've texted   b 've been texting
5 ___ my popcorn? The box is half empty!
   a Have you eaten   b Have you been eating
6 Is dinner ready yet? You ___ for hours!
   a 've cooked   b 've been cooking
7 I'm really enjoying this novel, but I ___ all of it.
   a haven't understood b haven't been understanding
8 My dad ___ his car. He goes everywhere by bike now.
   a has sold   b has been selling

4 Complete the replies with the present perfect simple or present perfect continuous form of the verbs in brackets.

1 A Have you finished that history project?
   B No, I haven't. And I _____
   (do) it all day!

2 A Why are your hands so dirty?
   B I _____ (try) to repair my
   bike.

3 A Did your brother forget about football practice?
   B Yes. And I _____ (remind)
   him three times this week!

4 A Did you write a letter to the town council?
   B Yes, but I _____ (not send)
   it.

5 A Are those potatoes ready yet?
   B No, they aren't. How long _____
   _____ (we / cook) them?

6 A Has Billy replied to your messages yet?
   B No, he hasn't. And I _____
   (text) him five times!

7 A You're nearly an hour late. What _____
   _____ (you / do)?
   B Sorry. I was asleep!

8 A This film doesn't make sense. Why are the police chasing that man?
   B I don't know. I _____ (not
   watch).

Compound nouns and adjectives

I can use compounds correctly.

1 Complete the sports venues with the words below. Then use six of them to label the photos.

basketball   bowling   boxing   court   football   golf
ice   room   studio   swimming   track   wall

1 _____ alley
2 _____ course
3 athletics _____
4 _____ rink
5 tennis _____
6 _____ ring

7 _____ court
8 dance _____
9 climbing _____
10 _____ pitch
11 weights _____
12 _____ pool

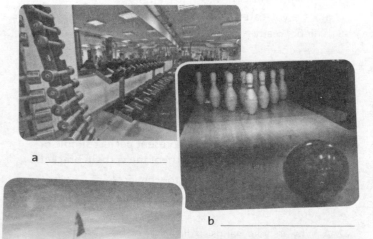

a _____

b _____

c _____

d _____

e _____

f _____

2 Match the words to make more compound nouns. Use each word only once.

1 mountain ☐
2 flood ☐
3 main ☐
4 sea ☐
5 tennis ☐
6 safety ☐
7 tower ☐

a road
b block
c net
d range
e player
f shore
g lights

3 Complete the table with compound nouns from exercises 1 and 2. Write two in column A, three in column B and four in column C.

A adjective + noun	B -ing form + noun
_____	_____
_____	_____
	_____

C noun + noun
_____
_____
_____
_____

4 Complete the compound adjectives in the sentences with the words below.

25   air   full   open   sound   well

1 It's an amazing house. There's a _____-sized bowling alley in the basement!
2 There's also a new _____-air swimming pool in the garden.
3 Is it healthy to spend all day in _____-conditioned offices?
4 The gym has a _____-equipped weights room.
5 She reached the top of the _____-metre climbing wall in less than a minute.
6 They record the podcasts in a _____proof room.

VOCAB BOOST!

Many compound adjectives are not in the dictionary because they are formed from other words. When you come across a new compound adjective, you need to work out the meaning by looking at the words which form it.

a three-wheeled motorbike = a motorbike with three wheels

a well-drawn picture = a picture which has been drawn well

---

5 Read the *Vocab boost!* box. Then complete the second part of each sentence with an explanation.

1 A three-headed monster is a monster with three heads.
2 A man-eating lion is a lion _____ _____.
3 A million-dollar apartment is an apartment _____ _____.
4 A five-storey house is a house _____ _____.
5 A well-prepared student is a student _____ _____.

2F Reading
Sport changes lives
I can understand a text about a sports charity.

Revision: Student's Book page 24

1 Complete the prepositions in the sentences.

1 We drove a_____ o_____r town looking for a chemist's that was open.
2 There are trees a_____ a_____g the road that goes to our school.
3 There's a post office b_____e the church in Kings Road.
4 Snow fell a_____s Britain last night, and temperatures were well b_____w zero.
5 Let's go to the café b_____ the river.

2 Read the article. Are the sentences true (T) or false (F)?

1 This sports organisation brings activities to school for young people. ☐
2 The organisation believes that sport helps young people in other areas of their lives. ☐

Reading Strategy

Multiple-choice questions may test:

• factual information (detailed or general).
• the writer's opinion.
• the writer's intention.

You can sometimes (but not always) see what a question is testing by reading the first part without the options (a–d). Turning it into a direct question can also help.

3 Read the Reading Strategy. Then circle the correct answers.

1 Nearly three quarters of teenagers
  a aspire to play better sport.
  b have found the sport they are looking for.
  c haven't played any sport.
  d would like to play sport if it was less expensive.
2 The aim of the charity is to
  a help communities to get fitter.
  b organise local sporting activities cheaply.
  c advise young people on how to succeed in life.
  d provide intensive sports training for teenagers.
3 Adventure sports were
  a chosen by boys only.
  b selected by both boys and girls.
  c more popular than dance classes.
  d not as popular as football.
4 The writer wants
  a to encourage teenagers to join the sports project.
  b young children to contact the organisation.
  c young people to pay for sporting activities.
  d to help young people at home.

StreetGames

Who are we?

StreetGames is a sports charity that changes lives and communities. We are proud to give young people exactly what they are looking for – the chance to enjoy sport, give back to their communities and aspire to greater things. Seventy-one percent of young people have said that they would like the chance to try more sporting activities, but that they can't afford to.

What do we do?

'Doorstep Sport' is what we do – we bring sport close to home in disadvantaged communities, at the right time, for the right price and in the right style. Sport is great! It provides fitness, fun and friendship opportunities, and since 2007 we have been using it to improve the lives of countless young people. It teaches them skills and knowledge which they can then use to make their own way in life.

What do we offer?

We have been speaking to a lot of young people about sports they would like to be involved in, and these are the answers: boys between the ages of 16 and 19 have voted for playing football, badminton and tennis, going swimming, cycling, running and to the gym and doing adventure sports. The girls have chosen similarly, except for netball rather than football, plus dance and fitness classes. Multi-sports sessions have also proved popular with everyone.

What do we want?

We are bringing sport to your neighbourhood, and we need some assistance. We are looking for young volunteers for this task. We need young people both to take part in our wonderful sporting activities and also to look after and coach the younger children. So, if you are aged 16–19, contact us if you would like to be involved. We need YOU!

2G Speaking

Stimulus-based discussion

I can discuss ideas for a day out and justify my opinions.

1 Complete the words with *a, e, i, o* and *u*. Then match them with the diagrams (A–L).

1 k__rt__ng
2 k__y__k__ng
3 __bs__ __l__ng
4 cl__mb__ng
5 sn__wb__ __rd__ng
6 s__rf__ng
7 b__ng__ __ j__mp__ng
8 b__dyb__ __rd__ng
9 p__rk__ __ __r
10 h__ng-gl__d__ng
11 h__k__ng
12 m__ __nt__ __n b__k__ng

 A
 B
 C

 D
 E
 F

 G
 H
 I

 J
 K
 L

2 Write four sentences using the phrases below and activities from exercise 1.

I like the idea of ...   I think ... would be (fun).
I'm quite keen on ...   I quite fancy ...

1 _____
2 _____
3 _____
4 _____

You are planning a day out with friends on your birthday. Discuss with your friend what you are going to do. Give reasons for your opinions. Agree on an activity.

3 🎧 **1.11** Read the task above. Then listen to two students doing the task. Answer the questions.

1 Why does the girl want to go bodyboarding?
_____

2 Why doesn't the boy want to go bodyboarding?
_____

3 Why does the girl prefer parkour to abseiling?
_____

4 In the end, they agree to _____

Speaking Strategy

When you have to reach an agreement, be sure to use a range of phrases for expressing preferences, raising objections and coming to an agreement.

4 🎧 **1.11** Read the Speaking Strategy. Complete the sentences. Then listen again and check.

1 I'm _____ _____ on bodyboarding.
2 Sorry, but I don't _____ that's a very _____
  _____.
3 I _____ _____ trying that.
4 I think parkour is a _____ _____ than abseiling.
5 Yes, I _____.
6 _____ _____ _____ on climbing, then?

5 You are going to do the task in exercise 3. Make notes about which two activities you would like to do and why.

Which activities would you choose? Why? _____
_____
_____
_____
_____

Which activities would you not like to do? Why?
_____
_____
_____
_____
_____

6 Now do the speaking task. Use your notes from exercise 5.

Writing

A blog post

I can write a blog post expressing an opinion.

Preparation

1 Match six school clubs below with the pictures (1–6) opposite.

art club   astronomy club   baking club
ballroom-dancing club   computer club   debating society
drama society   film club   fitness club   handball club
photography club   school choir   school orchestra
science club

 1 _____

 2 _____

 3 _____

 4 _____

 5 _____

 6 _____

2 At which of the other school clubs from exercise 1 could you:

1 sing with other students? _____

2 act in a play? _____

3 do interesting experiments? _____

4 draw and paint? _____

5 discuss important issues? _____

6 do physical exercises? _____

7 look at the planets? _____

8 play a musical instrument? _____

3 Read the task and the model text. Number the four points (a–d) in the order they appear in the text.

a Say who attended the meeting and what happened at it. ☐

b Give your opinion of how the first meeting went. ☐

c Say why you formed the new club and where and when the first meeting took place. ☐

d Describe your plans for the club. ☐

> You have organised a new after-school club and attended your first meeting. Write a blog post about it.

Last Thursday was the first meeting of the fitness club. This is a new club which I have organised with two classmates. We all love sport and PE and we thought it would be a good idea to encourage other people to be more active. We met in the gym after school and then we went out onto the playing field. Luckily the weather was good.

Fifteen students turned up for the club. Eight of them were girls and seven were boys, and we all spent an hour doing a variety of games and exercises. For example, we played volleyball in the gym and football on the playing field.

All in all, I think the meeting was a success. Fifteen students is a good number, especially for a first meeting, although it would of course be better with more. Everybody took part very enthusiastically, which is very encouraging.

In the future, I hope to organise a wider variety of games and sports. I also plan to advertise the club better, with posters on the main noticeboard and an article in the school newspaper. I'd also like us all to enter a fun run next spring. We could even wear special costumes!

 Posted today at 11:32

Writing Guide

> **Writing Strategy**
>
> Where there is a word limit for a writing task make sure you keep within it. If you go over the limit, decide which words you can delete. For example, there may be unnecessary adjectives or examples, or irrelevant details. When you have cut the words, make sure that a) the text still makes sense, and b) all of the points in the task are still covered.

4 Read the Writing Strategy. Which two of the five underlined sentences in the text could you delete?

1st sentence ☐   3rd sentence ☐   5th sentence ☐

2nd sentence ☐   4th sentence ☐

5 Read the task. Then make notes for each point (a–d). Use the questions (1–4) below to give you ideas.

> You have joined a new club at school and attended your first session. Write a blog post about it.
>
> a Say when and where it took place.
>
> b Say who attended the session and what happened.
>
> c Suggest how the club could improve its activities.
>
> d Make a request for some equipment.

1 What club is it? Where / When was the session? How many people were there? What did you do?

2 Did you enjoy the session? What was the best / worst thing about it?

3 What would make the club better?

4 What equipment does the club need? Why?

6 Write a blog post. Use your notes from exercise 5.

> **CHECK YOUR WORK**
>
> 👁 Have you ...
>
> ☐ covered all four points in the task?
> ☐ written clearly and concisely with no irrelevant details?
> ☐ checked your spelling and grammar?

Vocabulary

1 Complete the sentences with the verbs below.

collect   draw   hang out   make   text   use

1 My worst subject at school is art because I really can't
_____ .

2 All of my friends _____ social media several
times a day.

3 I usually _____ people instead of calling
them because it's far more convenient.

4 My uncle used to _____ stamps. He's got
hundreds of them!

5 Are you doing anything special tonight, or are you just
going to _____ with your friends?

6 Hannah is very good at sewing, so she is able to
_____ her own clothes.

Mark: ____ / 6

2 Read the definitions and write the sports and activities.

1 an activity where people sleep outside in tents
_____

2 an activity where people practise their acting skills
_____

3 a sport or activity where people ride a bike
_____

4 an activity where people dance with a partner using steps
and movements _____

5 a sport or activity where people do physical
exercise indoors, sometimes using bars or ropes
_____

6 a sport where two teams hit a ball over a high net with
their hands _____

7 an activity for people who love spending money
_____

8 an activity where people practise their skill with a camera
_____

Mark: ____ / 8

**3 Complete the sentences with the correct form of *play*,
do, or *go*.**

1 If it rains when we're on holiday, we usually stay in and
_____ board games.

2 Do you know anyone who _____ martial arts?

3 I _____ horse riding once when I was little and
I hated it!

4 My brother is quite fit. He _____ running every
morning before school.

5 Becky isn't at home right now because she
_____ basketball.

6 If you want to build up your muscles, you have to
_____ weights.

Mark: ____ / 6

Word Skills

4 Complete the sentences with compound nouns.

1 Do you have to be a member of the club to play on their
golf _____ ?

2 The new world champion ran around the athletics
_____ as the crowd stood up and cheered.

3 The main _____ to the stadium is closed to
traffic on the days when there's a match.

4 Last Saturday, we played a few games at the bowling
_____ before going out for dinner.

5 We don't often go skiing as the nearest mountain
_____ is over 300 km away.

6 They're building a new ice _____ , so we'll
be able to go skating in the future.

7 The match has been cancelled because the football
_____ is flooded.

Mark: ____ / 7

**5 Match the words in A and B to form compound adjectives.
Then complete the sentences.**

A air   open   six   solar   sound   well

B air   conditioned   equipped   heated   lane   proof

1 On Friday mornings, there's an _____
market in the square, where you can buy fresh fruit and
vegetables.

2 It was a relief to enter the _____ building
after walking around in the heat outside.

3 There's always a lot of traffic on the _____
motorway leading to the city centre.

4 The band are looking for a _____ room
where they can practise without disturbing anyone.

5 The hotel has a _____ gym with a wide
range of different machines.

6 The water in their _____ swimming pool
never goes below a certain temperature.

Mark: ____ / 6

6 Replace the underlined words with the words below.

agree   choice   like   overall   prefer to   settled

1 I think karting is a better <u>option</u> because it looks more fun.
_____

2 <u>In general</u>, the first activity would be better.
_____

3 I <u>quite fancy</u> the first activity. _____

4 We need to <u>make a decision together</u>. _____

5 That's <u>decided</u> then. _____

6 I'd <u>rather</u> go climbing than kayaking. _____

Mark: ____ / 6

Review Unit 2

Grammar

7 Complete the text with the correct past simple or present perfect form of the verbs in brackets.

> Twenty-three-year-old Sam Willoughby is a world champion BMX rider. He ¹_____ (get) his first bike when he was six, and since then he ²_____ (take) part in numerous competitions, including the 2012 London Olympics where he ³_____ (win) a silver medal. Although Sam is Australian, he ⁴_____ (not live) in the country of his birth since he ⁵_____ (leave) for the USA at the age of sixteen. During his first years in California, he ⁶_____ (not have) any money, but since then, his prize money ⁷_____ (make) him wealthy. Sam currently lives in San Diego, and he has an American girlfriend, Alise Post. Alise, who ⁸_____ (know) Sam for several years, is also a BMX champion.

Mark: ___ / 8

8 Complete the dialogues with the present perfect continuous form of the verbs in brackets.

Mark How long ¹_____ (your sister / play) the drums?
Holly For about two years.
Mark Does she practise every day?
Holly No, she ²_____ (not practise) recently. She ³_____ (study) for her exams.

Sarah Why are you so tired?
Paul I ⁴_____ (not sleep) well. I ⁵_____ (wake up) very early, and then I can't get back to sleep again.
Sarah Why do you think that is? ⁶_____ _____ (you / work) too much?
Paul Yes, I suppose that might be it.

Mark: ___ / 6

9 Complete the sentences with the correct present perfect simple or continuous form of the verbs in brackets.

1 We _____ (walk) for ages. I think we're lost.
2 Zach will have to walk to school because he _____ (miss) the bus.
3 Sorry I'm late. _____ (you / wait) long?
4 I _____ (go) to Paris twice, but I wouldn't mind going again.
5 She's hot because she _____ (play) tennis all afternoon.
6 You _____ (not have) that phone for long. Why do you want a new one?

Mark: ___ / 6

Use of English

10 Circle the sentence (a–c) that means the same as the first sentence.

1 It's five years since I went skateboarding.
   a I haven't been skateboarding for five years.
   b I learned to skateboard five years ago.
   c I've been a skateboarder since I was five.
2 A friend has just texted me.
   a I'm waiting for a text message from my friend.
   b I got a text message yesterday.
   c I got a text message a short time ago.
3 She's more relaxed because she's been on holiday.
   a She's away on holiday at the moment.
   b She's just got back from her holiday.
   c She went on holiday months ago.
4 I've been doing my homework in my room.
   a I've already finished my homework.
   b I haven't finished my homework yet.
   c I finished my homework hours ago.
5 Oliver has been collecting coins for ten years.
   a He doesn't collect coins any more.
   b He started collecting coins when he was ten.
   c He's still collecting coins.
6 My parents have gone to work.
   a They aren't at home right now.
   b They've been at home for ages.
   c They've just arrived home.

Mark: ___ / 6

Total: ___ / 65

I can ...

Read the statements. Think about your progress and tick one of the boxes.

★ = I need more practice.   ★★★ = No problem!

★★ = I sometimes find this difficult.

	★	★★	★★★
I can talk about likes and dislikes and leisure activities.			
I can use the past simple and present perfect tenses correctly.			
I can identify the context of a dialogue.			
I can use the present perfect simple and continuous correctly.			
I can use compounds correctly.			
I can understand a text about a sports charity.			
I can discuss ideas for a day out and justify my opinions.			
I can write a blog post expressing an opinion.			

Exam Skills Trainer

Reading

1 Read the Strategy. Then read the extract below and try to work out the meaning of any unknown words. Then circle the correct answer (A–D).

It is clear that interest in hobbies is changeable, but a few hobbies have stood the test of time. A conspicuous example of this is collecting. Anything is collectible if someone decides to collect it. And it is a curious fact that even objects with little intrinsic value can become exorbitantly priced if enough people demonstrate a desire for them.

What fact about collecting does the author point out?

A Very valuable objects are the most popular.

B All collectibles are extremely expensive.

C Objects of little value can become very expensive.

D Certain types of objects are popular collectibles.

2 Read three texts. Circle the correct answer (A–D).

For some reason, I was never thrilled by the hobbies my family and friends attempted to interest me in. When I was younger, my mum and sisters tried to get me into scrapbooking, but I failed to see the point. My friends' passion for skateboarding and martial arts like karate didn't catch my interest either. My dad tried to get me involved in his hobby, model planes, but I didn't have the patience for it. Then my mum and I started chatting with a neighbour who grew rare plants. One tour of her greenhouse, and I was hooked. Of course my friends were very surprised – and still are – but I am sure that plants will be a lifelong passion.

1 The writer suggests that

A his friends don't understand his hobby.

B he and his mother share the same interests.

C he used to be interested in skateboarding.

D he is keen on making things at home.

Hobby-related holidays are on the way to becoming one of the most lucrative forms of tourism, and younger people are definitely joining in. Of course, sports-related camps have been a huge part of tourism for ages, but what if you're someone with little interest in tennis or basketball? A good option for you might be a two-week photography tour – with stunning scenery, ancient buildings and sometimes even underwater photography. Alternatively, if you are interested in nature, you can spend two weeks in an exotic location helping to identify rare plants and animals – while soaking up some sun and meeting like-minded people.

2 What does the writer say about hobby-related holidays?

A They have existed for a long time.

B They are mainly sports-related.

C They are usually for young people.

D They are popular and varied.

MAPPLETON SCHOOL HOBBY DAY

Think you're too busy studying to make time for a hobby? Haven't found a hobby that interests you, but want to explore some possibilities?

Then come to Mappleton School's annual Hobby Day! Students and teachers will give presentations and lead hands-on workshops. Everything from collecting and crafting to photography and landscape painting will be covered. Come with an open mind, and there's a good chance you'll find an interest to last a lifetime! Saturday, 3 March from 10 a.m. to 5 p.m.

3 The purpose of the text is to

A help people find time for a hobby.

B encourage people to participate in an event.

C list hobbies that students might enjoy.

D remind people why it's good to have hobbies.

Listening

3 Read the Strategy. Then underline the key words in statements 1–3.

1 Jim's grandparents were ambitious for their children. ☐
2 Jim's grandparents both attended university. ☐
3 Jim's mother disappointed her parents. ☐

4 Read the extract from a recording. Are the statements in exercise 3 true (T) or false (F)?

🎧 **Jim** My mum's parents wanted a different life for their children. My grandparents didn't finish school, but they worked very hard so my mum could go to university. I'm not sure my mum really *wanted* to be a lawyer, but she knew it would thrill her parents, so she just got on with it.

5 🎧 **1.12** Listen to two young people talking about their family history. You will hear the recording twice. Are the statements true (T) or false (F)?

1 Lila has no memory of moving to the UK. ☐
2 Lila's mother made the decision to move to the UK. ☐
3 Most of Tim's family came to the UK from Norway. ☐
4 Tim's father grew up in the countryside. ☐
5 Tim admires his father's achievements. ☐

Exam Skills Trainer

Use of English

6 Read the Strategy. Complete the sentences with words from the pairs below.

didn't / don't   had / have   is / was   used / want

1 a Jim _____ disappointed. I could see.
  b Jim _____ disappointed. I can see.

2 a _____ you finished or are you still eating?
  b _____ you finished or were you still eating?

3 a Can you explain again? I _____ understand.
  b I felt very confused. I _____ understand.

4 a I _____ to live by the sea. I'd like the fresh air.
  b I _____ to live by the sea. I swam every day.

7 Complete the text with the words below. There are three extra words.

are   does   doesn't   don't   goes   going   had   have
is   isn't   used   was   when

Eleven-year-old Isabella Goudros and eighteen-year-old Boady Santavy ¹_____ two top-class weightlifters from Canada. They ²_____ both been weightlifting since they were young.

Isabella (who prefers to be called Izzy) started weightlifting when she ³_____ eight years old. At first, she practised lifting objects around the house. Now, she can lift an amazing 42 kg over her head. As well as weightlifting, Izzy swims and ⁴_____ ballet. She's tall and slim, and she ⁵_____ look like most people's idea of a weightlifter. 'People ⁶_____ understand,' says her coach. 'They think you need to be strong, but in fact that ⁷_____ so important. It's all about lifting the weights in the right way.'

On 16 May 2015, Boady competed at the Canadian weightlifting championships, and won a place at the 2015 Pan American Games in Toronto. He was wearing red trainers and a blue-and-white weightlifting suit. A friend of his father, Dalas, ⁸_____ given him the suit. Dalas ⁹_____ to be a weightlifter, and so did his grandfather, Bob. Bob and Dalas both took part in the Pan American Games when they were younger, and they have plenty of advice for Boady. 'There are ¹⁰_____ to be thousands of people watching you. Just keep cool and focus on the weights.'

Speaking

8 Read the Strategy. Then think of three words to describe each of the items in the list below.

People	Places
• age	• age
• build and height	• furniture
• feelings	• lighting
• general impression	• general impression

9 Photos A and B show people eating out. Compare and contrast them. Include the following points:

* your general impression of each place
* what the people are doing now
* what they have been doing before

10 You and your partner want to eat lunch out. Discuss the pros and cons of the two places (A and B) and come to an agreement.

Writing

11 Read the Strategy. Then complete the closing sentences with the words below.

all   hope   touch

1 That's _____ for now.
2 I _____ to hear from you soon!
3 I'll be in _____ again soon.

12 Read the task below and write the message.

Hi, how are you? I've been working hard for my exams. Hey, guess what? I'm coming over for the first week of next month! I'd really like to meet up with you. Are you free?

Write a message in reply.
* Tell your friend what you've been doing recently.
* Thank your friend for his / her invitation.
* Find out exactly where your friend is going to be.
* Explain why it will be difficult to meet up.
* Give your friend some advice about things to do in your country.

3 The human body

A Parts of the body

I can identify parts of the body and talk about injuries.

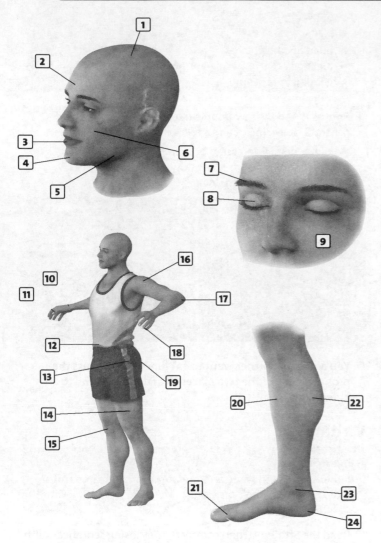

1 Complete the labels.

1 s_____	9 s_____	17 e_____
2 f_____	10 w_____	18 n_____
3 l_____	11 t_____	19 b_____
4 c_____	12 w_____	20 s_____
5 j_____	13 h_____	21 t_____
6 c_____	14 t_____	22 c_____
7 e_____	15 k_____	23 a_____
8 e_____	16 s_____	24 h_____

2 Complete the accidents and injuries with the verbs below.

bang   break   bruise   burn   cut
have   have   sprain   twist

1 _____ your ankle	6 _____ a black eye
2 _____ your wrist	7 _____ yourself
3 _____ a bone	8 _____ your head
4 _____ yourself	9 _____ yourself
5 _____ a bad nosebleed	

3 Match the words below with the definitions.

blood   brain   heart   intestine   kidneys   lungs
muscle   ribs   skull   spine   stomach   throat

1 You use it to think. _____
2 It allows you to move a part of your body. _____
3 It's made of bone and it runs down your back. _____
4 The red liquid in your body. _____
5 It's a bone that surrounds your brain. _____
6 The part of the neck where food and air go. _____
7 It's in your chest and it pumps blood around your body. _____
8 When you eat, the food goes down your throat to this place. _____
9 They're in your chest. You use them to breathe. _____
10 They are bones that go round your chest and protect your heart and lungs. _____
11 The long tube below your stomach that digests food and gets rid of waste. _____
12 They clean your blood. _____

4 🎧 **1.13 Listen to three dialogues. What problem does each person have? Choose from the illnesses and injuries in exercise 2.**

The patient has:

1 _____ .
2 _____ .
3 _____ .

5 Complete the treatments with *a, e, i, o* and *y*.

1 __nt__b__ __t__cs   ☐
2 b__nd__g__   ☐
3 cr__ __m   ☐
4 dr__ss__ng   ☐
5 m__d__c__n__   ☐
6 p__ __nk__ll__rs   ☐
7 X-r__ __   ☐

6 🎧 **1.13 Listen again to the dialogues. Which treatment or treatments in exercise 5 does the doctor give each patient? Write 1, 2 or 3 in the correct boxes.**

Speculating and predicting

I can speculate and make predictions about the future.

1 Look at the table. Then write sentences using the prompts.

100%	90%	70%	40%	10%	0%
will definitely	will probably	could / may / might	may not / might not	probably won't	definitely won't

1 it / rain / tomorrow (70%)
It might rain tomorrow.

2 I / go to bed late tonight (0%)
_____

3 Tom / pass all his exams (100%)
_____

4 Lisa / go to the doctor's tomorrow (70%)
_____

5 I / get the answer right (40%)
_____

6 Fred / see his girlfriend this weekend (90%)
_____

7 Jade / play computer games this evening (10%)
_____

2 USE OF ENGLISH Rewrite the sentence so that it has a similar meaning using the words in brackets.

1 I doubt scientists will find a cure for cancer in the near future. (probably)
_____
_____

2 I'm certain that doctors won't find a cure for the common cold. (definitely)
_____
_____

3 It's possible that millions of people will get ill from the flu virus this winter. (may)
_____
_____

4 I'm sure bio-printing of organs will become a reality. (definitely)
_____
_____

5 I'm fairly sure people will be healthier in the future. (probably)
_____
_____

6 It's possible that antibiotics won't be effective in the future. (might)
_____
_____

3 Match 1–6 with a–f to make predictions.

1 If you touch that hot saucepan, ☐
2 If you take painkillers, ☐
3 If you twist your ankle, ☐
4 If you break your arm, ☐
5 If you aren't careful with that knife, ☐
6 If you have a bad nosebleed, ☐

a you won't be able to walk.
b you'll have to go to hospital.
c you might cut yourself.
d you'll burn yourself.
e you could lose a lot of blood.
f your headache will disappear.

4 Complete the first conditional sentences with the verbs below. Use the present simple form and *will / won't* + base form.

be   be   not be able to   cut down   die out   find
get   get rid of   live   protect   rise   not use

1 If scientists _____ cures for most diseases, people _____ much longer.

2 If the climate _____ warmer, sea levels _____ .

3 Many endangered species _____ if we don't _____ them.

4 We _____ stop climate change if we _____ less fossil fuels.

5 If we _____ the rainforests, there _____ more carbon dioxide in the atmosphere.

6 If we _____ nuclear weapons, I think the world _____ a much safer place.

5 Some of the sentences are incorrect. Rewrite them correctly. Tick the correct sentences.

1 If you go to the cinema, I might to go too. ☐
_____

2 The weather could not be very good tomorrow. ☐
_____

3 I'll probably get up early tomorrow. ☐
_____

4 Sam won't probably be at home this evening. ☐
_____

5 You could be right. ☐
_____

6 I'll go to the concert if the tickets will be cheap. ☐
_____

3C

Listening
The body's limits
I can listen for specific information.

Listening Strategy

Some listening tasks may involve listening out for numbers, dates and measurements. Make sure you know how to pronounce these so that you can identify the information when you hear it.

1 🎧 **1.14** Read the Listening Strategy. Then listen and circle the number or measurement you hear.

1	a 115,000	b 100,050	c 150,000
2	a 3,700,000	b 37,000,000	c 3,000,700
3	a 2.07	b 0.27	c 2.70
4	a $3\frac{1}{10}$	b $\frac{1}{10}$	c $\frac{3}{10}$
5	a 35%	b 30.5%	c 13%
6	a 22–25	b 2–25	c 20–25
7	a 25°C	b -5°C	c -25°C
8	a 1930	b 1913	c 913

2 Read aloud all the numbers and measurements in exercise 1.

3 🎧 **1.15** Listen and complete the facts with the numbers and measurements you hear.

1 Your body makes _____ new blood cells every second.

2 There are nearly _____ kilometres of blood vessels in an average adult body.

3 Only _____ of the cells in our body are human; the other _____ are bacteria.

4 Your brain is only _____ of your body's weight, but it uses _____ of the oxygen.

5 Your temperature is usually about _____ lower in the morning than in the evening.

6 Blondes have about _____ more hairs on their head than people with black hair.

7 Adult humans have _____ bones, but newborn babies have a lot more.

8 The smallest muscle in the body is inside the ear; it is only _____ millimetres long.

9 Men usually stop growing when they are _____ years old, women when they are _____ .

4 **INTERNET RESEARCH** Find two more facts about the human body to add to the facts in exercise 3.

1 _____

_____

2 _____

_____

5 🎧 **1.16** Read the three short texts below about a Swedish woman called Anna Bågenholm, who had an accident. Then listen to an interview about her and decide which is the best summary of the accident. Underline the incorrect parts of the other options.

a Anna had an accident while skiing. Nobody found her for several hours and when they did, they believed she was dead. But when she arrived at the hospital, she came back to life. ☐

b Anna tried to rescue a colleague who had an accident in the mountains, but fell into some freezing water. She only survived because a helicopter took her to hospital. ☐

c Anna had an accident while skiing. She became so cold that her breathing and heartbeat stopped for hours, but she made a full recovery. ☐

6 🎧 **1.16** Listen again. Are the sentences true (T) or false (F)? Correct the false sentences.

1 About a third of people whose body temperature drops to below 28°C do not survive. ☐

_____

2 Anna's colleagues called for help seven minutes after the accident. ☐

_____

3 The first rescue team cut a hole in the ice and the second team pulled her out. ☐

_____

4 Anna's body temperature was 30.7°C when she arrived at the hospital. ☐

_____

5 Her heart did not begin beating again until her body temperature reached 36.4°C. ☐

_____

Future continuous and future perfect
I can talk about events in the future and when they will happen.

1 Make predictions about your future. Use the future continuous, affirmative or negative form of the verbs in brackets.

When I'm thirty years old,
1 I 'll be living (live) in New York.
2 I _____ (work) for a large company.
3 I _____ (earn) a lot of money.
4 I _____ (spend) a lot of time doing hobbies.
5 I _____ (drive) an expensive car.
6 I _____ (live) with friends.
7 I _____ (travel) a lot for work and pleasure.
8 I _____ (see) the same people I see now.

2 Look at the timeline for a new medical school. Write sentences using the affirmative or negative form of the future perfect and the prompts below.

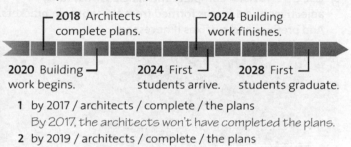

2018 Architects complete plans.

2024 Building work finishes.

2020 Building work begins.

2024 First students arrive.

2028 First students graduate.

1 by 2017 / architects / complete / the plans
  By 2017, the architects won't have completed the plans.
2 by 2019 / architects / complete / the plans
  _____
3 by 2019 / building work / begin
  _____
4 by 2023 / building work / finish
  _____
5 by 2025 / the first students / arrive
  _____
6 by 2027 / the first students / graduate
  _____
7 by 2029 / the first students / graduate
  _____

3 Complete the text with the future continuous or future perfect form of the verbs in brackets.

According to researcher Cadell Last from the Global Brain Institute, a completely new type of human [1]_____ (evolve) by 2050. We [2]_____ (live) much longer on average – perhaps to the age of 120. And we [3]_____ (enjoy) our old age much more because even when we are 90 or 100, we [4]_____ (lead) active lives. Mr Last believes that, by the middle of this century, scientists [5]_____ (invent) robots that can do most tasks, so humans [6]_____ (not do) boring housework or repetitive jobs. Instead, they [7]_____ (spend) more time living in virtual reality. But not everybody agrees with Mr Last's vision. Some scientists think that even by the end of the century, humans [8]_____ (not change) very much.

4 Complete the future time phrases with the words below.

at   by   from   in   into   ~~within~~

1 within 50 years
2 about 100 years _____ now
3 _____ some point in the future
4 _____ a million years' time
5 _____ the end of the century / millennium
6 a few thousand years _____ the future

5 Write your own predictions for the future using the prompts below. Use the future continuous or future perfect form and time phrases from exercise 4.

1 humans / live on Mars
  _____
  _____
2 scientists / accidentally create a new disease
  _____
  _____
3 all wars / end
  _____
  _____
4 robots / do most jobs
  _____
  _____
5 many people / have holidays in space
  _____
  _____

Word families

I can recognise different words formed from the same base.

1 Complete the related adjectives and nouns.

	Noun	Adjective
1	a_ _ _ _ _	angry
2	anxiety	a_ _ _ _ _ _ _
3	depression	d_ _ _ _ _ _ _ _ _ _
4	envy	e_ _ _ _ _ _ _
5	fear	af_ _ _ _ _
6	h_ _ _ _ _ _ _ _ _	happy
7	pride	p_ _ _ _ _
8	s_ _ _ _ _ _ _	sad
9	shame	a_ _ _ _ _ _ _
10	s_ _ _ _ _ _ _ _	surprised

2 Complete the sentences with adverbs formed from the nouns in brackets.

1 Angrily, (anger) he threw his bag onto the floor.
2 'It's broken,' she said _____ (sadness).
3 _____ (happiness), everyone passed the exam.
4 We looked _____ (anxiety) at the screen.
5 He looked _____ (surprise) calm as the exam began.
6 When she'd finished the painting, she _____ (pride) showed it to her friends.
7 I left my bag in the café. _____ (hope), it's still there!
8 The police officer looked _____ (suspicion) at the men on the street corner.
9 We stood outside the restaurant and stared _____ (hunger) at the menu in the window.

3 Complete the adjectives that are formed from the nouns below.

~~annoy~~ bore care disgust excite
help hope pain power surprise

A Form adjective with -ed or -ing.

annoyed   annoying

_____   _____
_____   _____
_____   _____
_____   _____

B Form adjective with -ful or -less.

_____   _____
_____   _____
_____   _____

4 Complete the sentences with adjectives formed from the words in brackets.

1 The leg injury was really _____ (pain) – in fact, I was _____ (surprise) it wasn't broken.
2 The shop assistant was very _____ (help) and gave me a refund.
3 I'm _____ (annoy) with my sister because she broke my sunglasses. She's so _____ (care)!
4 This TV has got really _____ (power) speakers, so action films are very loud and _____ (excite).
5 I enjoyed the play, but some parts of it were _____ (bore).
6 I'll never get these trainers clean. It's _____ (hope)! They're _____ (disgust)!

5 USE OF ENGLISH Complete the article with nouns, adjectives and adverbs formed from the words in brackets. Add prefixes and suffixes if necessary.

Everybody knows that smiling is a sign of [1]_____ (happy) and that we frown when we are feeling [2]_____ (happy). Our feelings affect our face. But scientists now believe that our face can also affect our feelings. In other words, smiling can actually help to create a feeling of [3]_____ (content). And one of the best ways to prevent [4]_____ (anxious) is to control your facial expression. In one study, volunteers looked at very unpleasant pictures. Some of the volunteers held a pen in their mouth so their face could not move easily. Those volunteers did not feel as [5]_____ (disgust) by the pictures as the others. Researchers also looked at women who were unable to frown because of botox injections. [6]_____ (surprise), these women were less likely to suffer from [7]_____ (depressed), even though they did not feel particularly [8]_____ (happiness) about the change in their appearance.

Revision: Student's Book page 36

1 Complete the sentences with the words below.
Use the same word in each pair of sentences.

exercise   hard   level   light
record   rest   show   work

1 a Usain Bolt set a new world _____ at the Olympic Games.
  b You can _____ a message for someone to listen to later.

2 a Look at _____ 3 on page 78.
  b You need to _____ to stay fit.

3 a This MP3 player doesn't _____ . It's broken.
  b Does your mum _____ at the hospital?

4 a There's a great quiz _____ on TV tonight.
  b Can you _____ me the way to the library?

5 a I'm exhausted. I need a _____ !
  b How will you spend the _____ of the day?

6 a I couldn't sleep because my bed was too _____ .
  b If I think _____ , I'm sure I'll work out the answer.

7 a It's getting dark. Switch on the _____ .
  b This suitcase is quite _____ – only 6 kg.

8 a There is a worryingly high _____ of CO_2 in the atmosphere.
  b The shelf isn't _____ so the books might fall off.

2 Read the text. Does the research support the theory that students perform better if school starts later?

Reading Strategy

When matching questions with texts, follow these steps.

1 Read the text to get a general idea of the meaning.
2 Read the task's lead-in line very carefully. (*In which paragraph* ...). Then read all the options carefully.
3 Read the paragraphs of the text carefully one by one and match them to the correct option.
4 If you can't find the answer, leave it for now and come back to it later when you have fewer options left.

Read the Reading Strategy. Then match paragraphs A–C with questions 1–4 below. One paragraph matches two questions.

In which paragraph does the author ...

1 suggest that students might be safer if the school start time were changed? ☐
2 refer to evidence that shows that adults' body clocks are different from those of teenagers? ☐
3 quote the results of a study that confirms the conclusions of British scientists? ☐
4 mention some practical problems that might result from a change in the start time? ☐

What time should school start?

A The debate in the USA about whether to start school later has been running for many years. Ask any American teenager arriving at school at 7.30 a.m. and they will tell you that it's difficult to memorise chemical formulae or lists of vocabulary so early in the morning. Is it just laziness, or is there a biological reason for this? Studies by scientists in the UK show that teenagers naturally want to go to bed about two hours later than adults and also get up later. This trend begins at about the age of thirteen and continues right through the teenage years. The scientists conclude that students inevitably feel tired in the morning and will therefore perform worse at school before lunch.

B Schools in some US states have tested this theory, and the findings back up the science. By delaying the start of school by just one hour, academic achievement has risen, absenteeism has declined and cases of depression among teenagers have also fallen. One study that involved 9,000 students revealed that grades in maths, English and science all rose when school began at 8.35 a.m. or later. Studies in other countries such as Brazil, Italy and Israel also show that later start times improve learning.

C However, not everyone advocates changing the school timetable. They claim that it would cause a huge amount of disruption. Others are opposed to the change because students won't have time for after-school activities or part-time jobs. However, one benefit of a later start time may yet convince the doubters. A study in Wyoming showed that car crashes among 16–18-year-olds fell by 70% after the start time was changed from 7.35 a.m. to 8.55 a.m. More studies need to be carried out before a definite link can be made between the number of accidents and the school start times, but it is undeniable that it is less safe to drive when you feel sleepy.

Photo description

I can describe photos and answer questions.

1 Circle the correct words. If both are correct, circle both. Then find the people in the two photos on this page.

1 The man **in / wearing** a baseball cap ...
2 The two women **in / with** ponytails ...
3 The girl **who is / with** sitting on the ground ...
4 The woman **in / with** long trousers ...
5 The man **in / with** his arms folded ...
6 The woman **wearing / with** a dress ...

2 Complete the sentences about photo A with the phrases below.

a sort of   I'd say   it looks like some kind of   I would say   most likely   or maybe   something like that

1 They're on a beach, _____ .
2 They're _____ in their twenties.
3 _____ the people in the background are a mix of ages.
4 _____ fitness competition.
5 There's _____ mat on the ground.
6 The bald man is doing push-ups or _____ .
7 The man with the cap is the judge _____ he's just a friend.

Speaking Strategy

Try to give your photo description a simple structure:
1) say what the photo shows in general. If you are unsure, use phrases like 'It looks to me as if ... ', or 'The photo appears to show ... '; 2) talk about some of the interesting details in the photo; 3) add a personal opinion or reaction.

3 Read the Speaking Strategy. Then look at photo B and prepare your description. Use the questions to help you.

1 Where are the women? What are they doing? What is unusual about the situation?

_____
_____

2 Is one of them the leader? Why do you think so?

_____
_____

4 Read the examiner's questions. Write notes for your answers.

1 Do you think the women are enjoying themselves? Why? / Why not?
2 What are the advantages and disadvantages of exercising outdoors rather than indoors?
3 Have you been in a similar situation when you enjoyed spending a lot of time outdoors? What were you doing?

1 _____
_____
2 _____
_____
3 _____
_____

5 Now do the speaking task. Use your notes from exercises 3 and 4.

3H

Writing

An opinion essay
I can write an opinion essay.

Preparation

1 Read the task and the essay. In which paragraph (A–D) does the writer ...

1 give his opinion? ☐   3 make his proposals? ☐
2 introduce the topic? ☐   4 sum up the essay? ☐

Some people think that the school curriculum should include subjects such as 'leading a healthy lifestyle'. Write an essay in which you give your own opinion on this issue and propose ways in which this subject might be taught in schools.

A If we can believe recent reports in the press, many teenagers are overweight and unfit. <u>Some people argue that</u> teaching children at school about a healthy lifestyle would help to solve this problem.

B <u>In my view</u>, it would be very sensible to teach students how to lead a healthy lifestyle. Health problems later in life often start because people get into bad habits during their teenage years. <u>It is sometimes said that</u> this is the responsibility of the parents and not the school. But <u>as I see it</u>, everyone in society would benefit from this.

C <u>In order to tackle this problem</u>, time should be set aside in the school timetable to teach children about the benefits of eating healthily and getting lots of exercise. <u>Moreover</u>, doctors could also play a part by coming into school and talking to students. <u>I suggest that</u> one or two hours a week should be spent on this topic.

D <u>To sum up</u>, I agree with those people who believe that healthy living should be taught in schools. <u>It seems to me that</u> the students themselves and society in general would benefit from this proposal.

2 Complete the gaps with the underlined phrases from the essay.

1 Introducing your opinions
in my opinion, ¹_____
²_____ ³_____

2 Introducing other people's opinions
It is a widely held view that   Most people agree that
It is a common belief that   ⁴_____
⁵_____

3 Making an additional point
What is more,   Not only that, but   Furthermore,
⁶_____

4 Introducing proposals and solutions
One solution might be to   What I propose is that
I would strongly recommend that   It is vital that
⁷_____ ⁸_____

5 Concluding
In conclusion,   To conclude,   ⁹_____

Writing Guide

Many people think that teenagers spend too much time using electronic gadgets. Write an essay in which you give your own view of the problem and propose ways of solving it.

Writing Strategy
1 Divide your essay into an introduction, main body and conclusion.
2 If the task has more than one element, deal with them in different paragraphs within the main body.
3 Use formal language.
4 Support opinions with evidence or examples.

3 Read the task and the Writing Strategy above. In which paragraph (A–D) of your essay will you ...

1 describe the problem? ☐
2 introduce the topic: mention the problem (using different words from the task) and say that you will propose solutions? ☐
3 sum up by saying that you are confident that your proposed solutions will help to solve the problem? ☐
4 propose solutions? ☐

4 Make notes about the headings below.

My view of the problem and its causes:_____
_____
_____
_____
_____

Solutions to the problem: _____
_____
_____
_____
_____

5 Write your essay. Follow the paragraph plan in exercise 3, and use your notes from exercise 4. Include some phrases from exercise 2.

CHECK YOUR WORK
Have you ...
☐ followed all the advice in the Writing Strategy?
☐ included phrases from exercise 2?
☐ checked your spelling and grammar?

3 Review Unit 3

Vocabulary

1 Match the words with the parts of the body where they are found.

1 brain ☐
2 calf ☐
3 cheek ☐
4 elbow ☐
5 heart ☐
6 heel ☐
7 throat ☐
8 thumb ☐

a arm
b chest
c face
d foot
e hand
f head
g leg
h neck

Mark: ☐ / 8

2 Complete the sentences with the treatments below.

antibiotics bandage cream dressing painkillers X-ray

Doctors often ...

1 put a _____ around your ankle if you sprain it.
2 prescribe _____ to cure an infection.
3 send you for an _____ when they need to see inside your body.
4 tell you to cover a cut with a _____ to protect it.
5 give you _____ if a part of your body is hurting.
6 recommend a _____ if you have a skin allergy.

Mark: ☐ / 6

3 Complete the sentences with the past simple form of the verbs below.

bang break bruise burn cut have sprain

1 My little sister _____ a bone in her leg when she fell off the wall.
2 Josh _____ a bad nosebleed after walking into a lamp post.
3 She _____ their heads on the shelf when she got up from the table.
4 He _____ himself when he was putting a pizza in the oven.
5 I _____ myself badly while I was opening a tin.
6 One of the players _____ his wrist as he was catching the ball.
7 You _____ yourself badly when you fell down the stairs.

Mark: ☐ / 7

Word Skills

4 Complete the sentences with the correct word formed from the words in brackets.

1 The captain of the team _____ lifted the trophy into the air. (pride)
2 All Ryan's friends are _____ of his new laptop. (envy)
3 He looked away _____ when she told him that his grandfather was very ill. (happy)
4 She's making a good recovery. The doctors are _____ that her knee will heal quickly. (hope)
5 It isn't _____ you have a cold. You haven't been looking after yourself recently. (surprise)
6 It was clear that something bad had happened because of the _____ in her eyes. (sad)
7 He's obviously _____ of his behaviour because he refuses to apologise. (shame)
8 Scarlett finds it hard to control her _____ when somebody offends her. (angry)

Mark: ☐ / 8

5 Complete the sentences with a suitable word. Sometimes more than one answer may be possible.

1 The girl _____ the red leggings is throwing a ball.
2 It looks _____ a race or something like that.
3 I think the man _____ the moustache is the instructor.
4 I'd _____ that all the competitors are quite young.
5 The boy _____ is on the ground looks exhausted.
6 It seems to be a competition of some _____ .

Mark: ☐ / 6

Grammar

6 Complete the sentences with will / may / might / could (not) and the verbs below. Sometimes more than one answer may be possible.

be close go out hurt like win

1 The doctor isn't completely sure, but he thinks that my leg _____ broken.
2 I don't think our team _____ today because our best player is injured.
3 I'm not sure if you should watch this horror film. You _____ it.
4 He's quite anxious about his operation, although the doctor has said it _____ at all.
5 I haven't decided yet, but I _____ tonight. I've got a lot of homework.
6 There are rumours that they _____ our local hospital. Very few people use it.

Mark: ☐ / 6

3 Review Unit 3

7 Complete the dialogues with the correct form of the verbs in brackets. Use the first conditional.

1. A What _____ (you / do) if somebody asks about your black eye?
   B I _____ (tell) them exactly what happened!
2. A Will you stop playing if your ankle _____ (start) to hurt?
   B Yes. The coach _____ (not let) me play if I'm injured.
3. A What will happen if I _____ (not take) the medicine?
   B Your cough _____ (get) worse.
4. A How will we get to the hospital if the bus _____ (not come)?
   B We _____ (walk). It isn't very far.
5. A _____ (the doctor / give) you antibiotics if you ask for them?
   B No, he'll only prescribe them if they _____ (be) really necessary.

Mark: _____ / 10

8 Complete the text with the future continuous or future perfect form of the verbs in brackets.

This is my final year at school. Six months from now, I ¹_____ (study) at university. It's a three-year course, so I ²_____ (finish) it by the time I'm 22. I'd love a career in nursing, but I want to do some voluntary work before I settle down. In four years' time, perhaps I ³_____ (help) the victims of a natural disaster somewhere. By the time I'm 26, I ⁴_____ (spend) enough time abroad, and I ⁵_____ (think) about coming home. In ten years' time, I hope I ⁶_____ (find) a good job in a hospital, where I ⁷_____ (work) with young children. Perhaps I ⁸_____ (start) a family by then, and I'll have my own baby to look after!

Mark: _____ / 8

Use of English

9 Circle the correct answers to complete the sentences.

1. You _____ not need antibiotics.
   a could   b have   c probably   d might
2. They'll _____ taken the bandages off her leg by the end of next week.
   a maybe   b have   c be   d likely
3. One hundred years from now computers _____ doing a lot of things that doctors do now.
   a will   b will be   c will probably   d are
4. You'll burn your hand if you _____ that saucepan.
   a touching   b touch   c might touch   d 'll touch
5. The doctors X-rayed his _____ after he hit his head in the accident.
   a lung   b rib   c skull   d shin
6. Will humans exist _____ a million years' time?
   a in   b within   c at   d until

Mark: _____ / 6

Total: _____ / 65

I can ...

Read the statements. Think about your progress and tick one of the boxes.

★ = I need more practice.

★★ = I sometimes find this difficult.

★★★ = No problem!

	★	★★	★★★
I can identify parts of the body and talk about injuries.			
I can speculate and make predictions about the future.			
I can listen for specific information.			
I can talk about events in the future and when they will happen.			
I can recognise different words formed from the same base.			
I can understand an article about teenagers and sleep.			
I can describe photos and answer questions.			
I can write an opinon essay.			

Vocabulary

A Describing houses and homes

I can describe houses and homes.

1 Complete the types of home with *a, e, i, o* and *u*.

1 m__ns__ __n
2 f__rmh__ __s__
3 v__ll__
4 m__b__l__ h__m__
5 fl__t
6 b__ng__l__w
7 h__ __ __s__b__ __ __t
8 t__rr__c__d h__ __s__
9 s__ m__ -d__t__ch__d h__ __ __s__
10 th__tch__d c__tt__g__
11 d__t__ch__d h__ __ __s__

2 Look at the picture and complete the labels.

1 f_____   10 s_____d_____
2 e_____   11 p_____
3 b_____   12 l_____
4 s_____   13 p_____
5 g_____   14 p_____
6 b_____   15 d_____
7 f_____b_____ 16 g_____
8 p_____   17 h_____
9 c_____

3 🎧 **1.17** Listen to someone describing their ideal home. Complete the description with the missing words.

My ideal home is in the city. It's a ¹_____
flat, in an ²_____, modern
building in a ³_____ .
It's ⁴_____ for shops,
restaurants and cinemas. Inside, it isn't at all
⁵_____ . In fact, it's very
⁶_____ .

4 Write a short description of your ideal home. Include the information below. Use words from exercises 1 and 2 and phrases from exercise 3 to help you.

- Where is it?
- What type of home is it?
- Rooms and other features
- Adjectives to describe it

_____
_____
_____
_____
_____
_____
_____
_____

Grammar
Comparison
I can make comparisons using a variety of structures.

1 Complete the sentences with a double comparative.

1 The weather is getting *colder and colder.* (cold)
2 This area is becoming _____ . (popular)
3 Jimmy is getting _____ . (tall)
4 Petrol was getting _____ . (expensive)
5 Maria is becoming _____ . (confident)
6 The film just got _____ . (silly)

2 Put the words in the correct order.

1 I thought / longer / The journey was / than
_____
_____

2 more spacious / The flat was / than / appeared / it
_____
_____

3 in Greece / hotter / it was / The weather here is / than
_____
_____

4 much more / it used to be / The house is / dilapidated / than
_____
_____

5 than / My grandad is / when he was a young man / shorter now
_____
_____

6 as popular as / it was / five years ago / This area isn't
_____
_____

3 Complete the sentence halves with the comparative form of the adjectives and adverbs in brackets. Then match 1–5 with a–e.

1 The _____ (long) I work, ☐
2 The _____ (spacious) the house, ☐
3 The _____ (fast) you drive, ☐
4 The _____ (carefully) you check your work, ☐
5 The _____ (long) you keep him waiting, ☐

a the _____ (expensive) it will be.
b the _____ (impatient) he'll become.
c the _____ (few) mistakes you make.
d the _____ (likely) you are to have an accident.
e the _____ (tired) I feel.

4 Write superlative sentences with the present perfect.

1 this / good / book / I / ever / read
This is the best book I've ever read.
2 this / remote / region of the UK / I / ever / visit
_____
3 those / expensive / jeans / I / ever / buy
_____
4 that / charming / cottage / I / ever / stay in
_____
5 this / lively / area of town / I / ever / live in
_____
6 that / pretty / flower bed / I / ever / see
_____

5 Complete the sentences with *less*, *the least*, *fewer*, or *the fewest*.

1 The kitchen is _____ spacious room in the house.
2 My flat is _____ conveniently located than yours.
3 This house has got _____ rooms of the three we've looked at.
4 Which costs _____ , the semi-detached house or the terraced house?
5 This is _____ popular area of the city.
6 Which room has got _____ furniture, the dining room, living room, or kitchen?
7 There are _____ flowers in the flower bed this year than last.
8 Wales is _____ remote than the north of Scotland.

6 Complete the sentences with the comparative and superlative form of the adverbs in brackets.

1 Dan drives _____ than Ed, but Sam drives _____ of all. (slow)
2 Amy works _____ than Kate, but Frances works _____ . (hard)
3 Adam speaks French _____ than Jason, but Chris speaks _____ . (fluently)
4 Jed walks _____ than Fred, but Tom walks _____ . (fast)
5 Ed writes _____ than Fran, but Susan writes _____ . (good)

Young and homeless
I can recognise paraphrases of simple verbs in a recording.

Revision: Student's Book page 43

1 Complete the paraphrases with the words below.

effort eye get give hand have
life make time touch turn word

1 to try hard
   = to _____ a big _____
2 to contact somebody
   = to _____ in _____ with somebody
3 to ignore something
   = to _____ a blind _____ to
   something
4 to talk to somebody
   = to _____ a _____ with somebody
5 to enjoy yourself a lot
   = to have the _____ of your _____
6 to help somebody
   = to _____ somebody a _____

Listening Strategy 1
When you listen to a recording, remember that many ideas
will be expressed differently in the task. For example, a
simple verb in the task may be expressed by a phrase in
the recording: *sleep well* → *get a good night's sleep.*

**2 🎧 1.18 Read Listening Strategy 1. Then listen to four
people and circle the correct summaries.**

1 For the past two weeks, speaker 1 has been ___ .
   a sleeping well
   b sleeping badly
2 He's got a new neighbour, but speaker 2 hasn't ___ .
   a seen him
   b spoken to him
3 Speaker 3's husband is in the mountains and nobody
   can ___ .
   a find him
   b phone him
4 Speaker 4 couldn't take part in the race, although he really
   ___ to be fit for it.
   a tried
   b expected

Listening Strategy 2
Pay attention to whether the language you hear is formal
or informal. This can be an important clue to the context.

**3 Read Listening Strategy 2. Match the phrases (1–6) with
similar meanings (a–f). Then circle the formal phrase in
each pair.**

1 increase sharply ☐   a gain employment
2 need help ☐   b at the moment
3 find a job ☐   c a high priority
4 currently ☐   d go up a lot
5 very important ☐   e suggest something
6 make a proposal ☐   f require assistance

**4 🎧 1.19 Listen to three recordings. Which two are formal?
Which formal phrases from exercise 3 did they include?**

Recording number ___ is formal and includes the formal
phrases:

1 _____
2 _____
3 _____

Recording number ___ is formal and includes the formal
phrases:

4 _____
5 _____
6 _____

5 🎧 1.19 Listen again and circle the correct answers.

1 In recording 1, we hear a man
   a asking for a form to complete.
   b asking for help in completing a form.
   c returning a form that he has completed.
2 In recording 2, what is the main intention of the speaker?
   a To persuade people to make donations to a charity.
   b To advise people against giving money to homeless
     people on the street.
   c To suggest ways of helping homeless people which do
     not cost money.
3 In recording 3, when the speaker took part in the Big Sleep
   Out, she
   a felt much colder than she had expected.
   b did not feel as cold as her friends.
   c did not feel as cold as she had expected.

4D Grammar
Imaginary situations
I can talk about imaginary situations and things I would like to change.

1 Complete the second conditional sentences with the correct form of the verbs below.

not believe   do   get   give   make   not spend   work

1 Your exam results would be much better if you _____ a bit harder.
2 If you moved to a new city, you_____ friends really quickly.
3 Homelessness wouldn't be such a big problem if the government_____ more to help.
4 I'd finish the housework a lot faster if you _____ me a hand with it!
5 Would she remember me if I _____ in touch after so many years?
6 You'd have more time for schoolwork if you _____ so long playing computer games.
7 If I told you the truth, you _____ me.

2 Complete the dialogue with the past simple and *would* + base form.

Tim I think we're lost. If this ¹_____ (be) the right path, we ²_____ (be) there by now.
Paul So which path should we be on?
Tim If I ³_____ (know) that, we ⁴_____ (not be) lost!
Paul If you ⁵_____ (have) your phone with you, we ⁶_____ (be able to) look at a map.
Tim We decided not to bring our phones, remember? A weekend without technology ...
Paul I know. I ⁷_____ (not be) so worried if we ⁸_____ (not be) so far from home. Next time, we should bring our phones, but only use them in an emergency.
Tim If you ⁹_____ (bring) your phone with you, you ¹⁰_____ (use) it all the time. You're addicted!

3 Rewrite the sentences. Use the second conditional.

1 Our house doesn't have a big garden, so we have to play football in the park.
If our house had a big garden, we wouldn't have to play football in the park.

2 I don't live in a detached house, so I can't play my music really loud.
_____
_____

3 We don't have a nine-bedroom mansion, so we don't invite lots of friends and family to stay.
_____
_____

4 Our flat is small, so my parents don't allow me to have a pet.
_____
_____

5 I don't close my bedroom shutters at night, so I wake up early in the morning.
_____
_____

6 They haven't got a fence. Their dog keeps running away.
_____
_____

7 They aren't interested in gardening. Their flower beds are a mess.
_____
_____

8 I share a bedroom with my brother. I can't watch TV at night.
_____
_____

9 Our house is near an airport. It's noisy in the garden.
_____
_____

4 Complete the sentences with the past simple or *would* + base form, depending on the meaning.

1 Our neighbours have still got my badminton net. I wish they _____ (give) it back!
2 I can't work with the TV so loud. I wish you _____ (turn) it down!
3 I love that new phone, but it's really expensive. If only it _____ (be) cheaper!
4 Unfortunately, I don't see my cousins very often. I wish they _____ (live) closer.
5 I want to go to bed, but our guests are still here. If only they _____ (leave)!
6 I wish it _____ (be) Friday today.
7 I really want to go skiing tomorrow. If only it _____ (snow) tonight!

4E Word Skills

do, make and take

I can use 'do', 'make' and 'take' correctly.

1 Complete the phrases with *do*, *make* and *take*.

1 _____ a look at something / a picture / a photo
2 _____ an appointment / up your mind
3 _____ yoga / karate / gymnastics / your best

2 Complete the dialogue with the correct form of *do*, *make*, or *take*.

Man   I love your house. It's really unusual.
Woman Yes, I designed it myself. You must ¹_____ a look at the basement. I'm really proud of it.
Man   Thanks. Wow! This is amazing. It's huge! Can I ²_____ a photo?
Woman Yes, of course.
Man   What are you going to use the basement for?
Woman It might be a guest room – or maybe a fitness room. I can't ³_____ up my mind. At the moment, my daughters ⁴_____ gymnastics down here. They love it!
Man   So, if you're happy to be in our magazine, I need some photos and an interview. Maybe one day next week?
Woman OK, I'll ⁵_____ my best, but I'm quite busy at the moment. Can you call my personal assistant and ⁶_____ an appointment?
Man   Yes, of course.

3 DICTIONARY WORK Read a short extract from a dictionary entry for *make*. How many example sentences does it include in total?

Answer: _____ example sentences.

> **make** /meɪk/ *verb* (pt, pp made /meɪd/)
> **1** CREATE to produce or create sth: *to make bread* ◆ *This model is **made of** steel.*
> **2** CAUSE to cause a particular effect, feeling, situation, etc.: *The film **made** me cry.* ◆ *Flying **makes** him nervous.* ◆ *I'll **make it clear** to him that we won't pay.*
> **3** FORCE to cause sb/sth to do sth: *You can't **make** her come with us if she doesn't want to.*

4 Match the examples below with the correct meaning of *make* from the dictionary entry in exercise 3: 1, 2, or 3.

1 If you're late for games, they make you run round the playing field three times. ☐
2 She never buys birthday cards; she makes them. ☐
3 At school, we're making a video about homelessness. ☐
4 I don't like theme park rides; they make me feel sick. ☐
5 It's a fascinating documentary that really makes you think. ☐
6 The robbers made the shop assistant open the till and hand over the money. ☐

5 Circle the correct verbs. Use a dictionary to help you.

1 How many goals have we scored? I **make** / **take** it six.
2 She could be a really good tennis player if she **made** / **took** it more seriously.
3 My neighbour works in London. I'm not sure what he **does** / **takes**, but it must be well paid.
4 My cousin refuses to **do** / **take** painkillers even when she's ill.
5 Don't **make** / **take** this the wrong way, but that jumper doesn't really suit you.
6 I like travelling, but flying **makes** / **takes** me anxious.
7 We only had three days in Paris, but we **did** / **made** the most of it.
8 The doctors were amazing and **did** / **took** everything they could to help.

> **VOCAB BOOST!**
> Common verbs like *do, make* and *take* often appear in everyday phrases and idioms. If you come across one, check its meaning in a dictionary and make a note of the meaning.
> it won't do any good = it won't help the situation
> it didn't make a sound = it was silent
> take it easy = relax

6 Read the *Vocab boost!* box. Then use a dictionary to complete the phrases with *do*, *make*, or *take*.

1 Can you _____ me a favour and hold my bag?
2 Try not to _____ a mess before the visitors arrive.
3 I can't understand his text – it doesn't _____ sense.
4 There's no hurry – _____ your time.
5 I don't mind you playing computer games, but you also need to _____ time for your homework.
6 Lisa looks really upset. I wish I could _____ something to help.

Alternative living

I can understand an article about alternative houses.

Revision: Student's Book page 46

1 Complete the compound nouns with the words below. Two are written as one word.

dining front housing rain rubbish
shipping sky sofa solar studio

1	_____ bed	6	_____ flat
2	_____ containers	7	_____ panels
3	_____ door	8	_____ scraper
4	_____ dump	9	_____ table
5	_____ estate	10	_____ water

2 Complete the sentences with compound nouns from exercise 1.

1 We've had _____ fitted on our roof.
2 Joe lives on the 20th floor of a _____.
3 There are about 200 homes on the _____.
4 Can you open the_____ for me?
5 Our guests slept on the _____.
6 My uncle's _____ is small, but cosy.

3 Read the texts. Look at the photo and match it with the correct text.

> **Reading Strategy**
> When you find evidence in the text that supports an answer, underline it and note which question it refers to. If you do that, you can find it again easily when you are checking all your answers at the end.

4 Read the Reading Strategy. Then match the texts (A–C) with questions 1–4 below. One text matches two questions. Underline the evidence in the text that supports your answers.

In which text does the author ...

1 mention that the house isn't built yet? ☐
2 refer to an indoor garden? ☐
3 make it clear that the house has more than one floor? ☐
4 suggest that the house will suit someone with a playful nature? ☐

Strange places to live in ...

A THE SLIDE HOUSE, JAPAN

Did you love going down the slide in the playground as a child? Perhaps you secretly wish you still could? If so, then the Slide House in Japan is the house for you!

Japanese architects have designed an unusual three-storey house with a huge slide that connects each level. This fun house has two staircases on one side going up, and the slide on the other going down, and together they form a circular route around the central area of the house.

The house is in the suburbs of Tokyo, and it functions as a real family home.

B THE SKATEBOARD HOUSE, USA

Are you a skateboarding fan? Would you like to live in a house where you could skateboard everywhere? This is exactly what a former skateboard champion wants to build in California. It will be the first house that can be entirely used for skateboarding as well as living in.

A prototype of the house is currently on display in a French museum. It has three spaces: a living area, a sleeping area and a skateboard practice area. However, you can skateboard everywhere because the floor becomes the wall and then the ceiling in a continuous curve. You can also skate on and off all the furniture!

C THE GIANT SEASHELL HOUSE, MEXICO

If you've ever wondered what it would feel like to live inside a seashell, then this house in Mexico City would be the home for you. This amazing shell-shaped house was designed and built in 2006. As strange as it looks, it's a real home built for a family. The parents were tired of having a traditional house and wanted to live in a home that was inspired by nature.

All the walls and furniture in the house are curved and all the surfaces are smooth. There are round windows and doors, coloured glass walls and even flowers growing in all the rooms.

Photo comparison and discussion

I can compare and contrast photos and discuss various options.

Compare and contrast the photos of holiday accommodation. Say which you would prefer to stay in and why.

1 **🔊 1.20** Read the task above. Then listen to a student doing the task comparing photos A and B. Which house did he choose?

Speaking Strategy
Learn phrases that create time for you to formulate opinions. They will also make you sound more fluent.

2 Read the Speaking Strategy. Then match 1–7 with a–g to make phrases for gaining time.

1 Actually, now I ☐
2 All things ☐
3 What ☐
4 Let me ☐
5 That's a good point. ☐
6 Thinking ☐
7 I suppose ☐

a What I'd say to that is ...
b else?
c considered, ...
d come to think about it, ...
e the thing is, ...
f see.
g about it, ...

3 You are going to do the task in exercise 1 about photos C and D. Make notes.

Photo C _____

_____

Photo D _____

_____

Your choice: C ☐ D ☐ Why? _____

_____

_____

4 Now do the task in exercise 1, comparing and contrasting photos C and D.

5 Read the task below. Write notes for your answers.

You are going to spend a week on holiday with friends. You can choose any of the four types of accommodation in the photos. Talk to your friend and agree on where you want to go. Discuss these points:
- location   • travel
- cost   • holiday activities

1 location _____

_____

_____

2 cost _____

_____

_____

3 travel _____

_____

_____

4 holiday activities _____

_____

_____

6 Now do the speaking task. Use your notes from exercise 5 and phrases from exercise 2.

An email
I can write an email to a friend about a new home.

Preparation

1 Read the task and the model email. In what order does Lisa cover the four points? Number them.

> You are moving in with relatives next week. Write an email to a friend. Include the following:
> - Explain the reasons for the arrangement. ☐
> - Describe your relatives' house. ☐
> - Describe the relatives. ☐
> - Ask permission to borrow something from your friend. ☐

✉ **To:** madison@email.com

Hi Madison,

I hope all is well with you. Did I tell you I'm moving house soon? We need to move out of our flat because the landlord is selling it, so we're going to live with my cousins for a few months. They don't live far away – in a small village about twenty miles from here. My cousin Joe is a really nice guy. He's the same age as me and he's got dark hair and brown eyes. My cousin Samantha looks a bit like you. She is tall, with curly hair and green eyes. She's great fun. You'd like them.

My cousins' house is quite large and includes a new extension, but it will still be a bit crowded. There are four bedrooms in the house and two in the extension, I think, but I'm going to sleep in the conservatory!

Better get back to my homework. Would it be OK if I borrowed your tennis racket this weekend? I've got one, but I can't find it. I think Mum might have already packed it!

Bye for now.

Lisa

Writing Strategy

When you write an informal email or letter:
- you should avoid formal language.
- you can use contractions (*you're, it's,* etc.).
- you sometimes omit words like *I, I'm* or *I've* at the start of a sentence (*Hope you're well, Got to go now,* etc.).

2 Read the Writing Strategy. Circle five different contractions in the model email. Then underline one sentence with a word omitted at the start.

3 Rewrite the sentences using *would rather* with the base form or past simple.

1 I want you to help me.
  I'd rather you helped me.
2 I don't want my sister to find out.
  _____
3 I want to be outside.
  _____
4 I don't want to go to bed yet.
  _____
5 I want us to spend more time together.
  _____

4 Complete the second sentence in each pair with *had better* (*not*) and the verb in brackets.

1 This milk smells bad. We had better not drink (drink) it.
2 The roads are icy. You _____ (drive) too fast.
3 This is my dad's laptop. We _____ (ask) before we use it.
4 It isn't safe to walk home at night. You _____ (get) a taxi.
5 That dog doesn't look friendly. We _____ (go) near it.
6 This is my sister's favourite chocolate. I _____ (save) some for her.
7 I haven't got any lights for my bike. I _____ (cycle) home before it gets dark.

Writing Guide

5 Read the task. Then make notes under headings 1–4 below.

> Imagine that you are moving house next week. Write an email to a friend. Include the following:
> - Describe your new home.
> - Give information about your plans for moving.
> - Describe someone you will miss after you move.
> - Ask permission to leave something at your friend's house.

1 What is your new home like?
  _____
  _____

2 What are the arrangements for moving?
  _____
  _____

3 Who will you miss?
  _____
  _____

4 What do you want to leave with your friend?
  _____
  _____

6 Now do the task. Write your email using your notes from exercise 5.

CHECK YOUR WORK
👁 **Have you ...**
- ☐ covered all four points in the task?
- ☐ used contractions and avoided formal language?
- ☐ checked your spelling and grammar?

Review Unit 4

Vocabulary

1 Match the definitions with the types of home below.

bungalow flat mansion semi-detached house
terraced house thatched cottage

1 a set of rooms usually on one floor, often in a tower block
   _____

2 a house which shares one wall with another to form a pair of houses _____

3 a house without stairs which is on one level _____

4 a small, old house with a roof made of straw
   _____

5 a house in a line of similar houses _____

6 a very large house _____

Mark: ☐ / 6

2 Complete the sentences with the words below.

attic basement conservatory drive
fence landing patio shutters

1 We often have lunch outside on the _____ when the weather is fine.

2 There's a wooden _____ around the garden to keep people out.

3 They're building a _____ onto the outside of their house.

4 His flat doesn't get a lot of light because it's in the
   _____ .

5 Go up the stairs to the _____ and the bathroom is on the left.

6 All of my old toys are up in the _____ .

7 It's dark in here because I haven't opened the
   _____ yet.

8 Our garage is full of old furniture, so we have to leave our car on the _____ .

Mark: ☐ / 8

3 Replace the underlined words with the adjectives below.

charming contemporary cosy
cramped dilapidated lively

1 We've just bought a <u>very attractive</u> old farmhouse which we're going to restore. _____

2 The living room looked extremely <u>warm and inviting</u> in the firelight. _____

3 I'm looking for a place in a <u>fun and exciting</u> part of town.
   _____

4 Nobody has lived in the family home for years, so today it looks <u>in very bad condition</u>. _____

5 Their living quarters are <u>uncomfortably small</u> because four of them are sharing the same room. _____

6 She lives in a flat in a <u>modern</u> building which is very conveniently located. _____

Mark: ☐ / 6

Word Skills

4 Complete the sentences with do, make, or take.

1 You can usually _____ one look at a house to know whether you want to live there or not.

2 You shouldn't _____ more than 120 km/h when you're driving on a motorway in Spain.

3 I can't _____ up my mind what to wear to the party tonight.

4 They're going to _____ the spare room into a nursery for their new baby.

5 We were prepared for last night's storm, so it didn't
   _____ a lot of damage.

6 I'd like to _____ French lessons, but I can't seem to find the time.

Mark: ☐ / 6

5 Complete the sentences with the correct form of the words below. The words may be used more than once.

consider feel suppose think

1 _____ about it, perhaps it isn't such a good idea.

2 I _____ the thing is whether you enjoy it or not.

3 Actually, now I come to _____ about it, that would definitely be the best option.

4 It's clearly a question which people have strong _____ about.

5 I'd have to give that some _____ .

6 All things _____ , I don't suppose it really matters.

Mark: ☐ / 6

Grammar

6 Complete the sentences with the correct form of the adjectives in brackets. It may be necessary to add an extra word to the sentence.

1 The _____ the house, the more expensive it is to heat. (large)

2 That's the _____ balcony I've ever seen. (tiny)

3 Houseboats are _____ today than they used to be. (common)

4 We'll have to look _____ if we want to find a house we can afford. (hard)

5 Our new flat has _____ rooms than our old one, so now I have to share a room with my sister. (few)

6 Your garden is _____ than ours because you haven't got as many flowers. (colourful)

7 They're worried that their cellar might flood as it's raining _____ now. (heavy)

Review Unit 4

4

8 This is the _____ room in the house because we haven't furnished it yet. (comfortable)

9 The grass on their lawn is growing _____ and _____ , but nobody seems interested in cutting it. (high)

Mark: / 9

7 Complete the dialogues with the correct form of the verbs in brackets.

1 A Where would you live if you _____ (have) the choice?
  B I _____ (buy) a villa on the coast.

2 A What would your parents do if you _____ (not clean) your room?
  B They _____ (not give) me any pocket money.

3 A How would you feel if you _____ (be) homeless?
  B I _____ (not like) it at all.

4 A If you could, _____ (you / make) any changes to your home?
  B Yes. I'd build an extension so that I _____ (can) have my own room.

5 A If your room _____ (need) painting, what colour would you choose?
  B I _____ (paint) one wall blue and the others white.

Mark: / 10

8 Complete the sentences with the correct form of the verbs in brackets.

1 I wish we _____ a swimming pool. It would be perfect in the summer. (have)

2 If only my brother _____ more in the house. Then I wouldn't have to do everything! (help)

3 If only you _____ so far away. We hardly ever see each other. (not live)

4 I wish my neighbour _____ his music so loud. I can't concentrate! (not play)

5 I wish you _____ the bathroom every time you have a shower. You make such a mess! (not flood)

6 If only I _____ older. Then I could leave home. (be)

Mark: / 6

Use of English

9 Complete the second sentence so that it has a similar meaning to the first. Use the words in brackets.

1 We haven't got enough money, so we can't buy a new house. (if)
  We _____ .

2 I didn't expect the mobile home to be so cosy. (than)
  The _____ .

3 She's stressed because she lives in the city centre. (be)
  If _____ .

4 I'm annoyed because you never make your bed. (wish)
  I _____ .

5 I've never seen such an ugly chest of drawers. (the)
  That's _____ .

6 I don't like my room. It hasn't got a desk. (only)
  If _____ .

7 The kitchen isn't as cramped as the bathroom. (less)
  The kitchen _____ .

8 There's a lift, so I don't use the stairs. (if)
  I _____ .

Mark: / 8

Total: / 65

I can ...

Read the statements. Think about your progress and tick one of the boxes.

★ = I need more practice.

★★ = I sometimes find this difficult.

★★★ = No problem!

	★	★★	★★★
I can describe houses and homes.			
I can make comparisons using a variety of structures.			
I can recognise paraphrases of simple verbs in a recording.			
I can talk about imaginary situations and things I would like to change.			
I can use 'do', 'make' and 'take' correctly.			
I can understand an article about alternative houses.			
I can compare and contrast photos and discuss various options.			
I can write an email to a friend about a new home.			

Reading

1 Read the Strategy. Then read the questions followed by the text. Which option is correct according to the text? Which options seem correct at first? Why aren't they correct?

Stephen bent down to pick up the fork, and when he stood up, he banged his head on the edge of the cupboard. It was not a light tap, but a powerful blow that nearly knocked him back down to the floor. Just managing to stay upright, he held his head with both hands and let out a shout. It wasn't pain he felt so much as surprise and, even more, anger with himself. When would he learn to be more careful?

1 The blow to Stephen's head
  A knocked him down.
  B almost made him fall down.
  C happened as a result of falling down.
  D occurred after he had fallen down.
2 What did Stephen feel as a result of the blow?
  A extreme frustration
  B extreme pain
  C no pain at all
  D embarrassment

2 Now read the extract from a story. Circle the correct answer (A–D).

The Pennine Way is a 469-kilometre walking path which runs from the Peak District in Derbyshire to just inside the Scottish border. Other trails go further, but it is known as the most challenging. This is because of the nature of the landscape, which is hilly, rocky and often very muddy. Some people see this trail as an opportunity to take a pleasant day's hike on a small section of the route, but eighteen-year-old David Lemming saw it as a challenge. 'I'd come across a great account of hiking the whole trail, written a few years ago, and I was determined to do it myself. A friend was going with me, but he changed his mind. So I promised my parents I'd check in daily on my mobile, and I'd also post pictures on my social media page. I didn't feel anxious – I was just excited to get going.'

Things went perfectly for the first week. David made good progress and was really enjoying the experience. Since many people use the trail, he was constantly meeting fellow hikers, so he never felt isolated. 'But then it got really stormy,' he says, 'so a lot of people gave up. I could go for hours without seeing anyone at all. But as long as I had my mobile, I wasn't really worried about anything bad happening.'

Unfortunately, something bad did happen. During a particularly heavy rain storm, David slipped in the mud, went off the edge of the trail and fell about ten metres down the hill. 'I realised I'd broken my arm immediately, but I knew my location and thought I could still call for help. Then I found that my mobile had fallen out of my pocket. And when I tried to get up to look for it, I couldn't stand up at all. My leg was injured too.'

All he could do was to shout for help. 'I yelled until my throat was sore,' he says. 'And nothing happened. But then I saw a head at the top of the hill – someone had heard me. A man came down, saw the state I was in and called for help. And really, that was the most amazing part of the whole experience. At the hospital, even the doctors were impressed at how much of the trail I'd covered. I felt really proud.' Will he try to walk the trail again? 'Absolutely,' he says. 'It's a fantastic place, and nothing can keep me away.'

1 The Pennine Way is
  A the longest trail in Britain.
  B located mainly in Scotland.
  C not popular with inexperienced walkers.
  D considered a difficult trail to walk.
2 Where did David get the idea of hiking the trail?
  A from reading about it
  B from his parents
  C from hearing an account of it
  D from being challenged by a friend
3 How did David get help after his accident?
  A He called for help on his mobile.
  B He spoke to a passer-by.
  C He called out until someone heard him.
  D He returned to the trail and found someone.
4 What is the best title for the article?
  A A Foolish Adventure
  B How a Mobile Saved a Boy's Life
  C Near Tragedy, But No Regrets
  D Fear and Tragedy on the Pennine Way

Listening

3 Read the Strategy above. Then read the extracts from five different recordings and complete the missing words in the sentences.

Liam	I made a big effort to meet new people and form new friendships.
Sally	I'm sorry, but I'd rather not empty the rubbish bins right now.
Arlo	We had the time of our life in Paris.
Julia	I'll have a word with the nurse.
Marty	I hate the fact that my bedroom has purple walls!

Exam Skills Trainer

1 Liam w_____ h_____ to make new friends.
2 Sally d_____ w_____ t_____ empty the rubbish bins at the moment.
3 Arlo and his friends really e_____ being in Paris.
4 Julia's going to t_____ t_____ the nurse.
5 Marty would rather h_____ b_____ d_____ have purple walls.

4 **🎧 1.21 You will hear a conversation about house moves. Complete each sentence with no more than three words.**

1 Steve now lives in _____ house in a village.
2 Liz's old flat was _____ than her new flat.
3 Steve would rather _____ spend so much time waiting for buses.
4 Steve's _____ enjoying doing DIY.
5 Liz _____ live in the countryside.

Use of English

Exam Strategy
When choosing a word which fits in two sentences, keep in mind that these are sometimes based on phrasal verbs (e.g. *turn off*) or collocations (e.g. *call a meeting*).

5 **Read the Strategy. Then circle the answer (A, B, C, or D) which completes both sentences.**

1 I can't ___ coffee without milk – it's disgusting!
  There were no more seats, so we had to ___ up.
  A stand   B make   C have   D take
2 The problem wasn't ___ to solve, but I finally found the answer.
  Take it ___ for a few days. You've been ill!
  A simple   B light   C quick   D easy
3 Can you check my list of guests? I don't want to ___ anyone out.
  If we ___ now, we'll probably catch the train.
  A put   B go   C leave   D run
4 You have to sit ___ to Grandma when you talk to her as her hearing isn't good.
  The sisters, who are very ___, don't keep any secrets from each other.
  A near   B next   C close   D tight

Speaking

Exam Strategy
Remember to ask questions, make suggestions and agree or disagree with your partner during a role-play.

6 **Read the Strategy. Then look at the role-play card and complete the dialogue with the words below.**

Student A
You and your partner don't like the living room in your flat. Suggest three changes you could make to the decoration.

could   good   keen   should   sure   would

A What do you think we ¹_____ do?
B We ²_____ paint the walls white.
A I think yellow ³_____ be better.
B I'm not ⁴_____. I'm not very ⁵_____ on yellow.
A How about cream?
B That's a ⁶_____ idea.

Read the role-play cards and decide who is Student A and who is Student B and role-play the discussion.

Student A
You and your partner want to get fit. Discuss different kinds of exercise. Suggest jogging in the park tomorrow morning.

Student B
You and your partner want to get fit. Discuss different kinds of exercise. Suggest going swimming tomorrow evening.

Writing

Exam Strategy
Learn a range of formal expressions to use in opinion essays.

8 **Read the Strategy. Complete the second sentence so that it has a similar meaning to the first. Use two or three words, including the word in brackets.**

1 I think it's very helpful.
  _____, it's very helpful. (view)
2 Lots of people think that it's difficult.
  It is _____ belief that it's difficult. (widely)
3 It also helps people sleep better.
  _____, it helps people sleep better. (more)
4 It's important to check your work.
  It's _____ you check your work. (vital)

9 **Read the task and write an opinion essay.**

Some people say that giving young people jobs to do around the home is good for them. Write an essay giving your own view, using examples to support your opinions.
• Describe some typical jobs around the house.
• Say how they might have a positive or a negative effect.
• Describe your own experiences.
• Make your opinion clear.

5 Technology

Vocabulary

A Computing

I can talk about computers and communication technology.

1 Complete the crossword.

Across

3 If you need information for your project, ___ online.

4 They've got Wi-Fi at the café in town, but I can never ___ to the network.

6 How many YouTube channels do you ___ to?

8 Can you show me how to ___ a video to YouTube?

10 Please ___ Joe's email to me as soon as you get it.

12 Please don't ___ on my status unless you have something nice to say!

13 I need to ___ my email account on my new computer.

Down

1 Can you ___ my contribution to the blog? Please give it five stars!

2 Can you help me ___ this new app on my phone?

5 In IT, we are learning how to create and ___ our own video games.

7 Why don't you ___ your Facebook profile? It's really old.

9 I can't ___ this document because we've run out of ink.

11 I'm going to ___ this photo on Facebook.

2 Complete the collocations with the nouns below.

a link   a new window   the trash
your username   your work

1 empty _____

2 follow _____

3 save _____ , a document, a file, a photo

4 enter your password, _____, your address, etc.

5 open / close an app, _____, a folder, a file, a document

an account   a box   a button   a page   text

6 check / uncheck _____

7 copy and paste _____ , a photo, a file, a link, a folder

8 click / double click on _____ , an icon, a link, a menu

9 scroll up / down _____ , a menu, a document

10 create _____ , a new document, a file, a link, a folder

3 🎧 1.22 Listen. What is the boy trying to do? Choose the correct answer.

1 update a Facebook account ☐

2 create a Facebook account ☐

3 delete a Facebook account ☐

4 🎧 1.22 Listen again. Choose the correct words.

1 Click on the 'Sign up' **icon** / **button** and **enter** / **save** the information.

2 You'll need to **confirm** / **create** your email address by **following** / **saving** the link in the email.

3 Let's create a **profile** / **password** for you.

4 You need to **copy and paste** / **upload** a photo.

5 **Open** / **Empty** the folder where your photos are stored.

5 Write instructions on how to do one of these things with a computer.

• download music

• update your status on a social networking site

• subscribe to a YouTube channel

• You choose!

_____

_____

_____

_____

_____

_____

5B

Grammar
Quantifiers
I can use quantifiers correctly.

1 Complete the rules with the headings below.

plural noun   singular countable noun   uncountable noun

1 every, each, either + _____
_____

2 all, most, some, much, little, a little, any, no + _____
_____

3 all, most, many, some, a few, few, no, both, any + _____
_____

2 Circle the correct answers to complete the sentences.

1 I've only used ___ my pocket money.
  a little   b a little   c a few   d a little of
2 ___ of the computers is broken.
  a Each   b Both   c Every one   d Every
3 There isn't ___ time before the film starts.
  a many   b few   c much   d little
4 Nearly ___ this software is out of date.
  a every   b all of   c each of   d every one of
5 ___ of the information is correct.
  a No   b None   c Any   d Either
6 The computer is very heavy. Pick it up with ___ hands.
  a each   b all   c either   d both
7 ___ teenagers use social networking sites.
  a Much   b Most   c Many of   d Most of
8 Have you bought ___ apps recently?
  a some   b any   c no   d few
9 Joe spends ___ his free time playing games online.
  a most   b most of   c much   d the most

3 Some of the sentences are incorrect. Rewrite them correctly. Tick the correct sentences.

1 No of my classmates did their homework. [X]
  None of my classmates did their homework.
2 Some of gadgets are difficult to use. [ ]
  _____
3 We had no time to lose. [ ]
  _____
4 Tom can write with every hand. [ ]
  _____
5 Not much games are easy to program. [ ]
  _____
6 There's a mistake in each sentence. [ ]
  _____
7 Kate doesn't like any these apps. [ ]
  _____
8 Jason spends few money on downloading music. [ ]
  _____

4 Complete the sentences with *few*, *a few*, *little*, or *a little*.

1 _____ people went to see the film, so it was only on at the cinema for a couple of weeks.
2 I'm tired because I got very _____ sleep last night.
3 I'll only need _____ more minutes to finish my homework.
4 'Is there any milk left?' 'Yes, _____.'
5 I posted that comment _____ days ago.
6 I had _____ subscribers to my video blog, so I removed it from YouTube.
7 Unfortunately they have _____ money to spend on holidays.

5 Look at the bar chart. Write a sentence for each activity with the words below. Use the present perfect.

all   almost all   ~~a few~~   most   none   some   very few

1 set up a new email account
2 play a computer game
3 download music
4 print a document from their phone
5 search within a specific website
6 install an app on their phone
7 update their profile on a social networking site

Students in the class

1 *A few of the students have set up a new email account.*
2 _____
_____
3 _____
_____
4 _____
_____
5 _____
_____
6 _____
_____
7 _____
_____

5C Listening

Navigation nightmare

I can distinguish fact from opinion.

Revision: Student's Book page 55

1 **Complete the gadgets in the sentences.**

1 He used a c___ ___ ___ ___ ___ ___ ___r to record the school play.

2 I need a new M___ ___ ___ ___ ___ ___ ___r so I can listen to music when I go running.

3 Without the s___ ___ ___ ___v, we would never have found the hotel.

4 She wears a B___ ___ ___ ___ ___ ___ ___ ___ h___ ___ ___ ___ ___ ___t so she can speak to the office while she's in her car.

5 His s___ ___ ___ ___ ___ ___ ___ ___h doesn't just tell him what the time is but also how far he's walked every day.

6 If I had a g___ ___ ___ ___ c___ ___ ___ ___ ___ ___ in my bedroom, I probably wouldn't do much homework.

7 Now that I've bought this t___ ___ ___ ___t, I hardly ever use my laptop.

8 My new d___ ___ ___ ___ ___ ___ ___ r___ ___ ___ ___ is also a B___ ___ ___ ___ ___ ___ ___ ___ ___ s___ ___ ___ ___ ___r, so I can use it to stream music from my s___ ___ ___ ___ ___ ___ ___ ___ ___ .

9 I've saved all of my school work onto a m___ ___ ___ ___ ___ ___ s___ ___ ___k.

Listening Strategy

You may have to distinguish fact from opinion in a listening task. Listen for clues to help you decide. An opinion might begin with a verb connected with thinking (e.g. *think*, *believe*, *expect*, *reckon*, etc.) or a phrase for introducing opinions (*in my view*, *as I see it*, etc.).

---

2 **🎧 1.23** **Read the Listening Strategy. Then listen to four short dialogues. Are the sentences below facts (F) or opinions (O)?**

	F	O
1 The best place to keep a copy of photos is on a memory stick.		
2 Smartwatches will get cheaper over the next few years.		
3 Watching films on a tablet is more popular than going to the cinema.		
4 People buy fewer gadgets now than they bought in the past.		

3 **🎧 1.23** **Complete the phrases for expressing opinions with the words below. Then listen again and check.**

as in opinion problem to

1 In my _____ , …

2 _____ I see it, …

3 _____ my view, …

4 The _____ is …

5 It seems _____ me that …

4 **Express your own opinions about these topics using the phrases from exercise 3.**

1 students using their phones in school

_____

_____

_____

2 drivers using satnav to find their way

_____

_____

_____

3 having hundreds of 'friends' on social media

_____

_____

_____

5 **🎧 1.24** **Listen to four dialogues. Circle the correct answers.**

1 In dialogue 1, which sentence is a fact, not an opinion?
   a They are driving along a road called West Way.
   b There can't be two hotels with the same name in the same part of town.
   c The Adelphi Hotel has two buildings.

2 In dialogue 2, why do they decide to use the paper map, not the phone?
   a There is no map app on their phone.
   b Mobile phone reception is not reliable.
   c The map on the phone is not big enough.

3 In dialogue 3, which sentence is an opinion, not a fact?
   a They can't drive along the High Street.
   b There's a market next to the park on Saturdays.
   c The fastest route to the station is along Park Avenue.

4 In dialogue 4, why will the man's mistake not make him late?
   a The train he is on is faster than the train he wanted.
   b He can still catch the train he wanted.
   c Both trains go to the same destination.

5D
Grammar
Modals in the past
I can use past modals correctly.

1 Circle the correct modals to complete the sentences.

1 She **can't have / might have / must have** left her phone at school. Or perhaps she left it on the bus.

2 There's no pizza left. They **can't have / could have / must have** eaten it all.

3 Juliet **can't have / may have / must have** gone on holiday. She was at school yesterday!

4 I didn't get your email. Do you think you **can't have / could have / must have** sent it to my old email address?

5 Your smartwatch probably isn't broken. It **can't have / could have / must have** run out of charge.

6 The school show is on YouTube. Our teacher **can't have / might have / must have** uploaded it.

7 You went 130 km in less than an hour? You **can't have / could have / must have** driven very fast!

8 Max isn't replying to my texts. He **can't have / might have / must have** taken his phone with him.

2 Complete the sentences with *must have* or *can't have* and the verb in brackets.

1 Jack is usually here by now. He _____ (miss) his bus.

2 Madison didn't know about the party. She _____ (get) your email.

3 Sam _____ (take) his phone with him; he isn't answering my text messages.

4 There's no bread. We _____ (eat) it all at breakfast.

5 They've left school already. Their lessons _____ (finish) early today.

6 He _____ (injure) his leg really badly. He cycled home!

3 Write the correct reply (a–f) after sentences 1–6. Use *should / shouldn't have* and the past participle form of the verb in brackets.

1 'My camcorder screen is damaged.'
'_____ ,'

2 'I think we're driving in the wrong direction.'
'_____ ,'

3 'I've spent a fortune on my phone this month!'
'_____ ,'

4 'My email account has been hacked again.'
'_____ ,'

5 'Mason is really angry with me.'
'_____ ,'

6 'My tablet is completely dead.'
'_____ ,'

a We (bring) the satnav.
b You (choose) a better password.
c You (charge) it overnight.
d You (drop) it on the pavement.
e You (make) those comments on Twitter.
f You (call) your friend when you were abroad.

4 Complete the dialogue with the modals below. You can use the same modal more than once.

can't have   may / might / could have
might not have   must have

Erica What's the matter, Jack? You look worried.

Jack   I can't find my phone. I ¹_____ left it somewhere.

Erica Did you have it on the bus?

Jack   Yes, I did. But I ²_____ left it there because I used it just after I got off. I sent you a text.

Erica You ³_____ dropped it when you were walking here from the bus stop.

Jack   Yes, that's possible. I was listening to my MP3 player.

Erica Somebody ⁴_____ found it by now and handed it in to the police.

Jack   Or they ⁵_____ handed it in. They ⁶_____ kept it.

Erica Shall I phone the police station and ask?

Jack   Yes, OK. But why don't you call my phone number first?

Erica OK, I will. I can hear your phone ringing.

Jack   Me too. I ⁷_____ dropped it in the street.

Erica No. You ⁸_____ put it down somewhere in the house.

Jack   That's a relief! But where is it?

5 Write replies for the sentences. Use the words in brackets.

1 'My back is really painful.' (might have)
_____

2 'Ellie has got a really expensive new phone.' (must have)
_____

3 'I failed my science exam.' (can't have)
_____

4 'I've deleted all my photos by mistake.' (should have)
_____

5 'Anna left a rude message on my Facebook page.' (might not have)
_____

6 'I haven't got enough money for my bus ticket.' (shouldn't have)
_____

7 'It took Ben two hours to get home from school.' (must have)
_____

8 'I was hungry all morning at school.' (can't have)
_____

9 'Molly seemed really disappointed with her exam result.' (might have)
_____

Word Skills

Adjective + preposition
I can use the correct prepositions after adjectives.

1 Circle the correct prepositions.

1 His eyes are very sensitive **at / to** bright lights.
2 Are you excited **about / for** your holiday?
3 She wasn't very pleased **in / with** her present.
4 Don't worry, nobody is angry **about / with** you.
5 I want 90%, but I'd be satisfied **for / with** 75%.
6 Who is responsible **about / for** all this mess?
7 I'm not familiar **to / with** this part of town, so it's easy to get lost.
8 If you were dissatisfied **from / with** your hotel room, you should have complained.

2 Complete the text with *about, at, in, of, on, to,* or *with.*

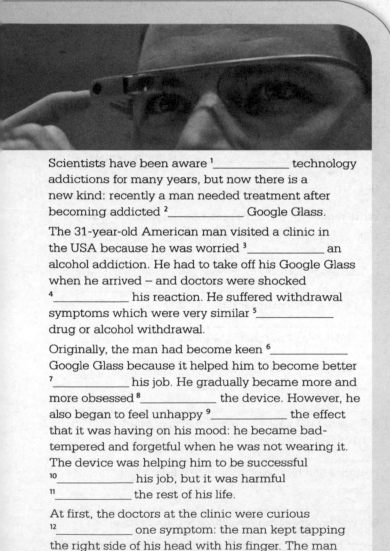

Scientists have been aware ¹_____ technology addictions for many years, but now there is a new kind: recently a man needed treatment after becoming addicted ²_____ Google Glass.

The 31-year-old American man visited a clinic in the USA because he was worried ³_____ an alcohol addiction. He had to take off his Google Glass when he arrived – and doctors were shocked ⁴_____ his reaction. He suffered withdrawal symptoms which were very similar ⁵_____ drug or alcohol withdrawal.

Originally, the man had become keen ⁶_____ Google Glass because it helped him to become better ⁷_____ his job. He gradually became more and more obsessed ⁸_____ the device. However, he also began to feel unhappy ⁹_____ the effect that it was having on his mood: he became bad-tempered and forgetful when he was not wearing it. The device was helping him to be successful ¹⁰_____ his job, but it was harmful ¹¹_____ the rest of his life.

At first, the doctors at the clinic were curious ¹²_____ one symptom: the man kept tapping the right side of his head with his finger. The man later explained that this was how you changed the view on Google Glass.

3 Tick the best summary of the text in exercise 2.

a A man in the USA developed an addiction to Google Glass while he was receiving treatment for another addiction. ☐
b A man in the USA became addicted to Google Glass after using it at work. ☐
c A man in the USA found it so difficult to break his addiction to Google Glass that he developed an alcohol addiction. ☐

4 Complete the questions with a preposition. Then write true answers about yourself.

1 Which friend or family member do you get angry _____ most often?

_____

_____

2 What kinds of thing do you get angry _____?

_____

_____

3 In what ways can social media be harmful _____ teenagers?

_____

_____

4 Which gadget are you most likely to become addicted _____, in your opinion? Why?

_____

_____

VOCAB BOOST!

Dictionaries often use abbreviations so that they can include a lot of information in a small space. Common abbreviations used in dictionaries include:

abbr (abbreviation)	etc. (and so on)
prep (preposition)	pron (pronoun)
sing (singular)	pl (plural)
pt (past tense)	pp (past participle)
C (countable noun)	U (uncountable noun)
BrE (British English)	AmE (American English)

5 Read the *Vocab boost!* box. Then study the dictionary entry and write the abbreviations below in full.

appropriate /əˈprəʊpriət/ *adj* **appropriate (for/to sth/ sb)** suitable or right for a particular situation, person, use, etc.: *The matter will be dealt with by the appropriate authorities.* ◆ *I don't think this film is appropriate for young children.* OPP **inappropriate** > **appropriately** *adv*

1 adj _____
2 sth _____
3 sb _____
4 OPP _____
5 adv _____

5F Reading
Intelligent footballers
I can understand a text about robot footballers.

Revision: Student's Book page 58

1 Complete the verb–noun collocations in the sentences with the words below.

an answer   break   competition   conversation
exchanged   pass   website   won

1 Who can **come up with** _____ to this question?
2 Did you _____ **the test** or fail it?
3 Ed **entered** a singing _____ and _____ first **prize**.
4 Mathematicians tried to _____ **the enemy code**.
5 I **searched** the Amazon _____ , but I couldn't find the book I was looking for.
6 My cousin and I _____ a few **text messages**, then **had** an interesting _____ on the phone.

2 Read the text. Are the sentences true (T) or false (F)?

1 RoboCup takes place every year. ☐
2 Twelve countries produce very strong teams. ☐

3 Read the Reading Strategy. Then circle the correct answers.

1 The movement of each robot is controlled by
   a the fans of each team.
   b itself.
   c the captain of the team.
   d the owner of the robot.
2 During the match, the robots can communicate with
   a any other robot on the pitch.
   b the people who created them.
   c other robots in the same team.
   d no other robots or people.
3 Before the robots can play against humans,
   a more countries need to get involved.
   b they need increased intelligence and better movement.
   c they simply need to become more clever.
   d the technologies need to be applied in areas other than football.
4 The main goal of the organisers is to
   a have the robots play in the real World Cup.
   b develop technologies that can help in search and rescue.
   c make it more fun to watch than real footballers.
   d eventually build robots that can play better than humans.

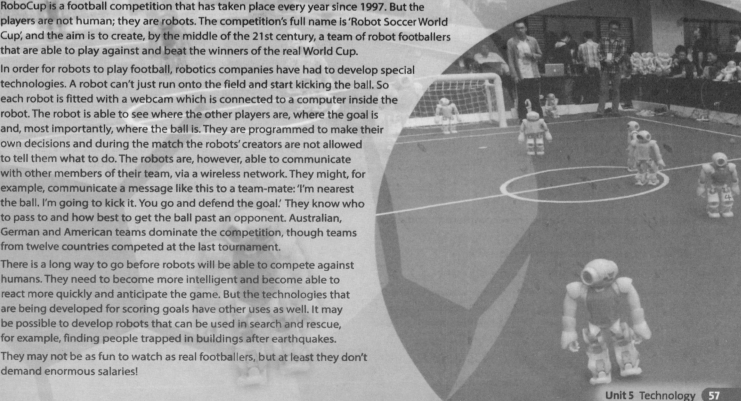

RoboCup

RoboCup is a football competition that has taken place every year since 1997. But the players are not human; they are robots. The competition's full name is 'Robot Soccer World Cup', and the aim is to create, by the middle of the 21st century, a team of robot footballers that are able to play against and beat the winners of the real World Cup.

In order for robots to play football, robotics companies have had to develop special technologies. A robot can't just run onto the field and start kicking the ball. So each robot is fitted with a webcam which is connected to a computer inside the robot. The robot is able to see where the other players are, where the goal is and, most importantly, where the ball is. They are programmed to make their own decisions and during the match the robots' creators are not allowed to tell them what to do. The robots are, however, able to communicate with other members of their team, via a wireless network. They might, for example, communicate a message like this to a team-mate: 'I'm nearest the ball. I'm going to kick it. You go and defend the goal.' They know who to pass to and how best to get the ball past an opponent. Australian, German and American teams dominate the competition, though teams from twelve countries competed at the last tournament.

There is a long way to go before robots will be able to compete against humans. They need to become more intelligent and become able to react more quickly and anticipate the game. But the technologies that are being developed for scoring goals have other uses as well. It may be possible to develop robots that can be used in search and rescue, for example, finding people trapped in buildings after earthquakes.

They may not be as fun to watch as real footballers, but at least they don't demand enormous salaries!

5G Speaking
Photo comparison
I can compare photos and answer questions.

1 Label the icons with the school subjects below.

art drama geography I.C.T. maths music P.E. science

1 _____ 2 _____ 3 _____ 4 _____

5 _____ 6 _____ 7 _____ 8 _____

4 🎧 **1.25 Listen to a student comparing photos A and B. Tick the phrases in exercise 3 which he uses.**

2 Look at the photo and the questions below. Complete the answers with your own ideas.

1 Where are the students?
  They might be _____ .

2 What is the boy with the headset doing?
  He could be _____
  _____ .

> **Speaking Strategy**
> When you have to compare and contrast photos, try to find at least two things the photos have in common and at least two differences. Learn some key phrases for expressing these similarities and differences.

3 Read the Speaking Strategy. Then complete the phrases with the words below.

kind   rather   theme   unlike   whereas

1 The common _____ in the photos is … ☐
2 Both photos show a … of some _____. ☐
3 In the first photo, … , _____ in the second photo … ☐
4 _____ the second photo, the first photo shows / does not show … ☐
5 In the second photo, they're … (-*ing*) _____ than … (-*ing*). ☐

Photos C and D show students in lessons. Compare and contrast the photos. Include the following points:
- the differences between primary and secondary school lessons.
- how technology can help students learn.

5 Look at photos C and D above and read the task. Prepare your answer. Use the questions to help you.

1 Which photo shows secondary students? Are they working alone or with a teacher?
  _____
  _____

2 How are the students in each class using technology? How do you use it at your school?
  _____
  _____

6 Now do the speaking task comparing photos C and D. Use your notes from exercise 5.

5H
Writing
An internet forum post
I can write an internet forum post about a new gadget.

Preparation

1 Circle the correct words to complete the concession clauses.

1 The image isn't very clear **in spite of / even though** the size of the screen.

2 **Despite / Although** I don't like video games, I bought the games console anyway.

3 It was quite expensive **even though / despite** it was in the sale.

4 I don't agree, **in spite of / although** it's obviously not a good idea to play for more than a few hours at a time.

2 Complete the internet forum post with three of the sentences in exercise 1.

CoolLisa01

I bought a new games console last week from a website.
1 _____

It's a handheld console with a large screen and controls for your thumbs on each end. Fifty games are built into the console, and you can download more from the internet.

Overall, I'm very happy with it. The games are certainly fun. I have one criticism: 2 _____

Some people think that teenagers should spend less time playing computer games because it's bad for their health.
3 _____

Writing Strategy
Each point in the task will ask you to do a different thing, such as *describe, recommend, relate, express an opinion, suggest,* etc. Read the task carefully and make sure that you understand exactly what you are being asked to do.

3 Read the Writing Strategy. Then read the points a–f below. Number four points in the order they appear in the text in exercise 2. There are two extra points.

The writer:

a compares it with another console. ☐

b presents the opinions of people who think teenagers spend too much time playing video games. ☐

c gives her opinion of the games console. ☐

d describes some of its features. ☐

e says when and where she bought the games console. ☐

f asks other forum contributors to react to her forum post. ☐

Writing Guide

You recently bought a new phone. Write a forum post in which you:

• <u>describe</u> to other forum contributors what you use it for.

• compare it with another phone which you have used.

• present the opinions of people who think that mobile phones should be banned in school.

• ask other forum contributors to react to your forum post.

4 Read the task above. Underline the verb in each point that describes what you should do. The first one is already underlined.

5 Make notes for each of the four points in the task.

1 _____
_____
_____

2 _____
_____
_____

3 _____
_____
_____

4 _____
_____
_____

6 Write your forum post using your notes.

CHECK YOUR WORK
Have you ...
☐ covered all four points?
☐ used one or two concession clauses?
☐ checked your spelling and grammar?

Review Unit 5

Vocabulary

1 **Complete the sentences with the verbs below.**

comment   forward   install   program
set up   subscribe   update   upload

1 If you receive a lot of spam emails, you probably need to _____ a new account.
2 She needs to _____ her profile because she's just got married.
3 I had to _____ on that post because it made me really angry.
4 Do you have any idea how to _____ a simple game?
5 If I made a video clip of myself, I wouldn't _____ it to YouTube.
6 Can you _____ that email to me, please?
7 I only _____ to a few YouTube channels because I haven't got time to watch all the videos.
8 What's the best app to _____ for measuring your calorie intake?

Mark: ☐ / 8

2 **Complete the instructions with the verbs below.**

check   click on   create   enter   log on
print   save   scroll down

🛒 **How to make an online purchase**

• Go to the website of the online retailer and type the item you're looking for into the search bar.
• ¹_____ the list of results until you find it.
• ²_____ the item you want.
• Go to the checkout. If you are an existing customer, ³_____ to the website. If you aren't an existing customer, ⁴_____ a new account.
• Read the terms and conditions and ⁵_____ the box.
• ⁶_____ your credit card details and pay for the item.
• ⁷_____ the confirmation document on your computer.
• ⁸_____ the document for future reference.

Mark: ☐ / 8

Word Skills

3 **Match the sentence halves.**

1	I'm pleased	a	about losing my tablet.
2	I'm worried	b	in most online games.
3	I'm shocked	c	with my new smartphone.
4	I'm aware	d	to negative comments on Facebook.
5	I'm sensitive	e	on making video clips.
6	I'm keen	f	at the price of some devices.
7	I'm successful	g	for running an online forum.
8	I'm responsible	h	of the dangers of social networking sites.

Mark: ☐ / 8

4 **Complete the sentences with the words below.**

like   look   see   seems   thing   think

1 The people look _____ they're enjoying themselves.
2 For me, the most important _____ is to know when to stop.
3 It _____ to me that internet addiction is growing.
4 They _____ as if they're concentrating very hard.
5 Personally, I _____ some gadgets are overrated.
6 The way I _____ it, many workers are exploited.

Mark: ☐ / 6

Grammar

5 **Complete the dialogue with the words below.**

all   any   every   a few   a little   many   most   much

Dave Emma, how long have you had your phone?
Emma It's quite new, actually. I've only had it for ¹_____ months.
Dave How often do you use it?
Emma I use it ²_____ the time! ³_____ of the people I know send me text messages, and I text a lot too, especially when I need ⁴_____ help with my homework. By the end of the day, my phone has no battery left, so I have to recharge it ⁵_____ night.
Dave Who pays your phone bill?
Emma My parents do, but it isn't a lot. I don't really spend ⁶_____ money on my phone because I never make ⁷_____ calls. If I want to speak to my parents, I text them and they call me back. I don't get ⁸_____ other calls really, except on my birthday.

Mark: ☐ / 8

6 **Complete the second sentence so that it has a similar meaning to the first. Use the words in brackets.**

1 There are no places left on the science trip. (all)
_____ on the science trip have been taken.
2 I don't get many important emails. (few)
_____ are very important.
3 I've lost my two phone chargers. (either)
I can't find _____ .
4 Her contacts were all deleted when she clicked on the button. (every)
When she clicked on the button, she deleted _____
5 The links on this website are all faulty. (none)
_____ on this website are working.
6 There are only a few apps on my phone that I use. (most)
I don't use _____ on my phone.

Mark: ☐ / 6

7 Complete the sentences with the past modal form of *must / might (not) / can't* and the verbs in brackets.

1 She _____ a fortune for that mobile – it's the very latest model! (pay)

2 I _____ my keys at home; I remember locking the door this morning. (leave)

3 The doctor wants me to have an X-ray because I _____ my arm. (break)

4 It's possible that your wallet is in the car; you _____ it. (lose)

5 I _____ that report properly. It isn't in the right folder. (save)

6 The test was really hard, but I think I _____ . I hope so, anyway. (pass)

7 He _____ my email yet because I only sent it last night. (read)

8 My phone is completely dead. It _____ itself off. (turn)

Mark: ___ / 8

8 Complete the dialogues with the past modal form of *should (not)* and the verbs below.

be   install   leave   put   take   write

1 A I've forgotten my password.
  B You _____ it down somewhere.

2 A I've dropped my phone in the shower.
  B You _____ it into the bathroom.

3 A I've spilled coffee on my computer.
  B You _____ the cup next to the keyboard.

4 A I think there's some malware on my laptop.
  B You _____ better antivirus software.

5 A I've cracked the screen of my laptop.
  B You _____ more careful.

6 A I think somebody's taken my e-reader.
  B You _____ it on the desk.

Mark: ___ / 6

Use of English

9 Circle the correct words to complete both sentences in each pair.

1 a Log ___ to the website and go to 'my account'.
  b Which button should I click ___ ?
  A at   B in   C on   D with

2 a I don't get as ___ emails as you do.
  b There aren't ___ Wi-Fi hotspots near here.
  A many   B most   C much   D any

3 a I'm usually very busy, so I spend ___ time playing computer games.
  b There's ___ information on this website; it isn't very useful.
  A few   B a few   C a little   D little

4 a He didn't answer his phone. He ___ not have heard it.
  b Let's call later, they ___ be having dinner now.
  A could   B might   C must   D can

5 a My phone battery ___ have run out yet. I've only just charged it!
  b Matt's games console ___ be working. He's reading a book!
  A can't   B may   C could   D must

6 a Old technical gadgets can be harmful ___ the environment.
  b My MP3 player is similar ___ my sister's. The only difference is the colour.
  A with   B of   C as   D to

7 a My friend is annoyed ___ me about the comment I posted on her wall.
  b How many people do you know who are obsessed ___ online games?
  A about   B in   C with   D at

Mark: ___ / 7

Total: ___ / 65

I can …

Read the statements. Think about your progress and tick one of the boxes.

★ = I need more practice.

★★ = I sometimes find this difficult.

★★★ = No problem!

	★	★★	★★★
I can talk about computers and communication technology.			
I can use quantifiers correctly.			
I can distinguish fact from opinion.			
I can use past modals correctly.			
I can use the correct prepositions after adjectives.			
I can understand a text about robot footballers.			
I can compare photos and answer questions.			
I can write an internet forum post about a new gadget.			

6 High flyers

A Describing character
I can describe people's character.

1 Complete the table.

Noun	Adjective
1 ambition	
2	cheerful
3 creativity	
4	enthusiastic
5 flexibility	
6	generous
7 honesty	
8	idealistic
9 intelligence	
10	loyal
11 maturity	
12	modest
13 optimism	
14	patient
15 pessimism	
16	punctual
17 realism	
18	self-confident
19 seriousness	
20	shy
21 sociability	
22	stubborn
23 sympathy	
24	thoughtful

2 Complete the phrases for describing personal qualities with the words below.

common communicating courage energy initiative lack sense skills

1 have a good _____ of humour
2 have lots of / no _____ sense
3 have good organisational _____
4 _____ self-confidence
5 have physical _____
6 be good at _____
7 show lots of _____
8 have lots of _____

3 Complete the sentences with adjectives and phrases from exercises 1 and 2.

1 Sue is very _____. She always thinks things will get worse.
2 Harry loves telling jokes. He has _____.
3 Try to be _____. It isn't good to be late.
4 She always tells the truth. She's very _____.
5 She's always telling everyone how clever she is. She isn't very _____.
6 He loves being with other people. He's the most _____ person I know!
7 She loves dangerous sports. She has great _____.
8 I can talk to her about my problems. She always listens. She's very _____.
9 He always knows what to do. You don't need to tell him. He _____.

4 🎧 1.26 **Listen to three people describing a friend or family member. Choose two adjectives below that best describe the people. There are two extra adjectives.**

ambitious cheerful generous intelligent optimistic patient punctual serious

1 _____ and _____
2 _____ and _____
3 _____ and _____

5 🎧 1.26 **Listen again. Match the descriptions 1–3 with sentences A–D. There is one extra sentence.**

This person:
A shows lots of initiative in planning his / her future. ☐
B lacks confidence in social situations. ☐
C has the opposite personality to the speaker. ☐
D likes to pass on knowledge to others. ☐

6 Write a short text describing someone you know. Give examples that show their personality.

My brother is very creative. He's really good at drawing and painting. He's also a bit ...

_____
_____
_____
_____
_____
_____

6B Grammar
Defining relative clauses
I can use defining relative clauses.

1 Complete the sentences with *who*, *which*, *where*, or *whose*.

1 That's the hospital _____ my dad works.
2 He is someone _____ face is familiar, but I can't remember his name.
3 Do you know a shop _____ I can buy printer paper?
4 The essay _____ Tom wrote got top marks.
5 The boy _____ sits next to me in class is from Warsaw.
6 I know a girl _____ plays tennis six times a week.

2 Circle the correct relative pronouns. If both answers are correct, circle both.

Amelia Humfress is a young entrepreneur ¹**who / which** has just turned 24, and ²**whose / who** aim is to make her company, Steer, the best in the world for teaching people how to make their own websites. The courses ³**which / that** she offers vary from web design to computer coding. The idea for the company came to her when she was looking for a course ⁴**where / which** she could learn about web design. It was a plan ⁵**that / which** grew slowly, and at first she lacked the confidence to start the company. But she found an office ⁶**where / that** she could start the business, and the business grew quickly. She thinks that more young people should set up their own businesses and that it's often a lack of confidence ⁷**that / who** holds them back.

3 Some of the sentences are incorrect. Rewrite them correctly. Tick the correct sentences.

1 A computer is a machine that can perform calculations. ☐
_____
2 This is the town where I was born there. ☐
_____
3 That's the woman who she dropped her handbag. ☐
_____
4 The cheese which I bought smell really bad. ☐
_____
5 That's the boy who his dad is a newsagent. ☐
_____
6 Where's the book which I left it on the table? ☐
_____

4 Join the two sentences with a relative pronoun (*who*, *which*, *where*, or *whose*).

1 I've lost the DVD. You gave it to me.
I've lost the DVD which you gave me.
2 Jo has an expensive car. She keeps it in the garage.
_____
3 Who's that man? He's looking at us.
_____
_____
4 I opened the cupboard. We keep the glasses there.
_____
_____
5 That's the girl. I saw you with her.
_____
_____
6 Who is the boy? You copied his homework.
_____
_____
7 Website designer is a job. It attracts young people.
_____
_____

5 Complete questions 1–8 with clauses a–h. Add a relative pronoun only where necessary.

1 Is this the phone *you used to text me*?
2 What's the name of the hotel _____
_____
3 Is Jake the boy _____
_____
4 This is the jacket _____
_____
5 Do you like people _____
_____
6 Can you fetch the DVD _____
_____
7 Is that the woman _____
_____
8 Is that the café _____
_____

a I wore to Beth's party.
b show lots of initiative?
c you used to text me?
d you introduced me to a few days ago?
e husband works in France?
f is on the shelf in the living room?
g we stayed last summer?
h you met Sam?

Listening
Margaret Fuller
I can listen for linking words and phrases.

> **Listening Strategy**
> When you listen to a more formal text, pay attention to linking words and phrases. These tell you how the pieces of information are connected: a contrast, a result, an example, emphasis, etc.

1 Read the Listening Strategy. Then complete the table with the headings below.

contrast   emphasis   example   result

1	2
indeed in fact	however mind you though
3	**4**
as a result consequently for that reason	for example for instance

2 Choose the correct linking word or phrase in the sentences.

1 She worked hard at school. **Consequently, / Mind you,** she did well in her exams.
2 The town has excellent leisure facilities. **For instance, / However,** there is a new sports centre.
3 The journey had been long and tiring. **For example, / For that reason,** they decided to get an early night.
4 The weather was extremely cold. **Indeed, / However,** it reached –12°C one night.
5 Ellie spent all afternoon at the beach. **As a result, / Mind you,** she got slightly sunburned.
6 The house is in a terrible condition – **in fact, / though** it would be impossible to live there.

3 Match sentences 1–6 with endings a–h. Use the linking words to help you. There are two extra endings.

1 She stayed up all night doing her homework. <u>As a result</u>, she ☐
2 He tried very hard to contact his parents. <u>For instance</u>, he ☐
3 They climbed the mountain in one day, <u>though</u> it ☐
4 She really disliked the film. <u>In fact</u>, she ☐
5 He applied for about twenty jobs. <u>However</u>, he ☐
6 He decided he wanted to be a journalist. <u>Consequently</u>, he ☐

a eventually managed to get in touch.
b needed more time.
c phoned and emailed them.
d sent his CV to all the national newspapers.
e left before the end.
f overslept and was late for school.
g was difficult and exhausting.
h only got two or three interviews.

4 You are going to listen to a radio interview about Margaret Fuller. First, read the sentences and circle the correct endings.

1 Margaret was an excellent student. <u>In fact</u>,
  a by the age of six, she was translating Latin poetry into English.
  b she always found Latin particularly difficult.
2 Boys often learned Latin, but girls learned different things: <u>for instance</u>,
  a girls usually started school at a later age.
  b how to behave in public.
3 She taught herself several languages and read great literature from around the world. <u>Indeed</u>,
  a novels from Germany, France and Italy.
  b many people considered her the best-educated person on the East Coast.
4 At that time, there were certain jobs which people thought of as suitable for women: <u>for example</u>,
  a being a teacher.
  b Margaret was not interested in these jobs.
5 Some of the reviews she wrote were very negative. <u>As a result</u>,
  a she was not always popular with novelists and poets of her time.
  b she praised good writing when she came across it.
6 She definitely tried to make the world a better place. <u>Mind you</u>,
  a she particularly wanted to help people who couldn't help themselves.
  b during her lifetime, she was actually best known for being bad-tempered!

5 🎧 1.27 Now listen to the interview. Check your answers to exercise 5.

6 🎧 1.27 Listen again. Are the sentences true (T) or false (F)?

1 Margaret Fuller was educated both at home and at school. ☐
2 In those days, most girls were expected to read great works of literature. ☐
3 She worked as a teacher before she became a journalist. ☐
4 She didn't become editor of the *New York Tribune* because she was a woman. ☐
5 She reviewed novels and poetry for the *New York Tribune*. ☐
6 As a journalist, she took an interest in groups of people whose lives were difficult. ☐

6D Grammar

Non-defining relative clauses

I can use non-defining relative clauses.

1 Complete the sentences with the relative pronouns below.

where   which   who   whose

1 The company's US offices are in Seattle, _____ is near the border with Canada.
2 I've applied for a job at the BBC, _____ my mum used to work.
3 At the job interview, she met Jack White, _____ father started the company.
4 The company has three hundred employees,_____ work in three different offices.

2 Complete the text with the relative clauses (a–f).

Google is famous for providing fantastic working conditions for its employees, ¹___ . But what qualities do you need to get a job at Googleplex in California, ²___ ? The answer may surprise you. Laszlo Block, ³___ , is in charge of finding new employees for Google, ⁴___ . He is not looking for people who describe themselves as 'intelligent and experienced', ⁵___ . In Block's opinion, people who describe themselves as intelligent think they know the answers already. This limits their curiosity and flexibility, ⁶___ .

a which are two qualities that most other companies value highly
b where the company has its main headquarters
c which receives around 2.5 million CVs every year
d who enjoy free leisure facilities (gyms, swimming pools, video games, etc.) and free meals
e which makes them unsuitable for a company like Google
f whose job title is 'senior vice-president for people operations'

3 Four of these sentences contain mistakes. Underline and correct the mistakes. Tick the two correct sentences.

1 For twenty years, I worked in New York, where is a really exciting city. _____ ☐
2 At the age of nineteen, she published her first novel, that won several awards. _____ ☐
3 At the party, I met Luke's wife, who's the CEO of a large cosmetics company. _____ ☐
4 After my degree, I did a professional qualification, which lasted two years. _____ ☐
5 The company's head office is in Tokyo, which house prices are extremely high. _____ ☐
6 On my first day, I became friends with a girl called Ava, who's desk was next to mine. _____ ☐

4 Rewrite the sentences as one sentence with a non-defining relative clause. Sometimes there are two possible answers.

1 My uncle worked on a farm. He lived in Italy.
   My uncle, who lived in Italy, worked on a farm. OR
   My uncle, who worked on a farm, lived in Italy.
2 The car factory is closing down. Three hundred local people work there.
   _____
   _____
3 He was very nervous during his first interview. It was at *The Times* newspaper.
   _____
   _____
4 My next door neighbour works as a gardener. She's a qualified doctor.
   _____
   _____
5 She had prepared well for the job interview. It lasted nearly two hours.
   _____
   _____
6 Our French teacher wants to move to France and open a hotel. Her husband is from Paris.
   _____
   _____
7 My cousin did a second degree in computer science. Her first degree was in maths.
   _____
   _____
8 I wrote an application letter. I forgot to post it.
   _____
   _____

Phrasal verbs (2)

I can use separable and inseparable phrasal verbs correctly.

1 Complete the text with the correct form of the phrasal verbs below.

come across   come up with   look up   look up to
run out of   throw away   turn into   work out

In Kelvin Doe's home in Sierra Leone, there is no reliable supply of electricity. So when Kelvin, at the age of ten, ¹_____ the idea of starting up his own radio station, few people took him seriously. But Kelvin began by making his own battery. He used things which people had ²_____, including a piece of metal and an old cup. Amazingly, it worked! But his battery soon ³_____ power – so he had to build a generator. He searched a rubbish dump until he ⁴_____ some old DVD players. He took them apart and used the parts. Next, he needed some electronic equipment for his radio station. How could he build that? He couldn't ⁵_____ it _____ online or in a library, so he ⁶_____ it _____ for himself. Other children in his town ⁷_____ him and call him DJ Focus. And his radio station has ⁸_____ _____ an important local facility. People take their phones there to charge them!

2 Complete the sentences with one verb and one or two particles below. You can use the words more than once.

Verbs   count   hold   look   take
Particles   after   down   on   up

1 Can you _____ my cat while I'm away?
2 Both girls _____ their aunt; they love art, and so did she.
3 I'd like to talk to you before you leave, but I don't want to _____ you _____ .
4 You shouldn't _____ people just because they are poor.
5 I need a reliable assistant, and I know I can _____ you.

3 Rewrite the sentences replacing the underlined words with a suitable pronoun (*it, him, her, them*). Remember, pronouns go before the particle if the phrasal verb is separable.

1 He needed a lot of courage to ask out <u>the girl next door</u>.
_____

2 I hope he doesn't bring up <u>those emails</u> when I see him.
_____

3 They called off <u>the match</u> because of the snow.
_____

4 The members are calling for <u>Mr Lewis</u> to resign as their leader.
_____

5 She's going to give up <u>eating chocolate</u> for a year.
_____

6 You should clean up <u>your skates</u> before you sell them.
_____

> **VOCAB BOOST!**
> When you learn new phrasal verbs, you need to remember if they are separable or inseparable. You can use *sth* or *sb* to show the position of the object. Put it between the verb and the particle if the phrasal verb is separable; put it at the end if it's inseparable.
> to work sth out (separable)
> to turn into sth (inseparable)

4 Read the *Vocab boost!* box. Then add the other phrasal verbs in exercise 1 to the table.

Separable	Inseparable
work sth out	turn into sth

5 Order the words to complete the sentences. Use the table in exercise 4 to help you.

1 Can you buy some more onions? We've (them / out / of / run) _____ .
2 I can't find my phone. (you / it / if / across / come) _____ , tell me.
3 If you don't know the meaning of a word, (up / it / should / you / look) _____
4 Listen to this idea. (up / my / came / friend / it / with)
_____
5 I can use these paper plates again, (don't / away / so / them / throw) _____

Out of work

I can understand a text about a young entrepreneur.

Revision: Student's Book page 68

1 **Complete the sentences with a verb and a preposition below. Use the correct form of the verb.**

Verbs appeal arrest complain employ respond search sit spend work worry

Prepositions about about as at for for for on to to

1 I usually _____ my pocket money _____ music downloads.

2 All I do is _____ _____ my desk all day. I need to get some exercise!

3 My dad has his own business, but he used to _____ _____ a big bank.

4 Working abroad doesn't really _____ _____ me. I'd prefer to stay in this country.

5 I _____ _____ my keys, but I couldn't find them. I wonder where they are.

6 I _____ _____ all the comments on my Facebook page. I think it's impolite to ignore them.

7 The café manager wants to _____ me _____ a dishwasher, but I want to work as a waiter.

8 Don't _____ _____ your exams. I'm sure you'll pass them.

9 Yesterday, the police _____ a teenager _____ shoplifting. They questioned him, but have let him go.

10 The neighbours always _____ _____ the noise when my little cousins come to stay.

2 **Read the newspaper article. Are the sentences true (T) or false (F)?**

1 Omar Bashir is in his twenties. ☐

2 He doesn't have a university qualification. ☐

3 He finally got a job. ☐

Reading Strategy

When you are doing a gapped-sentence task:

1 Fill in the easiest gaps first.

2 When you have filled all the gaps, try the extra sentences in each gap again to make sure they don't fit.

3 Read the whole text again, checking your answers.

3 **Read the Reading Strategy. Then match sentences A–F with gaps 1–4 in the text. There are two extra sentences.**

A It's important to do something that catches people's attention.

B He thought the job offer was too good to be true.

C He found a place at the top of the stairs at Bank Station in the heart of London's financial district.

D Although the first day had resulted in some interesting conversations, nothing had come of them.

E Omar used to help them at weekends.

F He was offered £5,000 more than his current job.

HOW TO SELL YOURSELF

WOULD YOU STAND OUTSIDE THE LONDON UNDERGROUND LOOKING FOR A JOB? THAT IS PRECISELY WHAT 23-YEAR-OLD OMAR BASHIR DID LAST SUMMER. ¹__ HE STAYED THERE FROM 7 A.M. HOLDING UP A BIG SIGN WHICH READ:

2:1 economics graduate with experience

Looking for career opportunities

Could you help me?

Grab my CV here!

Omar had qualified with a good degree in economics from City University, London, and had been working in a basic marketing job for some time. In order to further his career, he had applied for nearly 100 jobs, but without success. He said, 'The graduate job market is extremely competitive and good grades are not good enough. ²__'

So he took advice from his father, who he greatly admired. His father and uncle used to have market stalls in Petticoat Lane which sold women's clothes and mobile phone accessories. ³__ 'I picked up a lot of my selling skills from there,' Omar said. His father told him, 'You can sell anything.' So then Omar decided that the time had come to sell himself.

On the second day, Omar stood outside another underground station, this time Cannon Street, with the same sign. ⁴__ Early on the second day, however, he was noticed by the CEO of a top insurance firm, who took his CV. He was called in for an interview that afternoon, and at the end of the day he had a job. David Ross, who gave Omar the interview, said, 'Omar's work ethic, inclusive nature, willingness to learn and humility means that he has fitted straight into the organisation.'

Guided conversation

I can exchange information about jobs.

A Fruit picking

B Fruit packing

1 🎧 **1.28** Listen to a teenage boy enquiring about a job. Complete the information.

Job: A or B? _____

Responsibilities:

1 _____

2 _____

Salary: _____

Hours: _____

Accommodation included? _____

2 Complete the Speaking Strategy with the words below.

ask   question   reminds   something   speaking   thing

> **Speaking Strategy**
>
> Make sure that you refer to all four points in the task. You may need to move the conversation on in order to cover all four topics. Use phrases like:
>
> *Moving on to the* ¹_____ *of ...*
> *Another* ²_____ *I wanted to ask / know is ...*
> ³_____ *else I'd like to talk about is ...*
> *Could I possibly* ⁴_____ *you about ... ?*
> ⁵_____ *of X (if X has been mentioned)*
> *That* ⁶_____ *me, ... (if there is a link with something you want to say or ask)*

3 🎧 **1.28** Listen again. Tick the phrases in the Speaking Strategy that the interviewee uses.

4 Match 1–5 with a–e to make the start of indirect questions.

1 Could you ☐	a I ask ...
2 I'd be ☐	b tell me ...
3 I'd like ☐	c interested to know ...
4 May ☐	d wondering ...
5 I was ☐	e to know ...

5 🎧 **1.29** Listen to a teenage girl enquiring about a job. Complete the information.

Job: ¹_____

Responsibilities:

² _____

³ _____

⁴ _____

Salary: ⁵_____

Travel expenses included? ⁶_____

6 🎧 **1.29** Listen again. Complete the indirect questions with phrases from exercise 4.

1 _____ if I could ask you some questions.

2 _____ what the job involves?

3 _____ what experience is required.

4 _____ what the salary is.

7 Read the task. Prepare questions about the information below. Think of follow-up questions to find out more details.

> You have applied for a part-time holiday job as a sales assistant in a supermarket. You are going for an interview with the store manager. Prepare questions for the interview about these four points:
> • responsibilities
> • personal qualities and experience required
> • hours of work and salary
> • travel expenses.

1 Responsibilities?

_____

_____

2 Personal qualities?

_____

_____

3 Experience required?

_____

_____

4 Hours of work?

_____

_____

5 Salary?

_____

_____

6 Travel expenses?

_____

_____

8 Now do the speaking task above. Use your notes from exercise 7.

6H

A for and against essay

I can write a for and against essay about education and work.

Preparation

More university students should stay in education after their first degree in order to get another qualification. Do you agree?

1 Read the task and the model essay. Does the writer agree or disagree with the statement in the task?

Agrees ☐ Disagrees ☐

1 Nowadays, the number of students who do a second degree is increasing. In order to decide if this is a good thing, we must examine the advantages and disadvantages of taking a postgraduate course.

2 It is certainly true that there is fierce competition for employment, and candidates need something extra in order to get a good job. We should also remember that people with a second qualification can expect to earn more when they start work. Moreover, postgraduate courses offer the chance to focus on a topic which you find particularly interesting. What could be better than spending an extra two or three years studying something you find fascinating?

3 However, there are disadvantages too. Firstly, it is an expensive option. You often need to pay for your place at university and also support yourself financially during the course. What is more, many young people are understandably impatient to leave education by the time they finish their first degree.

4 On balance, I believe it is a good idea to continue your studies beyond a first degree, if possible. Although it may be expensive, an extra qualification allows you to find a better job and earn more money.

2 Study the model essay and answer the questions.

In which paragraph (1–4) does the writer ...

1 describe the arguments for? ☐
   How many does she / he describe? ☐
2 describe the arguments against? ☐
   How many does she / he describe? ☐
3 give his / her opinion? ☐

Writing Strategy

Rhetorical questions can make an opinion essay more persuasive, provided you only include one or two. You do not have to answer the questions, but always make sure that the expected answer is clear, e.g.

Some people work long hours for very low pay. How can this is be right? (Expected answer: *It can't be right.*)

3 Read the Writing Strategy. Find and underline a rhetorical question in the model essay. Choose the expected answer.

a everything ☐   **b** most things ☐   **c** nothing ☐

Writing Guide

More students should do their degree at a university abroad rather than in their own country. Do you agree?

4 Read the task above. Then plan your essay following the paragraph plan below. Use the questions to help you.

Paragraph 1: Rephrase the statement in the task.

_____

_____

Paragraph 2: What are the arguments for doing a degree abroad? Think of two or three.

_____

_____

Paragraph 3: What are the arguments against doing a degree abroad? Think of two or three.

_____

_____

Paragraph 4: Give your opinion.

_____

_____

5 Write your essay using your plan from exercise 4.

CHECK YOUR WORK

Have you ...
☐ followed your paragraph plan?
☐ included one or two rhetorical questions?
☐ checked your spelling and grammar?

Review Unit 6

Vocabulary

1 Complete the table with the related nouns and adjectives.

noun	adjective
1 _____	cheerful
2 _____	flexible
modesty	3 _____
idealism	4 _____
5 _____	shy
6 _____	thoughtful
pessimism	7 _____
honesty	8 _____

Mark: / 8

2 Complete the sentences with the adjective or noun form of the words in bold.

1 I don't expect any **sympathy** from my brother. He's never been very _____ .
2 My friend Hannah is always **cheerful**. Her _____ puts everyone in a good mood.
3 I haven't really got any **ambitions**. I guess you could say I'm not very _____ .
4 Some parents quickly lose _____ with their children. I think they need to be more **patient**.
5 If you want children to be **creative**, you have to encourage their _____ .
6 Our art teacher shows great **enthusiasm** for our pictures. I don't know how he can be so _____ .
7 My sister's **self-confidence** has grown since she was young. Now she's almost too _____ .

Mark: / 7

3 Circle the correct verbs.

1 To be a firefighter, you need to **be / have / lack** physical courage.
2 A career in politics is not for those who **be / lack / show** self-confidence.
3 A comedian needs to **be / have / lack** a good sense of humour in order to make people laugh.
4 It's important for a teacher to **be / have / show** good at communicating.
5 You need to **be / have / lack** lots of energy to work with small children.
6 You have to **be / lack / show** lots of initiative if you want to get a promotion.

Mark: / 6

Word Skills

4 Complete the sentences with the phrasal verbs below and a pronoun.

ask out   brought up   called off   came across
came up with   count on   look up to   take after

1 We were supposed to be playing a football match tonight, but they've _____ because of the rain.
2 I found some old photos this morning. I _____ when I was tidying my chest of drawers.
3 The person I admire most is my grandfather. I _____ because he's travelled so much.
4 My father has excellent organisational skills. People say I _____ .
5 We discussed the question of homelessness yesterday. Our teacher _____ at the start of the class.
6 I've thought of an idea for our project. I _____ when I was walking home from school yesterday.
7 Sam would like to go out with Cathy, but he's too shy to _____ .
8 The most reliable person I know is my sister. I know I can _____ whenever I need help.

Mark: / 8

5 Complete the sentences with the phrases below.

Could I ask   Could you   I'd be   I'd like   I was   May I

1 _____ tell me what the hours of work are?
2 _____ wondering if I would need any experience.
3 _____ to know which days I would have to work.
4 _____ ask what the job involves?
5 _____ interested to know how much the salary is.
6 _____ you if I would be paid weekly or monthly?

Mark: / 6

Grammar

6 Complete the dialogues with *who*, *which*, *where* and *whose*. Where it is possible to omit the pronoun, write 'no pronoun'.

1 A Who were you talking to on the high street?
  B The woman _____ owns the English Academy.
2 A What's in that package?
  B It's the book _____ I ordered online.
3 A Which restaurant are we going to tonight?
  B The one _____ we celebrated your birthday.
4 A Who's that?
  B She's the girl _____ mother works in the post office.
5 A Where are your notes?
  B I lent them to the student _____ I sit next to.
6 A Who is that letter from?
  B It's from a company _____ might give me a summer job.

Mark: / 6

7 Rewrite the sentences in a more formal style.

1 The girl he fell in love with was an old school friend.
_____

2 The subject most students complain about is physics.
_____

3 The room which we have our meetings in is not air-conditioned.
_____

4 The man who I gave the message to did not pass it on.
_____

5 The boy who I was telling you about no longer attends my school.
_____

6 The train we were travelling on did not serve meals.
_____

Mark: ____ / 6

8 Rewrite each pair of sentences as a single sentence with a non-defining relative clause.

1 A friend of mine helped me get a job. His mother is a company director.
_____
_____

2 The new shopping centre will open next month. It has over 200 different stores.
_____
_____

3 Next summer, we're going to Ibiza. My aunt and uncle have an apartment there.
_____
_____

4 My tennis coach was late today. He's nearly always on time.
_____
_____

5 My friend showed me a photo of her new boyfriend. He is a police officer.
_____
_____

6 That girl over there used to be in my class. I don't remember her name.
_____
_____

7 Thank you for your letter. It arrived yesterday morning.
_____
_____

8 The Grand Hotel has offered me a job. My brother works there.
_____
_____

Mark: ____ / 8

Use of English

9 Circle the correct answers.

There are few people for ¹_____ a job interview is enjoyable, but a little preparation can make a big difference. The most important thing is to ²_____ the company online and find out as much as you can about it. While you are reading, try to ³_____ some questions ⁴_____ will demonstrate the knowledge you have gained. You should also find out the name of the street ⁵_____ the company is located because you need to ⁶_____ how to get there in plenty of time. Make a note of the name of the person ⁷_____ will be interviewing you, and ask specifically for him or her when you arrive. During the interview, do not be afraid to ⁸_____ the subject of salary and holidays, but leave these questions until later. Obviously, the candidate ⁹_____ performance impresses the interviewer most will get the job, but with the right preparation it might ¹⁰_____ being you!

1 a who	b whom	c whose
2 a look after	b look up	c look up to
3 a come up with	b get away with	c go in for
4 a who	b whose	c that
5 a where	b which	c whose
6 a ask out	b come across	c work out
7 a whom	b who	c whose
8 a bring up	b give up	c hold up
9 a which	b who	c whose
10 a end up	b get up	c make up

Mark: ____ / 10

Total: ____ / 65

I can ...

Read the statements. Think about your progress and tick one of the boxes.

★ = I need more practice.   ★★★ = No problem!

★★ = I sometimes find this difficult.

	★	★★	★★★
I can describe people's character.			
I can use defining relative clauses.			
I can listen for linking words and phrases.			
I can use non-defining relative clauses.			
I can use separable and inseparable phrasal verbs correctly.			
I can understand a text about a young entrepreneur.			
I can exchange information about jobs.			
I can write a for and against essay about education and work.			

Reading

Exam Strategy
When matching headings with paragraphs, focus on the first and last sentences in each paragraph first. These often introduce and summarise the contents of a paragraph, so they may help you to identify the correct heading. It is still very important to read the whole paragraph carefully before making your choices.

1 Read the Strategy above. Then read the first and last lines of two paragraphs and match them with headings A and B.

> **1** Not everyone can manage a part-time job, interests and school work at the same time. ... So carefully consider your need for free time before deciding to take on a job.

> **2** Working while you're a student can broaden your view of the world. ... Learning that not everyone is thinking about school issues is a useful lesson.

A Work provides a wider experience of life. ☐
B Leisure activities may be more important than a job. ☐

2 Now read the article. Match the headings (A–F) with the paragraphs (1–4). There are two extra headings.

1 _____

A weekend job is an attractive idea for many of us. Weekend work is a break from school routine, and it provides some extra spending money. It can also give us a chance to explore the working world and gain a bit of experience.

2 _____

Unfortunately, there aren't many weekend jobs for school-aged people these days. Since the economic troubles of the early 2000s, many part-time jobs have been taken by adults who need the work – meaning fewer jobs for us.

3 _____

Young people can still find ways to earn money if they think creatively. Start by studying your house. Are there chores which no one seems to have time for? Offer to tidy the garden, paint the fence or clear out the garage – for a fee.

4 _____

Neighbours are a well-known source of income too. Babysitting is a traditional job, and if you're good at it, you can earn respect and money. Gardening, washing people's cars and cleaning windows are also dependable possibilities.

A The benefits of weekend work
B Some jobs are not right for us
C What's happened to jobs for young people?
D Traditional jobs in the community
E Get help in finding work
F Earning money can begin at home

Listening

Exam Strategy
Read the question stems carefully before listening in order to identify what you need to listen for. For example, if the stem is *The conversation takes place ...* , you need to listen for the setting of the conversation, and specific ideas or feelings are not relevant.

3 Read the Strategy. Then read the extract from a recording and sentences 1–3. What is the topic of each question?

> 🎧 Welcome back, listeners. I hope you enjoyed the last song. Now with us in the studio today we have a great musician and composer who I've looked up to my entire life. I am so thrilled to meet him at last, and I look forward to hearing about his latest album. So let's welcome ...

1 The conversation takes place in ... _____
2 The speaker feels that her guest is ... _____
3 The guest is going to discuss ... _____

4 🎧 **1.30** You will hear five extracts twice. Circle the correct answers (A–D).

1 What is the man doing at the moment?
  A interviewing someone for a job
  B offering someone a job
  C talking to a co-worker
  D preparing for an interview

2 The speaker is advertising something that
  A you must accept within a time limit.
  B will last for 24 months.
  C will give you free internet service for a short time.
  D is expensive but very good quality.

3 The girl admits that she
  A has arrived home late several times.
  B did not behave in the right way.
  C wanted to make her parents angry.
  D thinks her parents are right.

4 The conversation takes place
  A in a radio studio.
  B in a TV studio.
  C in a school classroom.
  D in a university classroom.

5 Which of the following statements is true?
  A You only need your password for the website.
  B You can only get help online.
  C You must change your personal information before you can speak to someone.
  D You can speak to someone without another phone call.

Exam Skills Trainer

Use of English

5 Read the Strategy. Then circle the correct answers (A–D) to complete the text.

Ever since the time when humans first began to study and describe personality, they have probably wondered ¹_____ personality can be changed. Can stubbornness be ²_____ into flexibility, or pessimism into optimism? You might have come ³_____ someone who used to ⁴_____ shy and modest, and who is now filled with self-confidence. How did this happen? Experts suggest that your basic personality cannot be altered. But you *can* change the behaviour ⁵_____ is connected to it. For example, you may see the least sociable of your friends laughing and chatting at a party. That doesn't mean that they are no ⁶_____ shy or introverted. But maybe they have learned to behave in a way that ⁷_____ them *appear* more comfortable in a social situation. Their real personality may not change, but with practice, they may be able to ⁸_____ up their unsociable behaviour for good.

1	A that	B about	C if	D which
2	A made	B turned	C put	D switched
3	A across	B apart	C along	D up
4	A be	B is	C being	D was
5	A what	B it	C who	D that
6	A later	B more	C less	D longer
7	A does	B leaves	C allows	D makes
8	A turn	B take	C give	D end

Speaking

6 Read the Strategy. Put sentences A–D in the correct order (1–4).

A I think the first photo might be a farm in Argentina. It's very beautiful. The second photo looks like France, or maybe it's Italy. ☐

B In this photo, the people are working with horses. ☐

C Both photos show people working on a farm. ☐

D In the second photo, the people are picking fruit rather than working with animals. ☐

7 Photos (A and B) show young people doing part-time work in their holidays. Compare and contrast them. Include the following:

- typical jobs that young people do part-time
- why young people do part-time work
- what skills people can learn by doing holiday work

8 In pairs, ask and answer the questions. If possible, use evidence from the photos in your discussion.

1 What kinds of skills and personality do people who work with young children need?

2 Which of the two part-time jobs shown in photos A and B would you rather do? Why?

Writing

9 Read the Strategy. Then complete the text with the words below.

addition   also   another   furthermore   other   overall

One issue with social media is that it can distract people from work or study. In ¹_____ , it can create unhappiness and anxiety when people compare their lives to other people's. ²_____ problem is that some people use it to spread unkind ideas about others.

On the ³_____ hand, thanks to social media, people can build friendships quickly and easily by sharing photos, links, ideas and opinions. Social media ⁴_____ allows people to ask for help and advice. ⁵_____ , it can educate people about things like health.

⁶_____ , I think social media has more positive than negative effects on everyday life.

10 Read the task below and write a for and against essay.

Teenage students should spend more time at school studying I.C.T. (Information and Communication Technology). Discuss.

Vocabulary

A **Talking about the arts**
I can talk about the arts.

1 Complete the art forms.

1 b_____
2 c_____ m_____
3 d_____
4 m_____
5 p_____
6 c_____
7 d_____
8 m_____
9 n_____
10 o_____
11 p_____
12 p_____
13 p_____ m_____
14 s_____
15 T_____ d_____

2 Complete the sentences with types of artist.

1 A playwright writes plays.
2 _____ choreographs dances.
3 _____ performs in operas.
4 _____ directs films and plays.
5 _____ sings in a band.
6 _____ conducts an orchestra.
7 _____ paints pictures.
8 _____ acts in plays and films.
9 _____ writes novels.
10 _____ carves statues and creates sculptures.
11 _____ writes poems.
12 _____ composes music.

3 🎧 **2.02 Listen to three speakers talking about art forms that they study. Match speakers 1–3 with sentences A–D. There is one extra sentence.**

Which speaker …

A already earns some money from his / her artistic skills? ☐
B describes an old and a new artistic skill that have a connection with each other? ☐
C wants to experiment with different performance ideas in his / her chosen art form? ☐
D says that his / her art form is not appreciated by many people? ☐

4 🎧 **2.02 Complete the sentences with the verbs below. Then listen again and check.**

carving choreograph compose create perform sing

Speaker 1
And I would like to _____ ballets as well as _____ them.

Speaker 2
a Firstly, I love _____ sculptures out of wood.
b I'm also fascinated by 3D modelling, where you _____ 3D models.

Speaker 3
a I _____ in two choirs.
b One day, I'd also like to _____ my own songs.

The passive

I can identify and use different forms of the passive.

1 Complete the sentences with the passive form of the verbs in brackets. Use the correct tense.

1 *Romeo and Juliet* _____ probably _____ between 1591 and 1595. (write)
2 '_____ these glasses_____ ?' 'No, they haven't.' (wash)
3 He told me that the show _____ two days before. (cancel)
4 I'm sharing my sister's bedroom because mine _____ at the moment. (decorate)
5 I walked into the office while a job applicant _____. (interview)
6 The exam results _____ by post next week. (send)
7 'What language _____ in Hong Kong?' 'Cantonese.' (speak)

2 Complete the text with the passive form of the verbs in brackets. Use the correct tense.

Until 2004, composer Mamoru Samuragochi ¹_____ (know) as 'Japan's Beethoven'. He is most famous for his Hiroshima Symphony No. 1, which ²_____ (compose) in 2003 in memory of the people who ³_____ (kill) by the atomic bomb in 1945. It ⁴_____ (perform) for the first time in 2008 in front of many of the world's most important politicians. But Samuragochi now admits that this piece and many others ⁵_____ in fact _____ (not write) by him, but by another musician. The real composer of the musician's works ⁶_____ yet _____ (not name), but a man called Takahashi Niigaki recently claimed to have written them. Although a talented composer, it is sad that in the future Samuragochi ⁷_____ (remember) as a fraud.

3 Write passive sentences with *by*.

1 Leonardo da Vinci painted the *Mona Lisa*.
_____
2 A group of young men will perform the dance.
_____
3 The Queen has opened a new art gallery.
_____
4 JJ Abrams directed *Star Wars: The Force Awakens*.
_____
5 In *The Theory of Everything*, Eddie Redmayne plays the role of Stephen Hawking.
_____

4 Make the active sentences passive. Use modal verbs. Don't use *by* + agent.

1 You shouldn't eat those mushrooms.
Those mushrooms shouldn't be eaten.
2 They might have cancelled the concert.
_____
3 You can often see foxes in my garden.
_____
4 We mustn't use mobiles during lessons.
_____
5 You have to write your name in capital letters.
_____
6 You can't trust Toby!
_____
7 We must hand in homework on time.
_____
8 You should leave dirty shoes by the door.
_____

5 Some of the sentences are incorrect. Rewrite them correctly. Tick the correct sentences.

1 I think we are been followed. ☐
_____
2 Peugeot cars make in France. ☐
_____
3 *Set Fire to the Rain* was written and performed by Adele. ☐
_____
4 The book must be returning to the library. ☐
_____
5 Was German teaching in your school? ☐
_____
6 Oh no! My mobile has been stolen! ☐
_____

Poetry in motion

I can listen for implications and subtext.

1 Complete the sentences with the words and phrases below.

apathetic era foolish lethargic the norm
peers quick fix straight

1 She was feeling _____ , so she spent the afternoon watching DVDs.
2 She loves classical music, though most of her _____ prefer pop.
3 Unfortunately, there is no _____ for the problem of homelessness.
4 Some people complete their degree in four years, though three years is _____ .
5 It's easy to become _____ about your future when there don't seem to be many opportunities on offer.
6 We need to get these things _____ to avoid similar misunderstandings in future.
7 It's quite an interesting play, but it isn't very relevant to our _____ .
8 I felt _____ when I realised that I had sent the email to the wrong person.

> **Listening Strategy**
> Sometimes the information you need for a listening task is implied rather than stated directly. For example, if somebody says 'I wish I was back home', it implies they are not happy with their current situation.

2 🎧 2.03 Read the Listening Strategy. Then listen to four monologues and circle the correct implication for each speaker.

Monologue 1
a Josh enjoyed the modern dance performance a lot.
b Josh didn't really enjoy the modern dance performance.

Monologue 2
a Hannah expected to get a part in the show.
b Hannah didn't expect to get a part in the show.

Monologue 3
a Ben is a big fan of modern art.
b Ben is not very keen on modern art.

Monologue 4
a Fatima prefers modern pop to 1980s pop.
b Fatima prefers 1980s pop to modern pop.

3 🎧 2.03 Listen again and complete the sentences from the monologues. Use them to help check your answers to exercise 2.

1 Let's _____ _____ this: I'm glad Katy liked it!
2 That was _____ _____ surprise – there was only one part.
3 With a lot of the pictures, it was _____ _____ _____ the point.
4 He claims it's much better than today's pop music, but _____ _____ .

4 🎧 2.04 Read the poem and listen to three speakers talking about poetry. Which speaker is talking about the poem below?

Our Meetings
BY ANDREW WATERMAN

As in the Underground there's no mistaking
the train's approach, it pushes air ahead,
whirls paper, the line sings, a sort-of dread
suffusing longing and my platform shaking –
so it is before our every meeting,
till you arrive. Hear how my heart is beating.

Speaker ___ is talking about this poem.

5 🎧 2.04 Listen again. Match speakers 1–3 with sentences A–F. There are two extra sentences.

The speaker:
A wanted a career in poetry. ☐
B used a poem to apologise to somebody. ☐
C made a new friend as the result of reading a poem. ☐
D tried to persuade somebody to like a particular poem, but failed. ☐
E enjoyed poems without really understanding them. ☐

Grammar

have something done

I can use the structure 'have something done'.

1 Order the words to make sentences with *have something done*.

1 You look different. (had / you / your / dyed / hair / have)?
_____

2 There's room for you all to stay at our house this year. (extension / we've / built / an / had).
_____

3 I can't text you. (phone / had / I've / stolen / my).
_____

4 He's started wearing glasses. (tested / eyes / had / his / he's).
_____

5 I couldn't open my parents' front door. (locks / they / had / the / changed)!
_____

6 This is a great photo. (can / copy / have / made / we / a)?
_____

2 Complete the text with the words in brackets and *have something done*.

The British TV show *10 Years Younger* helps members of the public to change their appearance and look younger. At the start of the show, the participants
¹_____ (their age / guess) by a hundred members of the public. They then
²_____ (their hair / do) by top hairdressers. They also ³_____ (new clothes / choose) by fashion experts. If necessary, they ⁴_____ (their teeth / fix) by a dentist. Some of them even ⁵_____
_____ (some work / do) on their face by a cosmetic surgeon. At the end of the show, they ⁶_____
_____ (their appearance / judge) by a hundred strangers again to see if they look younger. The show is popular, although it has also been criticised for focusing too much on appearance.

3 Complete the sentences with the words below, *have something done* and the words in brackets.

dye   paint   publish   remove   steal

1 My grandfather has written an interesting book.
He _____ (should / it).

2 The graffiti on our house looks terrible.
We really _____ (must / it).

3 She used to have blonde hair, but she
_____ (must / it).

4 Your bedroom looks too dark. You _____
_____ (should / the walls).

5 You shouldn't leave your bike unlocked.
You _____ (might / it).

4 Complete the sentences with the correct reflexive pronouns to add emphasis.

1 All the food at our café is home-made. We even bake the bread _____ .

2 It's a modern frame, but the painting _____ is nearly 300 years old.

3 I don't really like old buildings, but the designs _____ can be quite attractive.

4 I don't understand modern poetry. I'm sure the poets _____ don't know what they mean!

5 It doesn't have to be a professional photo. Just send them a photo that you took _____ .

6 She wrote the words and the music on her new album, and played all the instruments _____ .

7 It's a fantastic piece of music. The composer _____ thought it was his best work.

8 You and your friends can sing better than most people on this talent show. You should enter it _____ next year!

5 Complete the sentences with reflexive pronouns and the correct form of the verbs below.

feed   film   give   injure   see   tell

1 I can't walk. I _____ playing football yesterday.

2 It can be scary being alone in the house, but I _____ that there is nothing to be afraid of.

3 The twins are two years old now, and they can _____ with a spoon.

4 My sister _____ dancing and posted it on YouTube.

5 Turn that music down or you might _____ a headache!

6 I'm a good musician, but I can't _____ doing it professionally.

Word Skills
Indefinite pronouns
I can use indefinite pronouns.

Revision: Student's Book page 79

1 Complete the words with *a, e, i, o, u* and *y*. Are they musical genres or aspects of music?

		genre	aspect
1	b e a t	☑	☑
2	bl__ __s	☐	☐
3	ch__r__s	☐	☐
4	cl__ss__c__l	☐	☐
5	c__ __ntr__ __nd w__st__rn	☐	☐
6	f__lk	☐	☐
7	h__rm__n__	☐	☐
8	h__ __v__ m__t__l	☐	☐
9	h__p h__p/r__p	☐	☐
10	j__zz	☐	☐
11	l__r__cs	☐	☐
12	m__l__d__/t__n__	☐	☐
13	p__p/r__ck	☐	☐
14	rh__thm	☐	☐
15	sp__ __d/t__mp__	☐	☐
16	t__chn__	☐	☐
17	v__rs__	☐	☐

2 Complete the indefinite pronouns.

1 No_____ was listening when I spoke.
2 My phone must be some_____ in the house.
3 Did you notice any_____ different about Sam?
4 Does any_____ know the lyrics to this next song?
5 I know no_____ about modern classical music.
6 Did you go any_____ exciting during the summer?

3 Underline one mistake in each sentence. Then correct it.

1 We didn't see nothing we liked in the art gallery.
_____

2 I shouted, but anybody could hear me.
_____

3 It doesn't look as if somebody is home yet.
_____

4 Nobody saw you, did he?
_____

5 Has everybody got your tickets?
_____

6 I've looked anywhere, but I can't find my wallet.
_____

7 Everyone need to carry their own bags.
_____

4 Complete the sentences with indefinite pronouns.

1 Would you like _____ to drink before we leave?
2 He pressed the button, but _____ happened.
3 _____ knows why she resigned; it's a mystery.
4 When the ground floor flooded, we moved _____ upstairs to keep it dry.
5 They searched the sea for survivors, but they didn't find _____ at all.
6 The room was a mess: there were plastic cups and empty crisp packets _____.
7 There were a few people in the shopping centre, but _____ saw the robbery happen.
8 My sister is starting university in London next month and needs _____ to live.

5 Complete the dialogue with indefinite pronouns.

George Hi, Ellie. Did you do ¹_____ interesting at the weekend?

Ellie I went to a concert with my cousin on Saturday. It was at a tiny venue ²_____ in London.

George What was it like?

Ellie It wasn't like ³_____ I'd ever heard before. It was incredibly modern.

George Did you like it?

Ellie No, I hated it! But ⁴_____ else seemed to enjoy it. They all clapped at the end. Anyway, what did you get up to?

George I just stayed in and watched ⁵_____ on TV.

Ellie That sounds nice.

George It was OK. But I was a bit lonely. I didn't see ⁶_____ all weekend.

VOCAB BOOST!
Learn new words by making short, not long, lists. For example, make a list of five words related to music and write their translations. Learn the words. Then test yourself the next day by looking at one column and covering the other. Can you remember the covered words? Finally, swap columns and try again.

6 Read the *Vocab boost!* box. Then write translations for the words. Use a dictionary to help you if necessary.

English	Translation
1 to compose	_____
2 to rehearse	_____
3 to accompany	_____
4 to perform	_____
5 to improvise	_____

7 Test yourself. Cover one column of the table in exercise 6 and try to remember the words in the other column. Then swap.

Street art
I can understand a text about street art.

Revision: Student's Book page 80

1 Complete the definitions of things you can find in the street.

1 a place where you park your bike:
b_____ r_____

2 a piece of furniture on which a number of people can sit: b_____

3 the area at the side of the road where pedestrians walk: p_____

4 a tall post with a strong light on the top:
l_____ p_____

5 a place where you can ring somebody:
p_____ b_____

6 a model of somebody, usually made of stone:
s_____

7 a machine at the side of the road where you pay to park your car: p_____ m_____

8 a place where you catch a form of public transport:
b_____ s_____

9 something which tells drivers not to go:
s_____ s_____

10 a jet or stream of water usually coming from a pool:
f_____

2 Read the text. Are the sentences true (T) or false (F)?

1 Łódź was famous before the work of the Urban Forms Foundation. ☐

2 The Foundation's art project didn't cost anything. ☐

3 The project is now completed. ☐

Reading Strategy

1 Multiple-choice questions are always in the same order as the information in the text.

2 If there is a question testing the main idea of the text, or the writer's overall opinion, it will come last.

3 The correct option will match the meaning of the text but use different words. Make sure the other options are not right or are not mentioned in the text.

4 If you can't decide between the options, an intelligent guess is better than no answer.

3 Read the Reading Strategy. Circle the correct answers.

1 Two people started an organisation in Łódź to
  a provide more industry in the city.
  b rebuild the city centre.
  c hold more art exhibitions.
  d improve the look of the city.

2 The Urban Forms Foundation
  a asked the mayor to help.
  b needed the city council to agree to the project.
  c asked the council for money for their idea.
  d told the city council what to do.

3 Famous street artists
  a weren't interested at first in the project.
  b from abroad only were invited.
  c were asked to take part in the project.
  d asked the Foundation for work.

4 Because of the Foundation's work,
  a the city has become famous in the art world.
  b the city now has more street art than New York.
  c tourists are allowed to paint on the city walls.
  d there is no need for more artwork in the city.

A BRIGHTER CITY!

The city of Łódź in Poland was another unremarkable industrial city until a few years ago. In 2009, an organisation called the Urban Forms Foundation was set up by a well-known art historian and an actress. Their idea was to bring the tired urban landscape to life again.

The Foundation planned an art project that would change the city's image and regenerate the centre, and presented it to the city council. It wanted the council to ask street artists to paint on walls around the city centre as a permanent outdoor exhibition. The mayor of the city supported the idea and the Foundation was given permission to go ahead and raise the money needed. Famous street artists from all over the world were invited by the Foundation to come to Poland to work, including Os Gemeos from Brazil, Aryz from Spain and Remed from France, as well as local talent like M-City and Etam Cru. In total, artists from eight countries took part in the project over the next few years, and more than twenty huge murals were created on the sides of buildings in public spaces.

Łódź is now the second city in the world for street art after New York, and people visit there especially to see the amazing artworks. With a special map, tourists can walk round the city and view them all in a couple of hours. Now, once a year, the Foundation organises an art festival which attracts participants from all over the world. And in the future, the project will be continued with other pieces of urban art – statues, sculptures and 'street jewellery'. The transformation goes on!

Photo comparison and role-play

I can compare photos and role-play a discussion.

A

B

1 Look at photos A and B. What types of show are they? Match them with two of the types of show below.

an art exhibition   a circus   a classical concert
a comedy club   a magic show   a musical
an open-air theatre   a piano recital

> You are staying with an English friend and his family who have offered to take you to a show. Discuss with your friend which show is more appealing. Explain why you would choose one show and not the other.

2 Read the task. Then complete the sentences in your own words to compare the photos in exercise 1. Write one additional sentence to say which show you think is more appealing.

1 Both photos show _____
_____ .

2 Whereas photo B shows acrobats, photo A _____
_____
_____ .

3 Unlike photo A, in photo B the audience are sitting _____
_____
_____ .

4 _____
_____ .

> **Speaking Strategy 1**
> Try to use a variety of expressions instead of repeating the same common verbs too often. For example, make sure you know several different ways of saying *I like / I don't like*.

3 Read Speaking Strategy 1. Then complete the phrases with the words below.

absolutely do fan keen much quite stand thing

1 I'm (not) a big _____ of …
2 I'm _____ into … / I'm not really into …
3 I'm really / I've never been that _____ on …
4 I _____ love …
5 I really can't _____ …
6 I enjoy … very _____ .
7 … is not really my _____ .
8 … doesn't _____ anything for me.

4 Read Speaking Strategy 2. Complete the phrases with the words below.

afraid be frank I'm say

> **Speaking Strategy 2**
> We often use one of the phrases below to introduce a preference, particularly when it is negative.
> I'm ¹_____ … I must ²_____ …
> To be ³_____ … If ⁴_____ honest, …
> To ⁵_____ blunt, … Personally, …

5 Write two sentences about something you dislike (a type of music, sport, show, etc.). Use one phrase from exercise 3 and one phrase from Speaking Strategy 2.

1 _____
_____

2 _____
_____

6 You are going to do the task in exercise 2. Look at photos C and D below.

D

Your choice: C ☐ D ☐
Why this one? _____
_____
_____

Why not the other? _____
_____
_____

7 Now do the speaking task comparing photos C and D. Use your notes from exercises 5 and 6.

Writing
Article: a film review
I can write a film review.

Preparation

Your teacher has asked you to write a film review for the school magazine. Write your review describing the film and say what you liked and didn't like about it.

1 **Read the task above. Then read Writing Strategy 1 and the review below. Answer the questions.**

   a Where does each paragraph end?
   Paragraph 1: A ☐ or B ☐
   Paragraph 2: C ☐ or D ☐
   Paragraph 3: E ☐ or F ☐

   b Has the writer followed the second piece of advice in the Strategy? Yes ☐ No ☐

> **Writing Strategy 1**
>
> 1 Give your review a logical structure. Divide it into paragraphs, each with its own topic or focus.
>
> 2 The conclusion should restate the main idea given in the introduction, but using different words. It should also include the writer's opinion and, if appropriate, a recommendation.

An extraordinary film about an extraordinary man!

If you're looking for a film that has romance and drama and makes you think, this is the one for you! I loved *The Theory of Everything*, from start to finish. **A** And I have no doubt that it'll remain one of my favourite films for many years to come! I'd definitely recommend it. **B** It is mostly set in Cambridge, England, and it tells the story of Stephen Hawking, a physicist at Cambridge University, who was diagnosed with motor neurone disease while still in his early twenties. We see how, with the help of Jane – his girlfriend and then wife – he overcame great physical disabilities to become probably the world's most famous scientist. **C** What I really loved about the film is the way it involves you in the characters. I felt that I really got to know them, and found their story incredibly moving. **D** I thought the acting was first-class, with superb performances from Eddie Redmayne and Felicity Jones. The film was also beautifully filmed, with lots of atmospheric shots of Cambridge. **E** I have only one small criticism. We learn a lot about Jane and Stephen's relationship, but we learn nothing about Stephen Hawking the scientist, and what motivates him. **F** Overall, however, this is a fantastic film. If you haven't seen it yet, get the DVD. You won't be disappointed! I guarantee it.

> Choose a good title for your article.
>
> In the first paragraph, attract the reader's attention. You can do this by addressing him / her directly, especially with questions.
>
> Use an appropriate style and register for the target audience.

2 **Read Writing Strategy 2 and answer questions 1–3 below.**

   1 Underline the sentence that attracts the reader's attention in the first paragraph.
   2 Is the overall style formal ☐ or informal ☐?
   3 Has the writer addressed both elements of the task? Yes ☐ No ☐

3 **Tick the phrases for describing stories that the writer uses in the article. Which phrase cannot be used to describe a film?**

   1 It's set in (place and / or time). ☐
   2 There are lots of twists and turns. ☐
   3 It tells the story of (character). ☐
   4 I would definitely recommend it. ☐
   5 It's a real page-turner. ☐

   Phrase ☐ can't be used for films.

Writing Guide

4 **You are going to do the task in exercise 1. Make notes about a film of your choice.**

   What I liked: _____
   _____
   _____

   What I didn't like: _____
   _____

   Overall opinion: _____
   _____
   _____

5 **Write your review. Follow the structure of the model review in exercise 1, and use your notes from exercise 4. Use some phrases from exercise 3.**

> **CHECK YOUR WORK**
>
> 👁 Have you ...
>   ☐ given your article an interesting title and introduction?
>   ☐ attracted the reader's attention in the first paragraph?
>   ☐ divided your review into paragraphs?
>   ☐ included you opinion and a recommendation?
>   ☐ checked your spelling and grammar?

Vocabulary

1 Complete the sentences with the verbs below.

appeared in   carves   composes   creates
paints   performs   plays   writes

1 The actor Eddie Redmayne _____ Stephen Hawking in the film *The Theory of Everything*.
2 The American artist Brian Ruth _____ massive sculptures out of wood with a chainsaw.
3 The author JK Rowling _____ books for adults as well as children's stories.
4 Although he's still a child, Kieron Williamson _____ amazing pictures.
5 The singer Rihanna _____ in concerts all over the world.
6 Bradley Cooper and Jennifer Lawrence have _____ three films together.
7 The Italian musician Ennio Morricone _____ music for television series as well as films.
8 The sculptor Alonzo Clemons _____ incredibly realistic animal sculptures out of clay.

Mark: / 8

2 Complete the definitions with art forms.

1 A _____ is a piece of creative writing arranged in short lines, often about emotions.
2 A _____ is a funny drawing in a newspaper or magazine.
3 A _____ is a piece of writing performed by actors usually in the theatre.
4 A _____ is a figure or an object made out of stone, metal, or some other hard material.
5 A _____ is a book that tells a story about people who are not real.
6 _____ is a form of acting that uses body movements and facial expressions, not words.

Mark: / 6

3 Complete the sentences with the correct form of the words in bold.

1 Although Jane Austen only wrote six **novels**, she is an internationally recognised _____ .
2 The name of the Norwegian _____ who **painted** *The Scream* is Edvard Munch.
3 The most successful **play** written by the Irish _____ George Bernard Shaw is *Pygmalion*.
4 The Colombian _____ Fernando Botero is famous for his **sculptures** of large people and animals.
5 *The Divine Comedy* is a **poem** written by the Italian _____ Dante Alighieri.
6 The _____ Wagner **composed** both the words and the music for his opera *The Ring of the Nibelung*.

Mark: / 6

Word Skills

4 Complete the dialogues with the correct indefinite pronouns.

1 A Are you ready for your holiday?
   B Yes, I think I've got _____ I need.
2 A Did you manage to get some tickets for the play?
   B No, the ticket office was closed. There wasn't _____ there.
3 A Are you going to the music festival next month?
   B Yes, but I need _____ to stay.
4 A What's wrong?
   B I'm bored. I've got _____ to do.
5 A How much exercise do you do?
   B None at all. I go _____ by car.
6 A How are you getting home from the airport?
   B _____ is picking me up – probably my mother.
7 A Have you got any plans for tonight?
   B Not really. I'm not doing _____ special.

Mark: / 7

5 Complete the sentences with the words below.

anything   fan   into   love   much   on   stand   thing

1 Folk is not really my _____ .
2 I'm a big _____ of jazz.
3 I've never been that keen _____ rap.
4 I'm quite _____ classical music.
5 I really can't _____ country and western.
6 I enjoy techno very _____ .
7 I absolutely _____ heavy metal.
8 Hip hop doesn't do _____ for me.

Mark: / 8

Grammar

6 Complete the sentences with the passive form of the verbs in brackets.

1 This concert should _____ on TV so that everyone can see it. (show)
2 The new art gallery _____ by the mayor next Tuesday. (open)
3 That TV drama _____ by many people every evening. (watch)
4 How many *Hunger Games* films _____ so far? (make)
5 The painting *Sunflowers* _____ by van Gogh. (paint)
6 An opera _____ in the concert hall later this evening. (perform)

Mark: / 6

Mark: / 6

7 Complete the dialogues with the correct form of *have something done* using the verbs in brackets.

1 A Have you been to the optician's recently?
   B Yes, I _____ last week.
   (test / my eyes)

2 A How often do you have your flat cleaned?
   B We _____ twice a week.
   (clean / it)

3 A How long have you been wearing earrings?
   B I _____ since I was six.
   (pierced / my ears)

4 A Why can't you use your games console?
   B It isn't working, so I _____ .
   (repair / it)

5 A How old were you in that photo?
   B My mum _____ when I
   was ten. (take / it)

6 A When is your room being decorated?
   B I _____ next weekend.
   (decorate / it)

7 A Why are you calling the bank?
   B I _____ .
   (steal / my credit card)

8 A How often do you go to the hairdresser's?
   B I _____ every two months.
   (cut / my hair)

Mark: ___ / 8

8 Complete the sentences with the correct reflexive pronouns.

1 He cut _____ when he was making a sandwich.

2 My mother hasn't had time to iron my shirt, so I'll have to do it _____ .

3 If no one else is home, you and your brother will have to make dinner _____ .

4 When my sister's bike broke, she repaired it _____ .

5 Do you go to the hairdresser's, or do you dye your hair _____ ?

6 They were late for the match because they didn't give _____ enough time.

7 The only way the cat could have got out is by opening the door _____ .

8 Before we moved into our new flat, we painted it _____ .

Mark: ___ / 8

Use of English

9 Complete the text. Use one word in each gap.

American actress Shailene Woodley was born in California in 1991. She started acting when she was a child and first appeared on TV in 1999. In 2008, she [1]_____ given the part of Amy Juergens in *The Secret Life of the American Teenager*. Since then, she has appeared [2]_____ several films, including *The Descendants* with George Clooney and *The Divergent* series.

In 2014, Woodley played the female lead role in *The Fault in Our Stars*, a film about [3]_____ young couple called Hazel and Gus who are both suffering from cancer. The film, which was an enormous success, [4]_____ based on the novel of the same name. It was written [5]_____ John Green, a popular author of fiction for young adults.

'Everyone [6]_____ me "How did you prepare for the role of Hazel?"' says Woodley. 'I knew the book very well because I [7]_____ read it and loved it when it first came out. Ansel (who plays Gus) and I had the opportunity to meet several young cancer patients. It's funny, but we didn't actually spend a lot of time talking about cancer. We just talked about the normal things that teenagers go through. On a practical level, I also [8]_____ my hair cut very short.'

Mark: ___ / 8

Total: ___ / 65

I can ...

Read the statements. Think about your progress and tick one of the boxes.

★ = I need more practice.

★★ = I sometimes find this difficult.

★★★ = No problem!

	★	★★	★★★
I can talk about the arts.			
I can identify and use different forms of the passive.			
I can listen for implications and subtext.			
I can use the structure 'have something done'.			'
I can use indefinite pronouns.			
I can understand a text about street art.			
I can compare photos and role-play a discussion.			
I can write a film review.			

8 Messages

A On the phone
I can talk about using my phone.

1 Complete the dialogue extracts with the correct form of the verbs below.

disable   enter   make   save   send   text   top up

A Ben

I went abroad last month to Italy. I ¹_____ my mobile before I left with €40. I didn't ²_____ data roaming while I was away, and I ³_____ lots of calls. I checked my balance when I got back and found I'd been charged €30!

B Emma

I'll ⁴_____ you a text and you can ⁵_____ my number to your phone book. Then, when you want to ring or ⁶_____ me, you won't have to ⁷_____ the number.

call   leave   listen to   lose   put   put   recharge

C Ryan

I phoned Tom, but he must have ⁸_____ his phone on silent, so he didn't answer. I ⁹_____ a message, so hopefully he'll ¹⁰_____ his voicemail later.

D Zoe

Hi, Sally, we're on the train. I've ¹¹_____ the phone on loudspeaker so that Mike can speak to you too … No, it won't annoy the other passengers! … Oh, the train is about to go into a tunnel and I think we'll ¹²_____ the signal … Can you hear me? … OK, listen, I'm running out of charge too, I need to ¹³_____ the battery. I'll hang up now and ¹⁴_____ you later … Bye.

2 Complete the sentences with phrasal verbs.

1 Oh, no! My phone has r_____ _____ _____ charge! Can I borrow your charger?

2 'Did you speak to Jack?' 'No. I phoned him, and his mobile rang for ages, but he didn't p_____ _____ .'

3 Announcement on a plane: 'Would all passengers please s_____ _____ all mobile devices and computers.'

4 Can you please s_____ _____ ? I can't hear you very well. You are b_____ _____ because the signal isn't very strong.

5 I rang my dad's office and spoke to the receptionist, but I didn't g_____ _____ to my dad.

6 Message on an answerphone: 'Can you c_____ me _____ when you get this message? My number is 01548 956711.'

7 Recorded announcement: 'The number you have dialled does not exist. Please h_____ _____ and dial again.'

8 Message on an answerphone: 'Hi, Neil. I've been trying to call you all morning. Can you g_____ _____ to me on 01548 190684?'

9 'Why did you hang up during the call?' 'I didn't hang up. We were c_____ _____ .'

3 🎧 2.05 Listen and circle the correct answers.

Dialogue 1
Which of these sentences is a fact, not an opinion?
a Alex returned the charger to Jane.
b Alex borrows Jane's charger very frequently.
c Alex was the last person to use Jane's charger.

Dialogue 2
Daniel was cross because
a of something Sally said.
b Sally didn't return his call.
c he's too busy to go to the cinema.

Dialogue 3
Lucy's mum needs help with
a recharging her phone.
b saving a number to her phone book.
c understanding warning messages.

8B Grammar
Reported speech
I can use reported speech.

1 Complete 1–5 with the tenses below. Then complete 6–9 with the correct verb forms.

past continuous   past perfect   past perfect
past perfect   past simple

Direct speech	Reported speech
1 present simple	_____
2 present continuous	_____
3 past simple	_____
4 present perfect	_____
5 past perfect	_____
6 *can / can't*	_____
7 *will / won't*	_____
8 *might*	_____
9 *should*	_____

2 Circle the correct words.

Last weekend

1 John said he ___ ill.
  a is   **b** was

2 Maisie said that she ___ buy a new phone.
  a would   **b** will

3 Nathan said he ___ looking forward to summer.
  a is   **b** was

4 Harry said that Kay ___ gone to Italy.
  a has   **b** had

5 Emma told me that she ___ find her phone.
  a couldn't   **b** can't

6 Pete told me he ___ go to the party.
  a had to   **b** might have

3 How do these references to time and place change in reported speech?

Direct speech	Reported speech
1 today	_____
2 a week ago	_____
3 yesterday	_____
4 last year	_____
5 tomorrow	_____
6 next month	_____
7 here	_____

4 Complete the text with *said* or *told*.

Dan ¹_____ Bev that he had bought her a new phone. She looked at it and ²_____ him that it was too big. He ³_____ her that they were all that big nowadays. She ⁴_____ she wanted him to change it. He ⁵_____ that he couldn't change it and ⁶_____ her that it had cost a lot of money. She ⁷_____ she didn't care and ⁸_____ him she wouldn't use it.

5 Rewrite the sentences as reported speech. If necessary, change the pronouns, possessive adjectives and references to time and place.

1 John to Sue: 'I left a message for you yesterday.'
  John told _____
  _____

2 Mark: 'I'll top up my phone this evening.'
  _____
  _____

3 Jenny to Dave: 'I can't hear you.'
  _____
  _____

4 Ann: 'I've checked my balance three times this week.'
  _____
  _____

5 Jo to Si: 'You should turn off data roaming.'
  _____
  _____

6 Kate: 'I had already texted Harry at the weekend.'
  _____
  _____

7 Fran to Fred: 'I called Tom two days ago.'
  _____
  _____

6 Read the reported conversation between two identical twins. Write the direct speech below.

Imo was walking down the road when she slipped and fell. Her twin sister Zoe phoned just afterwards. Zoe told Imo that she had fallen over a few moments before. Imo told her that was an amazing coincidence because she had just done the same! Zoe said her leg was hurting so much that she couldn't walk. Imo told Zoe that her own leg was OK and that she could easily walk home. But Imo told Zoe that if she couldn't walk, she should call an ambulance. Zoe said that wouldn't be necessary and that she could phone their parents.

1 Zoe: _____
2 Imo: _____
  because _____
3 Zoe: _____
  _____
4 Imo: _____
  _____
5 Imo: But _____
  _____
6 Zoe: _____
  _____

Global network

I can identify the main idea of a listening text.

Revision: Student's Book page 87

1 Complete the sentences with the verbs and particles below.

Verbs call carry give go set work

Particles back off off on out up

1 If I'm going on a long car journey, I always check the traffic reports before I _____ _____.

2 I've got a new SIM card for my phone, but I can't _____ _____ how to install it.

3 If you make a mistake during the performance, don't stop – just _____ _____ .

4 When the weather got really bad, they decided to _____ _____ to their hotel.

5 They're going to _____ _____ the festival because of bad weather.

6 Although you failed your driving test, you shouldn't _____ _____ .

Listening Strategy 1

Sometimes you need to listen for the main idea (gist) rather than a specific piece of information. If this is the case, do not worry about a few unknown words. You can often understand the gist without understanding every word.

2 🎧 **2.06** Read Listening Strategy 1. Then listen to two mobile phone calls. Ignoring the words you cannot hear, circle the best summaries.

1 a Mary and Mike are going to meet up that day.
  b Mary and Mike are going to speak the next day to make an arrangement.

2 a Tom is going to buy some food for dinner.
  b Kirstie doesn't want Tom to buy any food.

Listening Strategy 2

When you do a multiple-choice task, do not choose the correct answer based only on one or two words. Remember that the incorrect options also have some connection with what you hear.

3 🎧 **2.07** Read Listening Strategy 2. Then listen to a radio programme and circle the correct answer.

What is the programme about, in general?
a The health effects of using mobile phones.
b The mobile phone network in the UK.
c The birth of the mobile phone industry.
d The best way to get a strong mobile phone signal wherever you are.

4 🎧 **2.07** Listen again and circle the correct answers.

1 The mobile phone network was built quickly in the UK because
  a two different phone companies were competing against each other.
  b two different phone companies were sharing the work.
  c a lot more people started using mobile phones than the phone companies had expected.
  d the government spent a lot of money on it.

2 The main difference between microcells and base stations is that microcells
  a are in cities, while base stations are in the countryside.
  b are smaller and less powerful than base stations.
  c are hidden, but base stations are visible.
  d are on the front of buildings, but base stations are on top.

3 Base stations are positioned in historic town centres because
  a they need to be close together in places with lots o buildings.
  b there are no rules to prevent it.
  c phone companies ignore the rules.
  d they can easily be disguised.

4 More research is being done into the health effects of base stations because
  a the results so far are not clear.
  b there have only been one or two studies so far.
  c some of the evidence suggests that there is a small risk to public health.
  d people do not always believe the results.

8D

Grammar
Reported questions
I can report questions correctly.

1 Order the words to make reported questions. Then write the questions as direct speech.

1 I / me / old / she asked / was / how
She asked me how old I was. 'How old are you?'

2 what / he asked / were / them / they / doing
_____
_____

3 afraid / you / you / were / I asked / if
_____

4 was / her / mum / why / she / we asked / angry
_____
_____

5 happening / I asked / what / him / was
_____
_____

6 where / would / me / stay / he asked / I
_____
_____

7 if / they asked / help / I / could / them
_____
_____

8 if / been / had / me / they asked / I / skiing / ever
_____
_____

9 how / we asked / spent / money / him / he'd / much
_____
_____

2 🎧 2.08 Listen to the direct speech and complete the reported questions.

1 He asked her _____ for dinner.
2 She asked him _____ on Sundays.
3 He asked her _____ the new Chinese restaurant.
4 She asked him _____ heavily.
5 He asked her _____ into town.

3 Rewrite the direct speech as reported questions.

1 'What are you doing?' Jake asked his sister.
_____

2 'Have you washed my jeans?' Poppy asked her mum.
_____

3 'When did you finish your homework?' my friend asked me.
_____

4 'Is it still raining?' Freddie asked Luke.
_____

5 'Can you play the saxophone?' Nadia asked me.
_____

6 'When will you give me back my laptop?' my dad asked my sister.
_____

4 Underline a mistake in each reported question. Then write the reported questions correctly.

1 She asked them why they are being so noisy.
_____

2 I asked her how she had hurt yourself.
_____

3 We asked them they wanted to travel with us.
_____

4 He asked me what was I listening to.
_____

5 They asked if who had told him the secret.
_____

6 She asked him why he had phoned her yesterday.
_____

7 I asked her that if she knew what was happening.
_____

8 I asked him how many brothers had he.
_____

5 Read the dialogue. Then complete the text below with reported statements and questions.

Zac Do you know Lily's email address? I want to invite her to my birthday party.

Ellie It's in my address book. I'll look in a minute.

Zac What are you doing?

Ellie I'm looking something up on the internet.

Zac What do you need to find out?

Ellie It's a secret.

Zac Can you give me a clue?

Ellie I don't want to spoil the surprise!

Zac asked Ellie if [1]_____ address.
He said that he [2]_____ to his birthday party. Ellie said [3]_____
address book. She said [4]_____ in a minute. Zac asked Ellie [5]_____ .
Ellie said that [6]_____ on the internet. Zac asked her [7]_____ .
Ellie said that [8]_____ . Zac asked Ellie [9]_____ a clue. Ellie said that
[10]_____ the surprise.

8E Word Skills

Verb patterns: reporting verbs

I can use a variety of reporting verbs correctly.

1 Circle the correct verbs to complete the sentences.

1 'OK. I'll feed your cat while you're away,' she ___ .
   a advised   b agreed   c encouraged

2 'You really must stay for dinner,' he ___ .
   a asked   b admitted   c insisted

3 'I'll definitely be there to meet you at the airport,' she ___ .
   a begged   b promised   c suggested

4 'It's dangerous to walk around that part of town at night,' he ___ .
   a denied   b offered   c warned

5 'Is the café still open at this time?' she ___ .
   a begged   b suggested   c wondered

6 'I'm the one who broke your laptop,' he ___ .
   a admitted   b apologised   c persuaded

7 'I could lend you some money,' he ___ .
   a denied   b proposed   c wondered

8 'You'd better say sorry,' she ___ .
   a advised   b apologised   c persuaded

2 Circle the correct reporting verb. Then complete the sentences with the infinitive or -ing form of the verbs in brackets.

1 My parents never **encouraged / suggested** me _____ (sing) when I was younger.

2 Did you **admit / apologise** to your teacher for _____ (miss) the class?

3 My Spanish friends **mentioned / told** _____ (come) to visit us this summer.

4 Why are you **accusing / blaming** me of _____ (copy) your homework? It isn't true!

5 The President has **denied / refused** _____ (answer) any more questions on this topic.

6 I **begged / offered** her _____ (pay) for our train tickets.

7 They **denied / insisted** _____ (stay) at the party until after midnight.

8 My cousin **encouraged / refused** me _____ (play) a few songs on the piano.

9 Why did you **agree / insist** on _____ (have) the end-of-term party at our house?

10 My parents **begged / refused** my sister not _____ (leave) school at sixteen.

11 My brother finally **admitted / apologised** _____ (tell) everyone my secret.

12 Our next door neighbour **accused / warned** us of _____ (make) too much noise late at night.

3 USE OF ENGLISH Complete the text with the missing words.

When I got home, my brother was singing loudly in the kitchen. I asked him ¹_____ to make so much noise, but he insisted ²_____ singing even louder. I accused him ³_____ being the worst singer I'd ever heard. Instead of getting cross, he thanked me ⁴_____ giving him an idea. Then he went upstairs, smiling. I wondered ⁵_____ asking him what he was doing, but I knew he would refuse ⁶_____ tell me. Two minutes later, he came downstairs again with a camcorder. He persuaded me ⁷_____ video him. 'If I'm that bad, we can make money on YouTube,' he told ⁸_____ .

VOCAB BOOST!

When you learn reporting verbs, it's a good idea to learn the related nouns at the same time. You can also learn what verbs these related nouns usually go with. **Tip:** the most common verbs that go with the related nouns are *give* and *make*.

agree – make an agreement

advise – give some advice

4 Use a dictionary to find the nouns related to the verbs below. Write them in the correct category.

accuse   apologise   encourage   promise   suggest   warn

give +	make +

5 Complete the second sentence so that it has a similar meaning to the first. Use the correct form of *give* or *make* and a noun related to the underlined verb.

1 They <u>warned</u> us about the dangerous cliffs.
   They _____ about the dangerous cliffs.

2 He rarely <u>encourages</u> his son.
   He rarely _____ his son any _____ .

3 She forgave him as soon as he <u>apologised</u> for his behaviour.
   She forgave him as soon as he _____ for his behaviour.

4 The police <u>accused</u> him of something serious.
   The police _____ a serious _____ against him.

5 Why do you never <u>suggest</u> anything?
   Why do you never _____ any _____ ?

88   Unit 8 Messages

Reading
Storytelling
I can understand a text about social media texts.

Revision: Student's Book page 90

1 **Complete the compound nouns with the words below.**

bestseller book contract culture high
love name phone social time TV

1 leisure _____
2 cell _____
3 _____ series
4 comic _____
5 _____ school
6 book _____
7 _____ list
8 pen _____
9 _____ media
10 pop _____
11 _____ story

2 **Complete the text below with compound nouns from exercise 1. Sometimes you need the plural form.**

My aunt writes novels, but not under her own name. She uses a
¹_____ _____ . She started writing in her
²_____ _____ , but now she does it full-time.
Her books are very popular and often appear on the
³_____ _____ . They are going to make one of
them into a ⁴_____ _____ . It's a ⁵_____
_____ about a teenage boy and girl. I can't wait to watch
it. My aunt has just got a new ⁶_____ _____ from
her publisher, and has already started to write her next novel.

3 **Read the text opposite. Are the sentences true (T) or false (F)?**

1 The author believes that Twitter is a very bad idea. ☐
2 A haiku is a type of modern short poem. ☐
3 The epistolary novel contains a series of letters. ☐

Reading Strategy
Read the missing sentences carefully. Then read the sentences in the text that come before and after each gap. Use these two strategies when selecting which sentence fits each gap.

1 Look for vocabulary links between the sentence and the surrounding text.

2 Look for pronouns, e.g. *he, she, it* and other references and check that they match your answer choice.

4 **Read the Reading Strategy. Then match sentences A–F with gaps 1–4 in the text. There are two extra sentences.**

A That's short!
B Nobody reads books any more, do they?
C They argue, for example, that fewer people read novels and write letters.
D There is, in fact, a lot we can learn from other cultures with a different writing tradition.
E Now writers are using this genre again, but with a modern day twist.
F Literature has suffered as a result.

SHORT AND SWEET

People complain nowadays that the popularity of media like Twitter has reduced our ability to read for long periods of time and to write properly. ¹___ It's also true that tweets are written by normal people, not professional authors, and that sometimes little attention is paid to correct grammar and spelling in digital messages. But are the new media only bad news for our literary tradition?

²___ In Japan, for example, the most popular form of poetry has long been the haiku, in which every word counts. A haiku is a poem with exactly seventeen syllables. Not words, but syllables. ³___ So with this method of writing, a lot of meaning has to be conveyed in a short space. This philosophy of 'less is more' made Japan the natural place for the birth of the cell phone novel with its very short chapters.

Other storytelling traditions using shorter forms have also been adapted to our modern tastes. The epistolary novel is a book written as a series of letters, or sometimes diaries. The genre used to be admired in Europe in the sixteenth and seventeenth centuries. ⁴___ Authors of teenage novels now often use emails, diary entries, text messages and cartoons to tell a story.

So perhaps these shorter styles of writing are not bad for literature as a whole. Perhaps they are just modern ways of expressing the age-old tradition of storytelling.

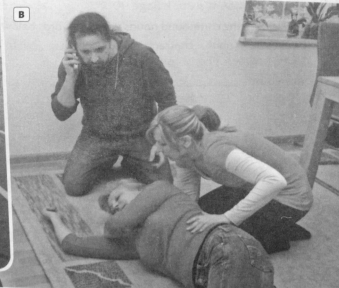

1 Look at photo A. What do you think has happened?

2 Complete the phrases for speculating with the phrases below. Then describe photo A.

as if   be (that)   but I'd say that   I'd say (that)
pretty certain that   say, but   that

1 I can't be sure, _____ ...
2 It could _____ ...
3 It's hard to _____ ...
4 It looks _____ ...
5 I'm _____ ...
6 It's clear _____ ...
7 Judging by (her expression), _____ ...

3 Compare and contrast photos A and B. Make notes.

1 Where are the people? What are they doing? What are they wearing?

_____
_____
_____

2 Similarities between the photos:

_____
_____

3 Differences between the photos:

_____
_____
_____

4 How do you think the people are feeling?

_____
_____

Do you think that people who call the emergency services without a good reason should be punished? Why do you think that?

4 🎧 **2.09** Listen to a student answering the questions above and complete the sentences.

1 Let me see. I'd have to give that some t_____ .
2 P_____ , I think it depends.
3 As I s_____ it, it depends on why they made the call.
4 I b_____ that they should be punished, maybe with a fine.
5 So, all things c_____ , you'd have to look at each unnecessary call individually.

5 Read the question below. Write notes for your answer.

What is the best thing to do in an emergency?

_____
_____
_____
_____

Speaking Strategy
• Speak in a loud, clear voice.
• Look at the other person when they are speaking to you and when you are speaking to them.

6 Read the Speaking Strategy. Now describe photo B, compare it with photo A and answer the question from exercise 5 using your notes.

8H

A narrative

I can write a story.

Preparation

1 Read the task and the story below. In which paragraph (A–D) does the writer ...

1 set the scene? ☐
2 describe the ending? ☐
3 describe the lead-up to the main event? ☐
4 describe the main event? ☐

> Write a story that involves a mobile phone.

A About two months ago, I was having a coffee with my cousin at a café in town. We were talking about my eighteenth birthday party. Ellie mentioned a friend of mine, Tom, and asked if he was going to be there. 'I haven't seen him for months,' I replied. 'I'm not even sure that I've got his number.' While we were chatting, I took out my phone and checked.

B About two weeks later, it was the day of my party and I was getting everything ready. To my surprise, I had a call from Tom. Naturally, I told him about the party. 'Why don't you come along?' I suggested. He accepted the invitation.

C When Ellie arrived for the party, I told her what had happened. 'It's such a coincidence,' I said to her. 'I hadn't spoken to Tom for months, but he phoned today. And he's coming to the party!' At the party that evening, Tom and Ellie got on really well together.

D In the end, Tom explained what had happened. 'You left a long message on my voicemail,' he said. 'You must have dialled my number by mistake when you were in the café. You were talking to Ellie about me. I heard everything!'

2 Put the time expressions in the correct groups. Tick the three that are in the story in exercise 1.

about two months ago   about two weeks later   after a while
eventually   in the end   one Saturday last month

A non-specific time expressions for starting a narrative
1 _____ ☐
2 _____ ☐

B expressions for ordering events
3 _____ ☐
4 _____ ☐

C expressions for bringing the narrative to an end
5 _____ ☐
_____ ☐

Writing Strategy

1 You can make your narrative more interesting by using comment adverbs such as *luckily, unfortunately, Thank goodness*, etc.

2 When you are narrating events, use a variety of tenses such as past simple, past continuous, present perfect, past perfect, *used to*, etc.

3 Read the Writing Strategy. Then, in the story in exercise 1, find and underline:

1 three comment adverbs.
2 an example of a) the past simple, b) the past continuous and c) the past perfect.

4 Complete the sentences with the comment adverbs below.

luckily sadly suddenly to my surprise wisely

1 It was cold and cloudy, but _____ there were lots of people on the beach.
2 I lost my wallet, but _____ I found it again.
3 _____ a car ran into us. I didn't see it coming because it happened so quickly.
4 _____ my grandmother is rather ill.
5 _____ , Joe saves a little of his pocket money each week.

Writing Guide

5 You are going to do the task in exercise 1. Make notes below.

1 Set the scene _____
_____
_____

2 Lead-up _____
_____
_____

3 Main event _____
_____
_____

4 Ending _____
_____

6 Write your story using your notes from exercise 5.

CHECK YOUR WORK

Have you ...
☐ used a variety of narrative tenses?
☐ used some comment adverbs?
☐ checked your spelling and grammar?

8 Review Unit 8

Vocabulary

1 Complete the sentences with the verbs below.

add enable leave lose make put recharge top up

1 Can I use your phone, please? I need to _____ a call.
2 We're supposed to _____ our phones on silent when we're in class.
3 You'll have to _____ data roaming if you want to make calls from abroad.
4 Tell me your number and I'll _____ it to my contacts list.
5 I need to _____ my phone because I haven't got much credit left.
6 Sam's not here. Would you like to _____ a message?
7 My battery has run out. Where can I _____ my phone?
8 This village is very remote, so you might _____ the signal.

Mark: ___ / 8

2 Replace the underlined words with the correct form of the phrasal verbs below.

break up call back cut off get through to
hang up pick up run out of speak up

1 I've been trying all day, but I can't establish contact with the hospital. _____
2 Sorry I didn't answer the phone, but I was driving. _____
3 Can you talk more loudly? I can't hear you. _____
4 I can't talk now, but I'll phone again later. _____
5 I didn't end the call until they had answered all my questions. _____
6 Tell me if I start to become difficult to understand and I'll go outside. _____
7 The signal is quite bad here, so we might get interrupted. _____
8 You won't be able to use your phone if you have no more credit. _____

Mark: ___ / 8

Word Skills

3 Circle the correct answers to complete the sentences.

1 Dave ___ me for breaking his phone, but it wasn't actually my fault!
   a accused   b blamed   c denied
2 My girlfriend wouldn't let me pay for the meal and ___ on paying herself.
   a insisted   b proposed   c refused

3 It was a beautiful evening, so I ___ having a barbecue.
   a begged   b suggested   c wondered
4 My friends ___ me to go to the concert although I didn't really want to.
   a admitted   b agreed   c persuaded
5 I ___ to lend you some money, but you said you didn't want it.
   a offered   b told   c warned
6 My sister ___ me to call my grandmother because it was her birthday.
   a mentioned   b promised   c reminded

Mark: ___ / 6

4 Rewrite the sentences using the verbs in brackets as a reporting verb.

1 'You should check your phone bill,' Fiona's mother said to her. (advise)
   Fiona's mother _____.
2 'I'll get back to you later,' Max told me. (promise)
   Max _____.
3 'I'm sorry I'm late,' said the student. (apologise)
   The student _____.
4 'Let's have a party!' my friend said. (propose)
   My friend _____.
5 'Why don't you join the debating society?' the teacher asked me. (encourage)
   The teacher _____.
6 'You've been reading my text messages!' Tina said to her brother. (accuse)
   Tina _____.

Mark: ___ / 6

5 Complete the sentences with the phrases below.

I can't   I'm pretty   It could   It looks
It's clear   It's hard   Judging by

1 _____ to say, but I think she might be crying.
2 _____ certain that no one else was involved.
3 _____ her expression, she appears to be in shock.
4 _____ be sure, but I'd say that it's quite late.
5 _____ that the bike is badly damaged.
6 _____ be that the roads are very icy.
7 _____ as if his car has broken down.

Mark: ___ / 7

Grammar

6 Complete the reported speech.

1 'I think my battery has run out.'
   Andy said _____.
2 'We don't want to go home now.'
   We said _____.

3 'Beth texted me an hour ago.'
Julia told us _____ .

4 'I can't hear what you're saying.'
My brother said _____ .

5 'I won't be going to school tomorrow.'
Peter said _____ .

6 'I didn't have time to call you.'
My dad said _____ .

7 'I was angry because you'd forgotten my birthday.'
She told him _____ .

8 'I'd like to get a new phone.'
Sue told her parents _____ .

Mark: ___ / 8

7 Complete the reported speech with *said* or *told*.

1 I _____ you I'd be late.

2 She _____ it didn't matter.

3 They _____ us they were moving abroad.

4 He _____ to me he wasn't sure.

5 We _____ we were very sorry.

6 You _____ me we didn't have an exam.

Mark: ___ / 6

8 Complete the reported questions.

1 'Do you have a signal?'
My friend asked _____ .

2 'How much credit would you like?'
The assistant asked her _____ .

3 'Have you switched off your phones?'
The examiner asked us _____ .

4 'Did you have a good time yesterday?'
My mum asked _____ .

5 'Where did you leave my tablet?'
Kate asked me _____ .

6 'When will you have finished the book?'
I asked Jack _____ .

7 'What are you doing tonight?'
Amy asked Mark _____ .

8 'Can I call you back this evening?'
Holly's boyfriend asked _____ .

Mark: ___ / 8

Use of English

9 Circle the answer (A, B, C, or D) which completes both sentences (a and b).

1 a At night, I always ___ my phone on silent.
  b Shall we ___ the call on loudspeaker for everyone to hear?
    A make   B get   C turn   D put

2 a The waiter asked ___ we wanted the bill.
  b I'd call him ___ I knew his number.
    A did   B what   C if   D that

3 a The other players accused my team ___ cheating.
  b I ran out ___ time in the exam.
    A of   B with   C in   D by

4 a I thought you ___ you weren't going out tonight.
  b Rob ___ to me he'd meet us outside the cinema.
    A said   B spoke   C told   D asked

5 a I can't ___ through to the sports centre. Nobody's answering.
  b I'll ___ back to you later with the final arrangements.
    A call   B go   C get   D be

6 a I apologised ___ forgetting his name.
  b You can only blame yourself ___ failing the exam.
    A in   B about   C to   D for

7 a I admitted ___ doing the previous day's homework.
  b We went out alone although we had been advised ___ to.
    A didn't   B don't   C not   D haven't

8 a I got cut ___ while I was talking to my friend.
  b You can't call her because she's switched ___ her phone.
    A on   B off   C out   D down

Mark: ___ / 8

Total: ___ / 65

I can ...

Read the statements. Think about your progress and tick one of the boxes.

★ = I need more practice.

★★ = I sometimes find this difficult.

★★★ = No problem!

	★	★★	★★★
I can talk about using my phone.			
I can use reported speech.			
I can identify the main idea of a listening text.			
I can report questions correctly.			
I can use a variety of reporting verbs correctly.			
I can understand a text about social media texts.			
I can describe a photo and answer questions about it.			
I can write a story.			

Exam Skills Trainer

Reading

1 Read the Strategy. Then read the text below. Are statements 1–4 true (T), false (F), or not given (NG)?

Anna Pavlova (1881–1931) was a famous Russian ballet dancer. She first fell in love with ballet when she was taken to see a performance of Tchaikovsky's *Sleeping Beauty*. She was eight years old at the time. Pavlova studied ballet at the Imperial Ballet School in St Petersburg. Students there had to get up early and have a cold shower. Lessons started after breakfast and continued until the evening, with very few breaks during the day.

1 Anna Pavlova was born in 1882. ☐
2 She was born in St Petersburg. ☐
3 She had her first ballet lesson when she was eight. ☐
4 Anna had lots of free time at the Imperial Ballet School. ☐

2 Read the text. Are the sentences true (T), false (F), or not given (NG)?

Still life

The other day, I was walking through the city when a silver statue caught my eye. It was a statue of a man in a suit looking into the distance. I wondered why so many people were standing there looking at it. Suddenly it turned its head and looked right at me before tapping me on the shoulder with its umbrella. I jumped and laughed. It was, of course, a living statue – and it had scared the life out of me!

Living statues are street performers who make their money by dressing up to look as if they're made of stone, metal, glass or wood. They stand still for long periods of time, moving now and then to remind people that they are actually real people. It's an artistic tradition that started more than five hundred years ago, when groups of actors started performing *tableaux vivants*. These were still and silent groups of people in costumes who were arranged to represent a particular scene or event.

Nowadays, most living statues work alone. Matt Walters has been working as a living statue for over 25 years. He usually dresses as a chimney sweep, covered from head to toe in very dark grey paint. He does all his make-up himself. 'Covering myself in paint and using the right stuff to get it all off again afterwards costs me about £10 a day,' he says, but he won't tell me how much he earns as a living statue when I ask him.

I hope it's a lot. Working as a human statue is a demanding job. Passers-by can be rude, and living statues are regularly pushed or even attacked by members of the public. Standing still for long periods of time isn't easy and it can cause health problems. Walters is helped by the fact that he's a marathon runner. He can drop his heart rate down to just 28 beats per minute, so people don't see him breathe.

Living statues have a lot of fun too. Chris Clarkson performs as a Greek statue who has a fountain of water. 'One day, I could see two children who wanted me to splash them,' he says. 'So I did, and the audience loved it. I got a lot of money. Then

their dad came to collect them, so I decided to get him too. It turned out not to be their dad – but a police officer! Luckily, he had a good sense of humour.'

1 The silver man with an umbrella was the first living statue the writer had ever seen. ☐
2 The only reason that living statues move is because they get so uncomfortable. ☐
3 A make-up artist covers Matt in paint. ☐
4 The writer asked Matt Walters how much money he makes as a living statue. ☐
5 People don't always treat living statues kindly. ☐
6 Matt Walters has trained as an actor. ☐
7 He can control how fast he breathes. ☐
8 The police officer was angry when Chris Clarkson threw water at him. ☐

Listening

3 Read the Strategy above. Then read statements 1–3 quickly and match them with extracts from recordings A–C. Then check your answers.

1 The speaker expresses dissatisfaction with a device. ☐
2 The speaker tells you how to communicate with someone. ☐
3 The speaker wants to convince you to buy something. ☐

🎧 A Please press three now to speak to an agent.
B It's so complicated that I can't get it to work at all!
C Call now, and we'll send you *two* for the price of one!

4 🎧 2.10 You will hear four speakers. Match the speakers (1–4) with the statements (A–E). There is one extra statement.

A The speaker describes what is wrong with a new device. ☐
B The speaker wants someone to make a decision about something. ☐
C The speaker wants to recommend something new. ☐
D The speaker describes a variety of communication devices. ☐
E You can hear this speaker in a classroom. ☐

Use of English

5 Read the Strategy. Then read the 'Lost and found' text below and answer questions 1–6.

1 What did Andrew lose?
2 Where did he lose it?
3 How did he try to find it?
4 Who found it in the end?
5 Where was it found?
6 Were there any problems with it?

6 Complete the text. Use one word in each gap.

Lost and found

In 2009, Andrew Cheatle and his friend were playing with Andrew's dog on a beach when Andrew dropped his phone. The phone wasn't ¹_____ silent, so Andrew rang it from his friend's phone, but he couldn't hear ²_____ at all. He looked everywhere, but he eventually accepted that the phone was lost for ever. Then, a week later, his girlfriend's phone started ringing. When she picked it ³_____, she noticed it was Andrew's number that was calling. Andrew was with her, so they realised that ⁴_____ had found Andrew's phone. She asked the caller who he ⁵_____. He told ⁶_____ that he was a fisherman and his name was Glen. He explained that he had been fishing ⁷_____ morning and had caught a big fish. When he had taken the fish to market, he had found a phone inside it. Yes, Andrew's phone had ⁸_____ eaten by a fish! Glen said he'd taken the SIM card out, put it into a dry phone and phoned the saved numbers. He was very pleased to get ⁹_____ to Andrew's girlfriend. When Andrew got his phone back the next day, it wasn't working, but he ¹⁰_____ it mended and started using it again. The biggest problem was getting rid of the fishy smell!

Speaking

7 Read the Strategy. Match A–E with 1–5.

1 So, what do the three photos have in common? ☐
2 What do you think of this one? ☐
3 Do you like that one? ☐
4 So, which one should we choose? ☐
5 Do you agree? ☐

A No, I don't. If I'm honest, I think it looks a bit boring.
B Yes, I do. 100%. I think we've made the right decision.
C They all show different kinds of presents.
D To be blunt, I think it's awful!
E don't know. Personally, I don't really think any of them are suitable.

8 Work in pairs. Compare and contrast photos A–C. Then do the task below.

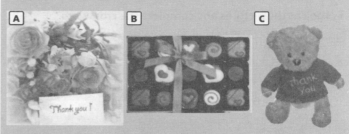

A
B
C

It's the end of term and you want to say 'thank you' to one of your teachers. First, decide which teacher you want to thank. Then decide which of the items in photos A–C would be most suitable and talk about when and where you will give the gift.

9 Work in pairs. Find out which 'thank you' from exercise 8 your partner would like to receive, and why. Then talk about other ways you can thank someone.

Writing

10 Read the Strategy. Then rewrite 1–4 replacing the underlined words with the words below. Combine the sentences if necessary.

either   this   which   who

1 *The Lion, the Witch and the Wardrobe* is set in Narnia. <u>Narnia</u> is a fantasy world.
2 Some people say the film is funny and some say it's clever. Personally, I didn't think it was <u>funny or clever</u>.
3 *The Life of Pi* tells the story of a boy. <u>He</u> is the only survivor of a shipwreck.
4 At 3 hours and 40 minutes, the film is rather long, but <u>the fact that the film is 3 hours and 40 minutes long</u> didn't spoil my overall enjoyment.

11 Read the task below and write the review.

Your teacher has asked you to write a review of a film or TV series for the school magazine. Write your review describing the film or TV series and saying what you liked and didn't like about it.

• Give your article a title and interesting introduction.
• Describe the plot and characters.
• Use an appropriate style.

Journeys

A Vocabulary
Travel and transport
I can talk about travel and transport.

1 Look at the pictures and complete the crossword.

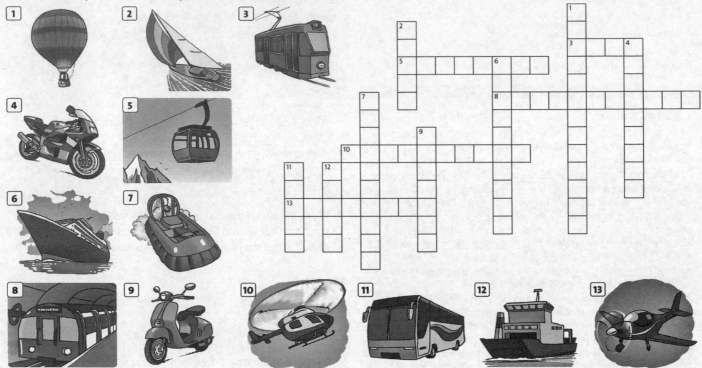

2 Divide the forms of transport into groups. (Do not include *cable car*.)

Air

_____ _____ _____

Sea

_____ _____ _____

_____

Rail

_____ _____

Road

_____ _____ _____

3 Complete the compound nouns with the words below.

barrier bay buffet check-in coach filling
gate hall level office park room station
taxi ticket train

1 arrivals _____
2 _____ car
3 car_____
4 _____ desk
5 coach _____
6 _____ station
7 departure _____
8 _____ station

9 lost property_____
10 _____crossing
11 service _____
12 _____rank
13 waiting_____
14 _____office
15 ticket _____
16 _____station

4 Complete the sentences with compound nouns from exercise 3.

1 After you get off a plane, you collect your baggage in the _____.

2 Where a road crosses a railway line, there's a _____.

3 If you lose something on a train or a bus, go to the _____.

4 If you get hungry on a train journey, buy something in the _____.

5 If you need petrol when driving in a city, stop at a _____.

6 Before you get on a flight, show your ticket and passport at the_____.

7 At many train stations you have to go through a _____ to get onto the platform.

8 If you need a rest while driving along a motorway, stop at a _____.

5 🎧 **2.11** **Listen to three conversations. Where are the people? Choose from the places below. There are two extra places.**

airport deck departure gate platform port

1 _____
2 _____
3 _____

Grammar
Third conditional
I can talk about imaginary events in the past.

1 Complete the third conditional sentences with the verbs in brackets.

1 If I _____ (be) hungry, I _____ (buy) a sandwich in the buffet car.

2 We _____ (book) a cabin if they _____ (not be) so expensive.

3 If we _____ (stop) at the filling station, we _____ (not run out) of petrol.

4 If you _____ (look) at the departures board, you _____ (know) which gate to go to.

5 What _____ you _____ (do) if the airline _____ (lose) your luggage?

6 We _____ (not go) out on deck if the weather _____ (not be) so lovely.

7 If you _____ (find) a bag on a train, _____ you _____ (take) it to the lost property office?

8 I _____ (not use) the car park if I _____ (can) park on the street.

9 If I _____ (need) a taxi, I _____ (wait) at the taxi rank.

2 Match the sentence halves. Then rewrite them as third conditional sentences.

1 We missed the ferry because ☐ e

2 We got lost because ☐

3 I couldn't get on the plane because ☐

4 The train was late because ☐

5 The car crashed because ☐

6 We didn't take the cable car because ☐

a I didn't have my passport with me.

b we wanted to walk up the mountain.

c you forgot the satnav.

d the driver didn't see the red light.

e ~~we were late setting off~~.

f there was snow on the line.

1 *We wouldn't have missed the ferry if we hadn't been late setting off.*

2 _____

3 _____

4 _____

5 _____

6 _____

3 Write questions using the prompts.

1 where / you / go / on holiday / last summer / if / you / have / the choice?
Where would you have gone _____
_____

2 what / you / do / if / you / feel ill / this morning?
_____

3 what / you / buy / last weekend / if / you / have / lots of money?
_____
_____

4 what / you / do / if / today / be / a public holiday?
_____
_____

5 what film / you / see / if / go / to the cinema / last night?
_____
_____

6 what / you / eat / yesterday evening / if / you / have / the choice?
_____
_____

4 Write answers to the questions in exercise 3.

1 _____

2 _____

3 _____

4 _____

5 _____

6 _____

Travel solutions

I can identify the context of a conversation and its register.

Revision: Student's Book page 99

1 **Complete the collocations with the verbs below.**

board   book   check in   check into
hail   hire   miss   reach

1 _____ your bags / your luggage
2 _____ a room / a flight / a holiday
3 _____ your destination
4 _____ a hotel
5 _____ a taxi
6 _____ a train / a ship / a flight
7 _____ a car
8 _____ your flight / your train

Listening Strategy 1

It is sometimes difficult to catch names and proper nouns when you listen. However, you can use the words around them (including collocations) to work out what they are (a person, a place, etc.). For example, if you hear 'We *stayed four nights* at the Grand Plaza', the underlined words tell you that the Grand Plaza is a hotel.

---

2 🎧 **2.12** **Read Listening Strategy 1. Then listen to three short dialogues and answer the questions.**

1 In dialogue 1, how are they planning to travel to their hotel?
_____

2 In dialogue 2, what is the Aurora?
_____

3 In dialogue 3, what does the man think he's lost?
_____

3 🎧 **2.12** **Listen again. Which verbs from exercise 1 helped you answer the questions in exercise 2?**

Dialogue 1: _____
Dialogue 2: _____
Dialogue 3: _____

Listening Strategy 2

Being aware of formal register can help you identify the context. Formal terms used in announcements include:

adjacent to (next to)   beverages (drinks)
to commence (to begin)   to depart (to leave)
due to (because of)   prior to (before)   to proceed to (to go to)
to purchase (to buy)   refreshments (food and drink)
to terminate (to end)

---

4 **Read Listening Strategy 2. Then complete the sentences with formal words from the Strategy that mean the same as the words in brackets.**

1 Will all passengers for Milan please _____ (go to) gate 7b, which is _____ (next to) gate 9.
2 A wide range of _____ (food and drink) are available to _____ (buy) in the departure lounge.
3 Passengers are advised that some flights will _____ (leave) later than scheduled. This is _____ (because of) the weather conditions.
4 This train _____ (ends) at Manchester. Please note that hot and cold _____ (drinks) are available from the buffet car.

5 🎧 **2.13** **Listen to three extracts. Which two are formal? Which formal terms from Listening Strategy 2 do they include?**

Extract ☐ is formal.
It includes these formal terms: _____
_____

Extract ☐ is formal.
It includes these formal terms: _____
_____

6 🎧 **2.13** **Listen again and circle the correct answers.**

1 What is the speaker's main purpose in extract 1?
a To make sure everyone has a map.
b To make sure nobody is late back to the coach.
c To make sure everyone has time to buy souvenirs.

2 Where is the announcement in extract 2 being made?
a On a train.
b At an underground station.
c In an airport terminal.

3 At what point in the flight is the announcement in extract 3 made?
a Just before take-off.
b Shortly after take-off.
c Shortly before landing at the destination.

9D Grammar
Participle clauses
I can use participle clauses correctly.

1 Circle the correct past or present participle form to complete the participle clauses.

1 We stayed in a villa **belonged** / **belonging** to my grandparents.
2 These scientists have designed a car **powered** / **powering** by solar energy.
3 He jumped from a train **travelled** / **travelling** at nearly 100 km/h.
4 The men **decorated** / **decorating** our house have made a real mess of the furniture.
5 They spent the night in a traditional Mongolian tent **known** / **knowing** as a *yurt*.
6 The police arrested a man **taken** / **taking** photos of the military base.
7 The tourists saw a message **written** / **writing** in large, white letters on the cliff.
8 His flat is full of old furniture **given** / **giving** to him by his grandfather.

2 Underline one participle clause in each sentence. Then write it as a full relative clause (defining or non-defining).

1 I bought a copy of *Twilight* <u>signed by the author</u>.
which had been signed by the author
2 I can see three cyclists not wearing helmets.
_____
3 She keeps getting emails from companies wanting to employ her.
_____
4 Three paintings stolen from the National Gallery have been found.
_____
5 This class is only for students studying nineteenth-century literature.
_____
6 His autobiography, published in 1931, was called *Far From Home*.
_____
7 I asked some girls standing outside the hotel to take a photo of us.
_____
8 We remind passengers that any luggage left on the platform will be destroyed.
_____
9 This book is a useful guide for students not living at home.
_____
10 We stayed in an amazing hotel room decorated to look like a space capsule.
_____

3 Complete the text with participle clauses with the same meaning as the clauses in brackets.

The largest man-made object in space is the International Space Station (ISS), ¹_____ (which was built) by the European Space Agency and the space agencies of America, Canada, Japan and Russia. These five agencies, ²_____ (who worked) together for many years, launched the ISS in 1998. Since then, they have all been sending astronauts, ³_____ (who have been trained) to carry out important scientific work, to the space station. Chris Hadfield, ⁴_____ (who was chosen) as one of Canada's astronauts, became well known for uploading photos ⁵_____ (which had been taken) in space to his social networking pages. He also recorded videos, ⁶_____ (which included) his own performance of the song *Space Oddity*, ⁷_____ (which was written) by pop star David Bowie. The video, ⁸_____ (which has been watched) by about 25 million people so far, made Chris Hadfield even more famous.

4 Combine the two sentences using a participle clause. Sometimes you need to add the clause in the middle of the sentence.

1 We visited a palace. The palace was built 400 years ago.
We visited a palace built 400 years ago.
2 Astronauts get homesick. They spend weeks in space.
_____
3 I lost a watch. It belonged to my cousin.
_____
4 A man sat down next to me. He smelled of coffee.
_____
5 The debates will help voters to decide. They will be shown live on TV.
_____
6 He gave me a small box. It contained a key.
_____

9E Word Skills

Verb patterns

I can identify and use verb patterns.

1 Complete the text with the infinitive (with or without *to*) or *-ing* form of the verbs in brackets.

Three years ago, an Australian couple from Perth decided
¹_____ (go) on holiday –
permanently. In other words, they hoped
²_____ (stay) on holiday for years
rather than days. So far, their trip has lasted for three years
and they're enjoying ³_____ (travel)
so much that they will keep ⁴_____
(do) it for as long as possible.

Before the trip, Nicole Connolly ran a successful business.
But the death of a family member made her
⁵_____ (think) about her life
in a different way. She spent some time
⁶_____ (discuss) her ideas
with Michael, her husband, and they ended up
⁷_____ (make) a decision: they
agreed ⁸_____ (give up) their home
and their jobs in return for freedom and adventure. But they
couldn't put their plan into action immediately. They went
on ⁹_____ (work) for a year and
managed ¹⁰_____ (save) some
money. They then sold their house and their possessions.
Finally, they could afford ¹¹_____
(begin) their journey.

They started ¹²_____ (travel) and
they've been on the road ever since. They've continued
¹³_____ (earn) some money by
managing an online business, including a successful blog
about their lifestyle. And although they miss their friends and
family, they don't miss their old life; they definitely prefer
¹⁴_____ (be) on holiday all the time.

2 Complete the sentences with the infinitive or *-ing* form of the verbs in brackets. **Your answers will depend on the meaning.**

1 She tried _____ (open) her suitcase, but it was impossible without the key.

2 I'm not surprised you found the film confusing – you didn't stop _____ (talk) all the way through!

3 I keep waking up at 3 a.m. I've tried _____ (go) to bed earlier, but it doesn't help.

4 I'll never forget _____ (visit) India when I was a child.

5 I don't remember _____ (buy) this T-shirt. Maybe somebody gave it to me.

6 We often forget _____ (turn) the computer off at night.

7 Before you go to bed, please remember _____ (lock) the front door.

8 There was an icy wind, so she stopped _____ (do) up her coat.

3 Complete the sentences so they are true for you. Use an infinitive in sentences 1 and 3 and an *-ing* form in 2 and 4.

1 I often forget _____
_____ .

2 I don't remember _____
_____ .

3 I stopped _____
_____ .

4 I stopped_____
_____ .

> **VOCAB BOOST!**
>
> When you learn verb patterns, you can write them like this:
> *fancy doing something*
> *let sb do something*
> Alternatively, write them in sentences which may be useful and underline the verb pattern:
> *Do you <u>fancy going</u> out this evening?*
> *Could you <u>let me see</u> that photo?*

4 Read the *Vocab boost!* box. Then write sentences which include these verbs. Underline the verb patterns.

1 (avoid doing sth) _____
_____

2 (choose to do sth) _____
_____

3 (not mind doing sth)_____
_____

4 (expect to do sth) _____
_____

9F Reading

Miscalculations

I can understand texts about mistakes.

Revision: Student's Book page 102

1 **Write the measurements using abbreviations for the units.**

1 six feet _____
2 nine inches _____
3 five feet ten inches _____
4 two metres sixteen centimetres _____
5 seventy-four kilometres _____
6 fifty-six millimetres _____

2 **Read the texts (A–C) and match the titles with the texts. There is one extra title.**

1 Side to side ☐
2 Safe and sound ☐
3 In and out ☐
4 There and back? ☐

Reading Strategy

When a statement can match more than one text, you need to make sure you have matched all of the possible texts to each statement. First decide which text matches with a particular statement. Then check that none of the other texts match the statement.

3 **Read the Reading Strategy. Then match the texts (A–C) with statements 1–4. One text matches with two statements.**

1 This mistake could have had fatal results. ☐
2 More than one person was responsible for this mistake. ☐
3 This problem took a long time to fix. ☐
4 The mistake was due to lack of knowledge rather than miscalculation. ☐

C In 1912, explorer Robert Scott fatally miscalculated the amount of food his team would need while trying to become the first to reach the South Pole. His team had rations of 4,500 calories per day. If Scott had known more about physical health at that time, he would have taken nearly double that amount of food. So the team must have lost about 25 kg of weight before they got to the Pole. The journey was doubly tragic for Scott. He was beaten to the South Pole by Norwegian explorer Roald Amundsen and, worse, he and his men died of starvation on the return journey, just eleven miles from their next food supply.

A

Imagine you were in the middle of a long-distance flight. How would you feel if you were told that your plane had run out of fuel? That's what happened to passengers on an Air Canada flight in 1983. The plane was the first to use metric measurements. However, the fuel gauge wasn't working, so the captain calculated the fuel needed – but in pounds, not kilograms. This resulted in the plane only carrying half the amount it needed. It ran out of fuel above a place called Gimli. Fortunately, the pilot was able to land there safely with minimal fuel, earning the plane the nickname the 'Gimli Glider'.

B Crossing the new Millennium Bridge for the first time in June 2000, the people of London got a more thrilling journey to work than they expected. As they passed over the River Thames, the footbridge started to swing. It was a beautiful, elegant bridge, designed especially for the new century. Unfortunately, the designers hadn't calculated the effect of thousands of people walking on it at the same time. Although it wasn't particularly dangerous, the bridge was very wobbly, especially when it was windy. It had to be closed for nearly two years while the design was modified, at great expense.

Speaking

Guided conversation
I can have a conversation about holiday plans.

Revision: Student's Book page 104

1 **Label the icons with six of the holiday activities below.**

fishing   hiking   horse riding   kayaking
mountain biking   scuba-diving   shopping
sightseeing   skiing   swimming

1 _____

2 _____

3 _____

4 _____

5 _____

6 _____

Speaking Strategy

In a guided conversation, it is important to interact appropriately with the other person. Do not just give your own opinions and ignore what the other person is saying.

2 **Read the Speaking Strategy. Then choose the correct reply question below for each statement. There are two extra questions.**

Are you   Do I   Don't I   Had I
Have you   Haven't you   Would I

1 I haven't got enough money for this holiday.

_____ ?

2 You need to book the train tickets soon.

_____ ?

3 You'd better check in that large bag.

_____ ?

4 You don't seem happy about the arrangements.

_____ ?

5 I'm booking a hotel for the first two nights.

_____ ?

You and some classmates are planning a day trip to celebrate the end of your exams. Discuss your plans with one of your classmates. Make a decision on these four points:

• choice of destination and your reasons
• the best way to get there
• what activities you want to do
• what you need to take with you.

3 🎧 **2.14** **Listen to a student and examiner doing the task after exercise 2. Which point do they forget to cover? Complete the table.**

1 Destination	
2 Form of transport	
3 Activities	
4 Take with them	

4 **Complete the sentences with question tags.**

1 It shouldn't be too far,_____ ?
2 The train is quite fast, _____ ?
3 It isn't too expensive, _____ ?
4 There are lots of other things we could do, _____ ?
5 Everybody likes swimming,_____ ?
6 Let's tell the others, _____ ?

5 🎧 **2.14** **Listen again. Check your answers to exercise 4.**

6 **Complete the sentences with question tags.**

1 You haven't booked a hotel, _____ ?
2 We shouldn't go away right at the end of the holiday, _____ ?
3 You'd rather stay at a campsite, _____ ?
4 I'm the only one of us who can drive,_____ ?
5 You never go on holiday with friends, _____ ?
6 Don't forget to pack the suncream, _____ ?

7 **Read the task and make notes for your answers.**

You and your cousin are planning a weekend away during the summer holiday. Discuss your plans with your cousin. Make a decision on these four points:

• choice of destination and your reasons
• accommodation
• when you want to go
• paying for the holiday.

1 Where do you want to go? Why?

_____
_____

2 Where are you going to stay? Why? (villa / hotel / campsite / youth hostel, etc.)

_____
_____

3 When is the best time to go? (beginning / middle / end of summer)

_____
_____

4 What activities do you want to do on holiday?

_____
_____

8 **Now do the speaking task. Use your notes from exercise 7.**

Writing

A formal letter

I can write a formal letter of enquiry.

Preparation

> **Writing Strategy 1**
> • If you know the name of the person you are writing to, start with *Dear Miss / Mrs / Ms / Mr ...* , and finish with *Yours sincerely*, followed by your signature and your full name.
> • If you don't know the name of the person, start with *Dear Sir or Madam*, and finish with *Yours faithfully*, followed by your signature and your full name.

1 Read Writing Strategy 1. Then write the two missing words at the start and end of the letter.

2 Underline in the letter more formal ways of saying:

1 to ask about	**5** tell me about
2 mum and dad	**6** make clear
3 we don't want to	**7** getting your answer
4 it would be good if	**8** soon

Dear Sir or ¹_____ ,

I am writing to enquire about the possibility of renting Hillside Cottage for three weeks in the summer.

I will be travelling to the Lake District with my parents and brother. We plan to arrive in London on 14 July, but do not wish to hire a car. I would be grateful if you could inform me of the best way to reach the cottage by public transport.

Although the advertisement states that the cottage has two bedrooms, it is not clear whether the second room is large enough for two people to share. I wonder if you could clarify this point.

Finally, I would like to know what leisure activities are available in the area surrounding the cottage. We are particularly interested in horse riding.

I look forward to receiving your reply in due course.

Yours ²_____ ,

Tom Baker

> Divide your letter into paragraphs.
>
> In the first paragraph, which can be a single sentence, say why you are writing.
>
> Each paragraph should have its own topic. It is usually best to deal with the four points in the task in four separate paragraphs.
>
> In the final paragraph, which can be a single sentence, say that you expect a reply.
>
> Avoid colloquial language and short forms.

3 Read Writing Strategy 2. Then read the task and answer the questions below.

> You are planning to visit the Lake District this summer with your family and have seen an advertisement for a cottage. Write a letter to the owner in which you:
> • give information about the people travelling.
> • ask about travelling to the cottage.
> • request information about the bedrooms.
> • ask about leisure facilities in the area.

1 How many paragraphs are in the model letter? ☐

2 Which two points in the task are covered in one paragraph in the model letter? ☐ and ☐

Writing Guide

> You are planning to visit the New Forest this summer with some friends and have seen an advertisement for a campsite. Write a letter to the campsite manager in which you:
> • give information about who will be travelling and when.
> • ask about prices and availability.
> • give information about leisure activities you would like to do.
> • enquire about a specific facility at the campsite.

4 You are going to do the task above. Plan your letter. Make notes using the prompts below to help you.

People travelling: _____

Dates of holiday: _____

Polite request to ask about prices: _____

_____

Polite request to ask about availability: _____

_____

Leisure activities: _____

_____

Campsite facility to ask about: _____

_____

5 Write the letter, using your notes from exercise 4.

> **CHECK YOUR WORK**
> **Have you ...**
> ☐ avoided contractions and informal language?
> ☐ divided the letter into paragraphs?
> ☐ checked your spelling and grammar?

Review Unit 9

Vocabulary

1 Match the definitions with the forms of transport below.

cable car coach ferry helicopter
hovercraft tram yacht

1 a boat that carries paying passengers across a river
_____

2 a vehicle powered by electricity that moves along special rails built in the road _____

3 a small aircraft without wings that can go straight up into the air _____

4 a vehicle that carries passengers up and down a mountain _____

5 a vehicle that sits on a pocket of air and can move over land or water _____

6 a large, comfortable bus used for long journeys
_____

7 a boat with sails used for pleasure trips and racing
_____

Mark: / 7

2 Match a word in A with a word in B to form places related to travel. Then complete the sentences.

A arrivals buffet check-in departure filling taxi

B car desk gate hall rank station

1 We had a lot of luggage, so we took it straight to the _____ when we got to the airport.

2 My sister's plane was delayed, so we spent hours in the _____ waiting for her.

3 Fortunately, we reached a _____ before our car ran out of petrol.

4 There was a massive queue at the _____ , so we caught the bus home instead.

5 When we got to the _____ , the flight was already boarding.

6 I went to the _____ at the back of the train to get myself a snack.

Mark: / 6

3 Complete the sentences with the verbs below.

board book check into hire reach

1 We can't _____ our hotel yet because it's too early.

2 The first thing I'm going to do when we _____ our destination is jump into the shower.

3 The best way to see Lanzarote is to _____ a car and drive around the island.

4 You usually have to show your passport when you go to _____ a plane.

5 I always _____ my flights online because it's much more convenient.

Mark: / 5

Word Skills

4 Circle the correct verb forms.

1 We hope ___ the Blue Mosque while we're in Istanbul.
   a see   b to see   c seeing

2 I don't mind ___ as long as the plane isn't delayed.
   a fly   b to fly   c flying

3 The driver didn't let me ___ on the coach until I'd finished my burger.
   a get   b to get   c getting

4 Ruby spent most of the journey ___ because she'd had a late night.
   a sleep   b to sleep   c sleeping

5 My dad offered ___ me a lift to the station.
   a give   b to give   c giving

6 The guard made me ___ another ticket when I told him I'd lost the one I had.
   a buy   b to buy   c buying

7 Callum agreed ___ his car on condition that they shared the driving.
   a take   b to take   c taking

8 We ended up ___ with friends because we couldn't afford a hotel.
   a stay   b to stay   c staying

Mark: / 8

5 Complete the sentences with the correct form of the verbs in brackets.

1 My cousin stopped _____ (use) his scooter when he bought a car.

2 She tried _____ (start) her car, but nothing happened.

3 Don't forget _____ (come) and see us if you're ever in the area.

4 I'll always remember _____ (visit) Menorca for the first time – it's such a beautiful island.

5 Tyler went on _____ (become) an airline pilot after he finished all his training.

6 We stopped _____ (admire) the view when we reached the top of the mountain.

7 I tried _____ (ask) the driver to turn down the heating, but he refused.

Mark: / 7

Grammar

6 Complete the third conditional sentences with the correct form of the verbs in brackets.

1 Ryan _____ (not be) late for the interview if he _____ (not miss) the bus.

2 If you _____ (wear) proper shoes, you _____ (not twist) your ankle.

3 If we _____ (stay) on the main road, we _____ (not get) lost.

4 She _____ (drive) to work if there _____ (not be) so much traffic.

5 You _____ (pass) your driving test if you _____ (remember) to look in the mirror.

6 If I _____ (not take) a guidebook, we _____ (not know) where to go.

7 If we _____ (go) by taxi, we _____ (arrive) by now.

8 They _____ (have) difficulty finding the street if they _____ (not use) a satnav.

Mark: ___ / 8

7 Rewrite the underlined clauses as participle clauses.

1 The train that is arriving at platform 4 is the 9.30 to London Paddington.

_____

2 My grandfather owns a vintage scooter, which was made in the 1960s.

_____

3 The new uniforms, which the flight attendants have designed, look extremely comfortable.

_____

4 She left the bag which contained all of her travel documents on the coach.

_____

5 Passengers who are travelling to Manchester will need to change at Birmingham New Street.

_____

6 Tickets which are booked a month in advance have a 10% discount.

_____

7 The three girls who were injured in the car accident have already been sent home from hospital.

_____

8 Commuters who wish to purchase a season ticket can apply for it online.

_____

Mark: ___ / 16

Use of English

8 Complete the text with words formed from the words in brackets.

Which Sydney?

Nineteen-year-olds Emma Nunn and Raoul Christian were very excited about their trip to Sydney. They'd never been to Australia before, and it was a big adventure for them.

The first six-hour [1]_____ (FLY) from London took them to Nova Scotia in Canada. Emma and Raoul had made their [2]_____ (BOOK) at the last minute, so they thought they must be taking an [3]_____ (USUAL) route to Australia. They thought they would have to wait in Canada for a couple of hours before continuing their journey, but then they were asked by airport officials to get on a small plane with just 25 seats.

'It was very [4]_____ (CONFUSE),' says Raoul. 'We couldn't understand what was going on.'

An hour later, they arrived in Sydney, a small town on an island off the coast of Canada. Not much happens in Sydney, Canada. It's a cold, quiet [5]_____ (LOCATE). There used to be work for people in the mines, but now it has the highest level of [6]_____ (EMPLOY) in Canada.

'Of course it was a big [7]_____ (DISAPPOINT),' says Emma, 'but we decided to make the most of the experience and to enjoy exploring the town. It would have been a waste of time if we'd just sat in the hotel feeling [8]_____ (HAPPY).'

Mark: ___ / 8

Total: ___ / 65

I can ...

Read the statements. Think about your progress and tick one of the boxes.

⭐ = I need more practice.

⭐⭐ = I sometimes find this difficult.

⭐⭐⭐ = No problem!

	⭐	⭐⭐	⭐⭐⭐
I can talk about travel and transport.			
I can talk about imaginary events in the past.			
I can identify the context of a conversation and its register.			
I can use participle clauses correctly.			
I can identify and use verb patterns.			
I can understand texts about mistakes.			
I can have a conversation about holiday plans.			
I can write a formal letter of enquiry.			

Exam Skills Trainer

Reading

1 Read the Strategy. Then read the text in exercise 2. Match the paragraphs with the descriptions below.

In this paragraph, the writer

A describes an option which involves exchanging something. ☐

B recommends getting to know the local way of life when you travel. ☐

C says that more adventurous accommodation can teach you more about local life. ☐

D talks about a change in what people want from travel. ☐

2 **Now read the text again. Complete the gaps (1–4) in the text with the missing sentences (A–F). There are two extra sentences.**

1 Staying in hotels and resorts has been a traditional part of travel since mass tourism began. But nowadays, many tourists want a more intimate experience. ¹___ This often means staying in the kinds of places that local people inhabit. In big cities, try staying with the friend of a friend. You may end up sleeping on the couch or the floor, but the advantages outweigh the discomfort. The biggest plus is that you'll be staying with a local and seeing the city from a local perspective.

2 Another option is house-swapping. ²___ It's usual to exchange emails about favourite places in the city before the swap, meaning you can have a truly local experience. But of course, you can only do this if you don't mind having strangers staying in your house.

3 For the more adventurous, staying in a native structure in an African village or a hut on the water in Vietnam or Thailand can be a real thrill. ³___ The experience of dealing with oil lamps and carrying water really gives you a sense of how the people live.

4 No matter how unadventurous you feel, you might want to consider crossing hotels off your list. ⁴___ And what better way is there to do this than staying where the local people actually live?

A Unfortunately, these areas are becoming increasingly tourist-orientated.

B For this reason, they are choosing to 'go native'.

C Several websites allow you to connect with people who want to trade living situations.

D Of course this type of accommodation is not for everyone.

E Getting to know the local way of life is the most valuable part of travel.

F These might not even include plumbing or electricity, and that is part of the charm.

Listening

3 Read the Strategy. Then read the extract from a recording and statements 1–6. Which statements match the information in the extract and are true? Which of the statements contain information that is not given in the extract? Why are the other statements false?

🎧 **Liam** So Tony, do you think you'd ever try to organise something like the 'Run for Life' again?

Tony I really doubt it. It was an amazing experience, and I don't at all regret that I took it on. I got loads of help from both friends and complete strangers, and that kept me going. But I kept worrying that if it didn't go well, it would be *my* responsibility. That put pressure on me. Next time, someone else can do the organising and I'll just volunteer.

1 'Run for Life' raises money for charity. ☐
2 Tony is sorry that he decided to organise the event. ☐
3 Tony appreciated the help that he got from others. ☐
4 Tony felt that it would be his fault if the event failed. ☐
5 Tony knows he worries too much about things. ☐
6 Tony plans to organise the next 'Run for Life'. ☐

4 🎧 **2.15** You will hear an interview with a young person who has done something amazing. Are the statements true (T), false (F) or not given (NG)?

1 Lindsay's bike ride from Aberdeen to Brighton was about six hundred miles. ☐
2 Lindsay's friend Stella was born blind. ☐
3 The idea for a bike ride was inspired by something that Lindsay did with Stella before the accident. ☐
4 Lindsay collected all the donations through the internet. ☐
5 Lindsay met people who do voluntary work with blind people. ☐
6 Almost £250,000 has already been donated. ☐

Use of English

5

Exam Skills Trainer

5 Read the Strategy. Then complete the word families in the table using the prefixes and suffixes below.

-al -dom im- -ing / -ed -ness un- -y

noun	verb	adjective	opposite adjective
¹happ_____		happy	²_____happy
	rock	³rock_____	
		patient	⁴_____patient
nation nationality		⁵nation_____	
⁶bore_____	bore	⁷bor_____ ⁸bor_____	

6 You are going to read an article about a motorbike trip. Some words are missing from the text. Use the words in brackets to form the words that fit in the gaps. Use only one word for each gap.

Desert adventure

Travelling by motorbike across the Gobi Desert in Mongolia was the experience of a lifetime. My group were all experienced off-road bikers, which was important as a lot of the route was on rocky trails and ¹_____ (SAND) tracks.

We did a circular eight-day trip, starting from the capital, Ulaanbaatar, going south through Middle Gobi, then on to South Gobi, before returning to Ulaanbaatar. The journey ²_____ (IT) was 1,500 km. Each night, we stayed at a different camp in a ³_____ (TRADITION) round tent. I had an amazing sense of adventure and ⁴_____ (FREE).

We passed through mountains and deserts, and we met a family travelling with lots of camels, horses, goats and sheep. The family was very ⁵_____ (FRIEND). At first, communication seemed ⁶_____ (POSSIBLE), but after a lot of smiling and pointing, I think we all understood each other.

Ulaanbaatar seemed ⁷_____ (INTEREST), but we didn't have long there. If we'd had more time, I'd have definitely done some ⁸_____ (SIGHTSEE).

Speaking

Exam Strategy
Remember to use a range of phrases for describing similarities and differences between photos.

7 Read the Strategy. Then complete the sentences with the words below.

both rather unlike whereas

1 _____ photos show forms of transport.
2 The first photo shows a yacht, _____ the second photo shows a cruise ship.
3 In the first photo, the people are working hard on the boat _____ than relaxing.
4 _____ in the first photo, the sea in the second photo is very calm and blue.

8 Photos A and B show holiday destinations. Compare and contrast them. Include the following points.
- what makes each destination appealing
- popular holiday destinations in your country
- holiday activities that are popular with young people

9 Now talk for one or two minutes on the topic below. First, prepare what you are going to say (you have one minute). Make some notes to help you if you wish.

Describe a holiday you enjoyed. Include:
- where you went
- who you went with
- why you enjoyed it
- how you travelled
- what you did there

Writing

Exam Strategy
In formal letters of enquiry, you usually need to ask more than two questions. It's best to use a combination of direct and indirect questions to do this.

10 Read the Strategy. Then complete the direct and indirect questions.

1 Is there a swimming pool nearby?
Could you tell me _____ ?
2 I'd also like to know how much a double room costs.
How much _____ ?
3 Can you tell me if the hotel has a garden?
_____ a garden?
4 Can we check in before midday?
I'd like to know _____ .

11 Read the task below and write the letter.

You have been asked to organise a half-day event for about 150 people from your school. The school has invided a popular TV star to talk about his/her trip to India. You are thinking of booking a meeting room at the Victoria Hotel. Write a letter in which you:
- give information about why you'd like to book a room.
- inform them of the time and date you'd like to have the room, and ask about availability.
- ask about equipment in the room.
- ask for suggestions about cheap places to eat in or near the hotel.

B2 Exam Skills Trainer

Reading

1 **Read the Strategy. Quickly read the extract and question below and try to eliminate the incorrect answers. Then go back and choose the correct answer.**

Families often try to give career advice based on what they believe is best for you, but blindly following their advice may lead to issues in the future.

Allowing family to influence your career choice

A is never a good idea.
B may produce positive results.
C can have negative consequences.
D can be a good idea.

2 **Read the text. Choose the correct answers, A, B, C or D.**

Volunteer blog

When I signed up to volunteer at a local hospital last year, I didn't have any real expectations. I decided to do it mainly because my friends were planning to do volunteer work, and our class attended a volunteer job fair that October, which made it easier to choose something interesting. I knew the experience would look good on my college applications, and that was a plus too.

On my first day, I was given a tour of the hospital. Then I was given a tablet computer with maps and some basic information. I was then told to stand next to an information sign and to answer any questions that came my way. I'm sure I sent a few visitors in the wrong direction that first day, but I did my best. It wasn't a big deal, and my second time there was much the same.

But on the third day, everything changed. I was in the middle of my shift when I noticed a wheelchair speeding in my direction. A young boy of about six with one of the biggest smiles I have ever seen was sitting in it. The boy stopped in front of me and said, 'Who are you? You're in *my* hospital and I don't even know you!'

I have to say that I've never been known for self-confidence. But this boy with his irresistible smile completely disarmed me. I introduced myself and explained that I was new. 'Like you know anything!' the boy said. 'I've been coming here for the past two years, so I know every inch of this hospital.'

David's parents caught up with him and introduced themselves. They explained that he was there for his weekly check-up, and they sat down for a bit while they waited. David began to tell me about his medical history, his favourite football player and other details of his life. Our conversation transformed my view of young children, illness and hospitals.

In fact, after David had gone to his appointment, one of the administrators came up to me and said, 'That was amazing.

You were a different person when you were talking to him!' She went on to explain that they needed volunteers to work in the children's department. 'And I think you'd be great at it,' she added.

This led to my becoming a regular in the children's department, and also to my decision to study medicine at university and become a paediatrician. It was a career path that hadn't crossed my mind before. Volunteering might not do the same for everyone, but in my case it was a life-changer.

1 When the author decided to do volunteer work, she
   A didn't know anyone else who was interested in it.
   B persuaded her friends to do it too.
   C was influenced by her friends.
   D thought it would be an amazing experience.

2 The volunteer job fair
   A helped her decide which volunteer job to do.
   B was an event that she went to on her own.
   C was, she believed, an experience that would look good on her college applications.
   D was organised by her class that October.

3 During the first couple of days at the hospital, she
   A had to give people tours of the building.
   B didn't find the work too challenging.
   C didn't know where some hospital facilities were located.
   D was informed she was giving wrong directions.

4 On her third day, she met a young boy
   A who demanded to know who she was.
   B when she was leaving work.
   C who was walking towards her in the hospital.
   D who seemed very sad.

5 The author spoke to the boy because
   A she felt he'd been rude to her.
   B she was curious to know why he was in hospital.
   C he asked her something about the hospital.
   D she found him very charming.

6 Why did David tell the author his medical history?
   A Because his parents told him to.
   B Because he told her lots of things about himself.
   C Because he thought she was a doctor.
   D Because she asked him about it.

7 What led to her volunteering in the children's ward?
   A feeling sorry for David
   B someone observing her conversation with David
   C her ambition to become a medical professional
   D a suggestion from the boy's parents

8 Before working at the hospital, the author
   A had regularly visited the children's department.
   B had always wanted to be a doctor.
   C hadn't thought about studying medicine.
   D had sometimes thought about becoming a paediatrician.

B2 Exam Skills Trainer

Listening

Strategy
Before you do a true or false listening task, read the statements and underline the key words or information.

3 🎧 **2.16** **Read the Strategy. You are going to hear three recordings twice. Read the statements and underline the key words or information. Then listen and choose the correct option, *True* or *False*.**

1 The majority of the London Underground's tracks are above the ground. **True / False**
2 Victoria is the busiest Underground station. **True / False**
3 The new principal is a famous dancer. **True / False**
4 The students will be able to prepare a performance with help from visiting choreographers. **True / False**
5 The speaker is telling young people to feel good about themselves. **True / False**
6 The 'Better You' programme is an after school club for young people that runs all year. **True / False**

Use of English

Strategy
Before you complete the gaps in a cloze task, read the whole text through to get a general sense of what it is about. When you've finished the task, read the whole text again to check the words you've added are correct in context.

4 **Read the Strategy above. Then complete the gaps with a suitable word. Write one word in each gap.**

Over the last century, public health messages have focused ¹_____ the dangers of exposing the body to too much sunlight. However, the best way for the body to produce vitamin D ²_____ to expose the skin to sunlight. If people don't have ³_____ of vitamin D, their bones become weak and it can become painful for them to move around. So just ⁴_____ bad is sunlight for us? Sunlight is ⁵_____ up of two kinds of ultraviolet rays, UVA and UVB. Both UVA ⁶_____ UVB rays can be harmful to the body, but in different ways. UVB rays burn the top layer of the skin, ⁷_____ can lead to sunburn. UVB rays go deeper into the skin, resulting in the skin aging more quickly. Exposure to UVA and UVB rays can increase the risk ⁸_____ someone developing cancer. It's important, therefore, to ⁹_____ care when outside on a sunny day. Avoid spending too much time in the sun ¹⁰_____ the hours of 11 a.m. and 3 p.m., when the sun's rays are strongest, and use suncream that has the right level of protection.

Speaking

Strategy
Sometimes you will be asked to do a role-play in which you have to suggest and discuss different options before reaching agreement. Don't reach a decision too quickly! Make lots of suggestions and think of reasons to disagree with your partner's ideas.

5 **Four people from Australia are coming to visit your school. They are all about the same age as you. You and your classmate have been asked to give them a tour of the town or city you are in next Friday. You need to take them to some interesting places, go for lunch with them and then take them to some shops. Talk together and reach a decision on the following points:**

- which three places (e.g. museums, bridges, parks) you will take them to
- how you will travel from place to place
- where you will go for lunch
- which shops you will take them to

Writing

Strategy
The introduction to an article should introduce the topic of your article and encourage people to read it. Refer to the situation described in the instructions, mention an interesting fact or incident, or ask the reader a question.

6 **Read the Strategy. Then read the question and choose the best introduction for the article. Explain why the other two introductions are not as good.**

A school newspaper has asked its readers for articles about the positive influence of some hobbies on school work. Write an article in which you describe such a hobby and someone who, thanks to their hobby, has been more successful at school.

A Did you know that the average secondary school student spends between 25 and 40 hours a week at school? And that isn't all – at home, most students have to do homework. This leaves little time for hobbies.
B It is believed that happiness is the key to success: if you love what you're doing, you will be successful. This is true of school work and hobbies.
C Teenagers have a lot of useful and fascinating hobbies which they do after school. I strongly believe this has advantages, and it can help students to get better results at school.

7 **Read the task in exercise 6 again. Then write an article on the topic. You can use the best introduction from exercise 6 or write your own.**

Reading

1 Read the Strategy above. Then read the questions and match them with the type of information in the box that they are asking you for.

advice   direct speech   a number   an opinion

In which paragraph does the author
1 refer to statistics to make a point? _____
2 give their personal reaction to a situation? _____
3 recommend what people should do? _____
4 quote an expert to support an argument? _____

2 Now read a text divided into three parts (A–C). Match the correct question (1–6) to the correct part of the text. Each part matches two questions.

A Device-centred communication has become almost universal over the past twenty years. More than three quarters of people in the world now own or have access to a mobile device, and more than half communicate via social networking. But no matter which format people favour – text, social media, photo- or video-sharing – there is a worry that people are becoming less and less comfortable with face-to-face communication. Just recently, I found myself in the same room with two people who were both tapping away on their mobile phones. Later, I discovered that not only did the two people know each other, but that they had actually been communicating with each other online while they were sitting there in the same room. Situations like this may be amusing on one level, but on a deeper level they could be real cause for concern.

B Of course it is now hard to imagine a world without mobile devices like mobile phones and tablets. They are wonderful tools, allowing us to stay in touch with a large network of friends, no matter where they are. But many experts say that communicating with a device is nothing like talking to someone in person. 'Body language, eye contact and tone of voice can tell us so much,' psychologist Mary Peters says. 'And none of those exist on a device. Even video chat removes many subtle clues.' She adds that there is no proof that this damages a person's ability to communicate effectively. But she worries that people might lose the ability to read non-verbal signals if they aren't frequently exposed to them.

C We don't know to what extent these technologies will permanently change the way people interact. Undoubtedly, people will always want to meet up with others in small and large groups just as they have always done. Indeed, it is fair to say that social media makes it easier than ever before for people to organise social events like festivals and parties. However, in my view, there is still a danger that device-centred communication may have a negative long-term impact on the way people interact with each other on a day-to-day basis.

We must not, therefore, lose sight of the need to focus on the actual people around us, and remember that they deserve our real – not virtual – attention. The idea of a culture where people always have a screen between them is not reassuring. 'Deep understanding comes when we see the reactions on other people's faces,' Mary Peterson says. 'With all the misunderstanding in the world today, face-to-face encounters are increasingly important.'

In which paragraph does the author
1 accept that online communication can lead to face-to-face communication?
2 refer to statistics to make a point?
3 explain the difference between types of communication?
4 give an example of two friends choosing online communication instead face-to-face communication?
5 recommend doing something?
6 report a psychologist's concerns about the dangers of device-based communication as well as the acknowledgement that this is still just a theory?

Listening

3 Read the Strategy above. Then read the extract and sentences 1–4, which could all be correct options in a multiple-choice task. Note the words and phrases which give the same information in the extract and sentences.

Travelling across Canada by train was a dream come true for me. I adore train travel, but in the UK, even the longest trips seem to end too soon for my taste. I was pleased to find the Canadian passengers more willing to chat than the British.

1 The trip was the achievement of a long-time goal.
2 The speaker is very fond of travelling by rail.
3 The speaker is dissatisfied by the length of train journeys in the UK.
4 Other people on the train were more sociable than the speaker was used to.

4 **2.17** You are going to hear an interview with a student twice. Choose the correct option, A, B, C or D.

1 The speakers
A met when they were both exchange students.
B both go to the same school.
C have both lived in the US.
D are meeting for the first time.

2 Kevin says that travelling to the US
- **A** made him very anxious.
- **B** did not go smoothly.
- **C** felt like the first time he had flown.
- **D** was very enjoyable.

3 Kevin was very surprised by
- **A** how easy it is to travel in the US.
- **B** how different the US and Canada are.
- **C** how friendly people are in the US.
- **D** the huge distances people can travel inside the US.

4 About school itself, Kevin felt
- **A** that all the subjects were too easy.
- **B** that it was quite challenging.
- **C** that he received valuable help in some subjects.
- **D** that maths and science are poorly taught.

5 In general, how did Kevin feel about his stay in the US?
- **A** He was disappointed by the experience.
- **B** It was better than expected and he'd like to go back.
- **C** He found that all his ideas about the US were wrong.
- **D** He would rather have stayed in the US the whole time instead of going to Canada too.

Use of English

> **Strategy**
>
> Banked cloze tasks often test discourse markers that highlight, link or contrast ideas within sentences, between sentences and across paragraphs. Look carefully at the information that comes before and after each gapped item to discover the function of the missing word – for example comparison, emphasis, or addition.

5 Read the Strategy above. Then complete each gap in the text with one of the words below. There are two extra words.

and   considering   in fact   instead   once
provided   though   whatsoever   whereas   while

Attending art exhibitions is an important part of my job
¹_____ I enjoy it a lot. It must be said, ²_____ , that they are often fairly predictable. They usually focus on a single artist, period, or theme, and visitors are given all the information about who created what, their dates and so on.

The new show at the Atley Art Museum, *Artists in their Youth*, is very different. ³_____ all of the works are by very famous artists, all of them were made before the artists were eighteen years of age. ⁴_____ most museums label all the works at an exhibition, here there is no information ⁵_____ about who created each piece. ⁶_____, each one has been assigned a number, and viewers are invited to guess who the work is by.

⁷_____ that I'm an art critic by profession, you might assume that I would have scored very highly. However, the work of young artists is often very different from their mature work, and I admit with no embarrassment that I didn't do very well. ⁸_____, I got fewer than 50% of them right.

Speaking

> **Strategy**
>
> You may be asked to compare and contrast two photos. As well as describing their overall content, look for details in the pictures that you can speculate about.

6 Read the Strategy. Then compare and contrast the two photos. Include information about the points below.
- where the people are
- what they are doing there
- how they are feeling about the activity
- what role music plays in their lives

Writing

> **Strategy**
>
> Learn appropriate phrases to perform the functions that you need when writing a formal letter, e.g. starting a letter, expressing an opinion, adding ideas and ending a letter.

7 Read the Strategy above. Then match the functions below with phrases A–E.

adding another argument   ending a letter
expressing an initial opinion   expressing a strong reaction
introducing the topic of a letter

- **A** Furthermore, I believe …
- **B** I am writing in connection with …
- **C** I must say that I disagree with the idea that …
- **D** Yours faithfully
- **E** I was shocked to read that …

8 Read the task below and write the letter.

You read an article in yesterday's local newspaper. Its author claims that playing computer games does more harm than good to young people. Write a letter to the editor in which you either agree or disagree with the author's point of view. Give examples of how playing computer games has either helped or harmed you and/or other people you know.

Cumulative Review 1 (Units I–1)

Listening

1 🎧 **2.18** Listen to four speakers talking about their memories of family holidays. Match the speakers 1–4 with the adjectives describing attitude a–d.

Speaker 1 ☐
Speaker 2 ☐
Speaker 3 ☐
Speaker 4 ☐

a bitter
b grateful
c nostalgic
d sarcastic

2 🎧 **2.18** Listen again. Match speakers 1–4 with sentences A–E. There is one extra sentence.

Speaker 1 ☐
Speaker 2 ☐
Speaker 3 ☐
Speaker 4 ☐

A He/She didn't get on with the rest of the family on holiday.
B He/She had to put up with a lot of discomfort while they were away.
C He/She used to create problems when the family went on holiday.
D He/She looked forward to going on holiday each year.
E He/She didn't mind travelling with his/her family.

Speaking

3 Work in pairs. A family that you know is planning their summer holiday. The family is composed of the parents, who are in their forties, their children, a teenage daughter and an eight-year-old son, and the children's seventy-year-old grandfather. Give the family some advice about the holiday. Discuss the following points:

- where they could go
- where they could stay
- how they could travel
- what they could do together

Reading

4 Read the article. Match sentences A–G with gaps 1–5 in the article. There are two extra sentences.

A She asked Ann and Elizabeth to take part in her research, and they agreed.
B The thing that most twins always want to know is which of them was born first.
C When she was an adult, she made several attempts to locate her, but without success.
D There she met her husband and went back with him to settle in the USA.
E The reason for so much emotion is that twin sisters Ann Hunt and Elizabeth Hamel have not seen each other since they were babies, 78 years ago.
F She doesn't think her adoptive mother had any idea she was a twin.
G In 2001, Ann collected a copy of her own birth certificate from the register office and the search began.

Together again – after 78 years!

Imagine the scene: two sisters in their seventies running to greet each other with tears in their eyes. 'Lizzie, Lizzie, how lovely!' shouts one. 'How lovely to see you in the flesh!' cries the other. ¹_____ According to the Guinness World Records, the two women are the longest separated twins ever.

The twins' mother, Alice Lamb, was unable to bring up both girls because she was a domestic cook in the house of an employer. She gave Ann up for adoption because she was the healthier of the two. Ann was fourteen when she found out she was adopted, and once her adoptive mother died, she decided to start looking for her birth mother. ²_____ With the help of her daughter, she also found a copy of Alice's birth certificate, and later the two discovered that Alice had married a man who already had a son called Albert.

5 Read the text again with the missing sentences. Underline the word or words in the sentences before or after the gap that link with vocabulary in the missing sentences.

Alice's stepson had died, but his son was able to tell them that Alice had a daughter in the USA. That was how they found out about Elizabeth.

Alice Lamb had originally intended for both of her daughters to be adopted, but in the end, she had to keep Elizabeth because of her poor health. At first, Elizabeth stayed with an aunt and then with a woman who did not care for her properly, prompting Alice to take Elizabeth to live with her in the house where she worked. Elizabeth remembers her mother telling her when she was fifteen that she was a twin, but at the time she thought it would be impossible to find her sister. ³_____ So she was more than delighted to received Ann's letter in 2014, and minutes after reading it, the two were talking on the phone.

The reunion was arranged in Los Angeles at the invitation of psychologist Nancy Segal, who has been studying twins separated at birth for nearly forty years. During her studies, Ms Segal has discovered that twins growing up in completely different families can share many similar attitudes. ⁴_____ At first glance, the sisters appeared to have quite a lot in common: both had married men called Jim, who had recently died, so both women became widows. Both of them were grandmothers and evidence from photos shows that they both like to pose in front of the camera.

However, there were also big differences in their lives. After leaving school, Ann worked for a printer until she got married, and remained all her life in the town where she was born. Elizabeth left school to work in a sweet shop, but after going to night school, she joined the navy and moved to Malta. ⁵_____ Ms Segal is going to take a DNA sample from each twin and study all their similarities and differences to establish whether Ann and Elizabeth are identical or non-identical twins. As for the sisters themselves, the most remarkable thing for them is that after such a short time, they feel like they have known each other all their lives.

Grammar and vocabulary

6 Choose the correct answers.

Happiest age

They say that good things come to those that wait and, according to a recent survey, the saying appears to be true. The survey, carried out by ¹_____ electronics company, found that the happiest age for working people in the UK is 58. The results revealed that people generally ²_____ find happiness until this time because there is so much going on in their lives. ³_____ most stressful age seems to be the thirties because it is the time when couples often decide to ⁴_____ a family. Although it is obviously a joyful occasion when a baby ⁵_____ , it can take a little time to ⁶_____ having an infant in the house. ⁷_____ with sleepless nights is one thing if you don't have to get up early the next morning, but it is quite another if you need to ⁸_____ your boss's expectations at work. Analysing the study reveals that things get easier as children ⁹_____ , and by the time parents reach their fifties, they are feeling better about their lifestyles. Of course, the prospect of retiring in the near future may be one reason for this. And for some, a further cause for celebration may be the news that they ¹⁰_____ become grandparents.

1 a an	b the	c a
2 a doesn't	b don't	c isn't
3 a A	b An	c The
4 a do	b make	c start
5 a is born	b born	c are born
6 a be used to	b get used to	c used to
7 a Getting away	b Getting on	c Putting up
8 a live up to	b get up to	c look up to
9 a bring up	b grow up	c make up
10 a are	b are going to	c will

Writing

7 You have received a letter from a cousin you haven't seen since you were a young child. In the letter your cousin says he/she wants to visit you. Write a reply in which you:
* apologise for not writing back sooner.
* say how happy you are about the visit and remind your cousin about the last time you met.
* explain what you are doing now.
* request a recent photo of your cousin.

2 Cumulative Review 2 (Units 1–3)

Listening

1 **2.19** Read the sentences and practise saying the numbers. Then listen to an interview with an endurance cyclist. Are the sentences true (T) or false (F)?

1 The distance an endurance cyclist usually cycles is between 50 and 100 kilometres. ☐

2 Participants in the Paris–Brest–Paris event have to complete the course in 90 hours. ☐

3 The French event started back in 1871. ☐

4 The winners of the Race Across America sleep for less than two hours a day. ☐

5 In the American event, the fastest cyclists ride around 800 km per day. ☐

Speaking

2 **Work in pairs. Look at the photo and answer the questions.**

1 How do you think the people are feeling?

2 Do you think cycling is a good way of keeping fit?

3 What do you do to keep fit? Do you think this is enough? Why? / Why not?

Reading

3 **Read the text and choose the correct answers.**

1 The participants of the study were asked to run
a for a certain amount of time a day.
b for a certain distance a day.
c for a certain amount of time several times a day.
d for a certain distance several times a day.

2 The results of the study suggest that
a anybody can win a sports event.
b an athlete's success can depend on the time of their event.
c 'larks' are more likely to win sports events than 'owls'.
d only the best athletes can break records.

3 Athletes can take advantage of these results before an event to
a choose the time that they compete.
b adjust the number of hours they sleep.
c work out a bedtime schedule.
d create a suitable training programme.

4 According to the article, talent spotting would be more effective if
a testing happened at different times of the day.
b teenagers got more sleep.
c schoolchildren started doing sport at a younger age.
d high performers were more enthusiastic.

5 The most successful football teams in Europe appear to have players
a who get a good night's sleep before a match.
b whose body clock coincides with the time of the matches.
c who are used to playing in international competitions.
d whose bedtime schedule never changes.

WHAT TIME IS THE MATCH?

Most of us are aware of the power of our body clock, the internal rhythms that turn us into 'larks' or 'owls', depending on when we prefer to sleep. But what effect does this biological phenomenon have on our sporting ability?

A study published recently in the journal *Current Biology* suggests that a competitor's sleeping habits can have a dramatic impact on their performance. Researchers asked 20 female hockey players to take part in the research. At six different times of day, the players had to perform a series of 20-metre runs in shorter and shorter times. The results revealed that as a group, the players performed better in the late afternoon. But when the individual player's performances were analysed, the figures told a very different story.

Researchers discovered a gap of around 26% between the best and the worst times achieved by the hockey players, depending on when they did the test. The early risers – the larks – performed best at 12.00, approximately eight hours earlier than the late risers – the owls – who peaked at around 20.00. The findings suggest that in every sports event, some athletes may be at a disadvantage because their bodies are not at their best at the time they compete. Their hearts could be pumping more slowly, their blood may be thicker and their muscles might not be as strong. Apparently, even a small divergence can be the difference between fourth place and producing a record-breaking performance.

Athletes can, however, benefit from the results of the study to improve their chances of winning. This is because the body clock can be adjusted. If they know when they perform best, competitors can adapt their sleeping time to the hour of their event in order to ensure their best performance, be it on the basketball court, the athletics track or in the swimming pool.

The study may also have implications in the selection of future sportsmen and women. Talent spotting among adolescents usually takes place during school hours, although it is a well-known fact that at least half of teenagers are 'owls'. This means that a huge number of high performers will only just be waking up when they are being observed and they won't have reached the point at which they perform best. This means that they may be missed by talent spotters who are testing at the wrong time of day.

But the place where the study has the greatest implications is on the football pitch. The findings suggest that problems with body clock could be the reason for England's struggles in the Champions League. These matches are usually played late in the evening, which gives an advantage to teams from countries such as Spain, which are more used to performing later in the day. This news will be reassuring for English football fans, who often despair at the performance of their players in international competitions.

Grammar and vocabulary

4 Choose the correct answers.

Paralysed man walks again

A paralysed man [1]_____ to walk again, thanks to a new technique developed by British scientists. Bulgarian Darek Fidyka, who [2]_____ be a fireman, was injured during a knife attack. He was left with no feeling or movement from the waist down, and he [3]_____ that he would ever walk again. But then he had surgery to repair his spinal cord, which his attacker's knife [4]_____ through completely. A top Polish surgeon, Dr Tabakow, performed [5]_____ operation, which involved using cells from inside the patient's nose to reconnect his spinal cord. As a result, Darek is now back on his feet with the help of a frame, and is delighted that he [6]_____ the treatment. The scientists who developed the technique are [7]_____ that more patients will benefit from the treatment soon. Over the next three to five years, the medical team [8]_____ three more patients if there is enough money. Meanwhile, they [9]_____ the new technique with other researchers to create an international team. They hope that in the near future, the team [10]_____ a cure for paralysis to help the millions of people in the world who suffer from this condition.

	a	b	c
1	has started	have started	had started
2	got used to	used to	was used to
3	didn't think	hadn't thought	wasn't thinking
4	cut	had cut	was cutting
5	a	an	the
6	fitted in with	got away with	went through with
7	hopeful	hopefully	hopeless
8	treat	treated	will treat
9	share	will be sharing	will have shared
10	find	will be finding	will have found

Writing

5 Some people believe that learning how to lead a healthy lifestyle is a skill that students should learn at school. Write an essay in which you give your own opinion about this issue and propose how students should learn this skill.

Cumulative Review 3 (Units I–5)

Listening

1 **📢 2.20** Listen to five texts and choose the correct answers.

1 Listen to speaker 1. What is special about the new headphones?
  a They are worn over the ears.
  b They are bigger than usual.
  c They have no cables.

2 Listen to dialogue 2. What is the girl's first instruction?
  a to find a number
  b to turn on the phone
  c to unlock the phone

3 Listen to speaker 3. What is the gadget?
  a a tablet
  b a games console
  c a camcorder

4 Listen to dialogue 4. What does the girl like most about the smartwatch?
  a the size
  b the battery life
  c the design

5 Listen to speaker 5. Which part of the 'tree' is the turbines?
  a the leaves
  b the branches
  c the trunk

Speaking

2 Work in pairs. Look at the photos. You are looking for something to do on a free afternoon and have three options. Choose the best one in your opinion, and justify your choice. Say why you are rejecting the other options.

Reading

3 Read the text and match paragraphs A–E with the questions below. There are two extra questions. Underline the evidence in the text that supports your answer.

In which paragraph does the writer mention

1 a rule that sets the time limit for the use of gadgets each day? ☐
2 a tactic for putting electronic devices out of sight? ☐
3 a technique for making a venue a technology-free zone? ☐
4 a tip for getting a good night's sleep? ☐
5 a strategy for protecting the privacy of guests at a party? ☐
6 a method for preventing impolite phone behaviour in restaurants? ☐
7 a way to promote communication among families for a limited time each day? ☐

The society that can't switch off

A Los Angeles dancer, Brian Perez, was eating out with his friends one evening when suddenly everyone went quiet. To his horror, he saw that the reason for this was that people were checking their phones. Realising he had to do something to stop this, Brian made a rather daring suggestion. What if they all put their gadgets in a pile in the middle of the table until they had finished the meal? If anyone picked up their phone, that person would have to pay the whole bill. And so, it is said, the game of 'phone stacking' was born.

B The necessity for action like this highlights a major problem in today's society: our inability to disconnect from technology. But while Brian's idea deals with the obsession in a social context, measures also need to be taken at home. Some people drop their smartphones into a box the moment they arrive home, which gives them the chance to interact with the people they live with. The fact that the phone cannot be heard – it is on silent – nor seen – the flashing lights are hidden by the box – means that they are no longer tempted to use it.

C A less drastic solution is to ban electronic devices at certain times of day when the whole family is likely to be together, for example at meal times. This can be hard for everyone, from teenagers desperate to text friends to parents unable to switch off from work. On a normal day, however, dinner takes less than an hour, and the benefits of exchanging opinions and anecdotes with the rest of the family certainly makes up for the time spent offline.

D Taking a break from technology is one thing, but knowing when to turn off a device is another. Time seems to stand still in the virtual world, and before you know it, you find that it is three o'clock in the morning. This is where a digital curfew comes in handy, a set time when all devices must be put away. Evenings without technology are usually nice and peaceful and make a more agreeable end to the day.

E And then it's time for bed. One of the best ways of ensuring you can sleep at night is to ban electronic devices altogether from the bedroom. Lying next to a machine bursting with information is far from relaxing, and the sounds it emits during the night can easily wake you up. With technology out of the room, a line has been drawn between daytime and sleep time, which enables us to switch off ourselves and drift off to sleep.

Grammar and vocabulary

4 Choose the correct answers.

ROBOTS IN THE KITCHEN

When it comes to cooking, current trends show that people are spending ¹_____ time in the kitchen than ever before. Even those who know how to prepare a meal have moments when they wish they ²_____ to make the dinner. Of course, if these people ³_____ a robot at home that could cook, they wouldn't have to do it themselves. However, that is easier said than done. It ⁴_____ a long time to program a robot to cook, basically because there are so ⁵_____ different decisions involved. The biggest of these is ⁶_____ up your mind what to cook in the first place! However, a team of American and Australian scientists has come up with a new idea for teaching a robot to cook: by showing it videos on YouTube. Now, not everyone is aware ⁷_____ the educational values of YouTube, but the site has thousands of videos that teach all sorts of things. One of ⁸_____ useful skills you can learn is cooking, and this is what caught the researchers' attention. After using data from 88 different YouTube videos, their robot was successful ⁹_____ identifying all of the objects and actions on the screen. Although the team is pleased ¹⁰_____ these results, they admit there is still a long way to go before the technique is perfected.

	a	b	c
1	fewer	less	little
2	don't have	didn't have	wouldn't have
3	had	has	have
4	does	makes	takes
5	many	most	much
6	doing	making	taking
7	about	for	of
8	more	most	the most
9	about	in	on
10	for	to	with

Writing

5 You recently saw somebody using their mobile phone irresponsibly (for example, being rude or dangerous) in a social situation. Write a forum entry in which you:

- relate what you saw.
- compare social situations in the past to those in the present.
- recommend how you think people should behave in this kind of situation.
- ask other contributors to react to your post.

Listening

1 **🎧 2.21** Listen to four speakers talking about memorable art exhibitions. Match speakers 1–4 with sentences A–E. There is one extra sentence.

Speaker 1 ☐
Speaker 2 ☐
Speaker 3 ☐
Speaker 4 ☐

A He/She doesn't remember anything about the exhibition itself.

B He/She remembers the exhibition because it was very boring.

C He/She remembers the exhibition being rather amusing.

D He/She only remembers one of the pieces in the exhibition.

E He/She remembers something embarrassing happening at the exhibition.

2 **🎧 2.21** Listen again. Which words or phrases helped give you the information that you needed to match the speakers with the sentences?

Speaking

3 Work in pairs. You are staying with your English penfriend and want to go to an exhibition where you will learn more about British culture. Express your opinions about the three exhibitions. Which one will you go to see? Justify your choice and say why you are rejecting the other options.

Reading

4 Read three texts connected with films and choose the correct answers.

56 Up

On ITV tonight, there's another chance to see part of the latest documentary in the *Up* series. Since the first instalment in 1964, director Michael Apted has been following the lives of fourteen British citizens from all walks of life, catching up with them every seven years to see what has changed. The participants were first filmed aged seven, when their social differences were already noticeable: some were living in children's homes while others were attending expensive private schools. The aim of the documentary has been to explore the idea that a child's future is already decided by the time he or she is seven years old. To find out how far the theory is true, you will have to watch tonight's programme, which shows the participants aged 56. Viewers who have seen the previous documentary may be in for some surprises!

1 The author of the text wants to
   a encourage readers to watch a TV programme.
   b find out if children's backgrounds affect their futures.
   c explore the differences between the classes in the UK.

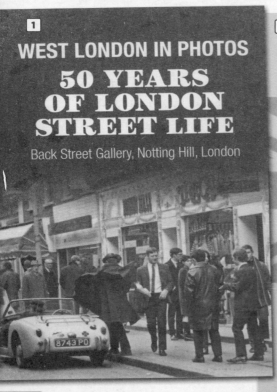

1

WEST LONDON IN PHOTOS
50 YEARS OF LONDON STREET LIFE
Back Street Gallery, Notting Hill, London

2

Objects that shaped a nation

100 objects important to the British from the last 100 years
Bradford Street, London

3

CONTEMPORARY BRITISH ARTISTS

Paintings, sculptures and installations from today's important artists
THAMES SIDE GALLERY, HAMMERSMITH, LONDON

4DX: THE ULTIMATE CINEMA EXPERIENCE

If you thought 3D films were the latest in the world of cinema, then it's time for you to think again. A UK cinema chain is currently investing millions in new technology to bring 4DX films to their screens. The audience will sit in seats that move forwards and backwards and from side to side to simulate the action on screen. Meanwhile, water, air and smoke will be used to provide the rain, wind and fog of weather conditions, and special lighting will be used to create a storm. Aromas such as coffee will be pumped into the cinema to complete the experience, which will result in the audience being much closer to the drama in the film. The company's first 4DX cinema, complete with a curved screen measuring 10.5 m by 5.8 m, is already open for bookings.

2 What is remarkable about the new technology?
  a The films will be shown in 3D.
  b The special effects will appeal to more of the senses.
  c The audience will take part in the action.

Becoming a film extra

If you want to get into acting, then working as a film extra can help you on your way. Like any job, it can take a little while to find the first one. The best way to go about it is to register with an online extras directory. Complete your profile with details about your appearance, personality and experience, and send in some photos of yourself in natural poses. Check the adverts on the site regularly and apply for any that seem interesting. Once you get your first job, make sure you turn up on time and find your contact person immediately. Pay attention at all times and follow the directions of the film crew. Being an extra requires a lot of patience, but it also gives you valuable experience, a little cash and maybe a chance to meet some of the stars.

3 The purpose of the text is to
  a explain what film extras have to do.
  b provide a list of requirements to be a film extra.
  c give advice on finding work as a film extra.

Grammar and vocabulary

5 Choose the correct answers.

Bibliotherapy: a novel idea

We often think of novels as places in [1]_____ to lose ourselves, but the truth is that reading can have a much more far-reaching effect. If you find [2]_____ in trouble, there's always a book to remind you that others have been there before. It's just a question of finding the right book. And that is where bibliotherapy comes in: the use of books to help people deal with their problems, whatever they [3]_____ be. The treatment has become more [4]_____ more common in recent years, and today it is practised [5]_____ psychologists – and librarians – all over the world. There is also scientific evidence in favour of the technique. Researchers at Sussex University in the UK have found that reading is a more effective way of relieving stress than listening to music, going for a walk or sitting down [6]_____ with a cup of tea. After just six minutes with a book – any book – the people in the study found their stress levels [7]_____ reduced by up to 68%. This suggests that the therapy could help people [8]_____ lives have become meaningless leading them to fall into depression. If they have the right book recommended to [9]_____ , they may get over their illness quicker. Bibliotherapy can certainly [10]_____ no harm. At the very least, a patient will discover some great new titles to read.

1 a where	b which	c who
2 a you	b your	c yourself
3 a can	b may	c will
4 a and	b in	c than
5 a by	b for	c of
6 a anywhere	b everywhere	c somewhere
7 a are	b been	c were
8 a which	b whose	c who
9 a themselves	b they	c them
10 a do	b make	c take

Writing

6 Your teacher has asked you to write a film review for the school magazine. Write your review describing the film and say what you liked and did not like about it.

Alternative commuting

Listening

1 🎧 **2.22** Listen and choose the correct answers.

1 Listen to speaker 1. What is the reason for the announcement?
   a to explain what to do in an emergency
   b to tell passengers how to fasten their seat belts
   c to give the necessary safety information

2 Listen to dialogue 2. Where does the woman's train leave from?
   a platform 3
   b platform 8
   c platform 11

3 Listen to speaker 3. How long will the flight be delayed for?
   a less than an hour
   b about an hour
   c more than an hour

4 Listen to dialogue 4. Where is the bus stop?
   a outside the cinema
   b in the car park of the shopping mall
   c outside the front entrance of the shopping mall

5 Listen to speaker 5. Which route only has one sailing per week?
   a Portsmouth to Santander
   b Plymouth to Santander
   c Portsmouth to Bilbao

Speaking

2 **Work in pairs. Look at the photo and answer the questions.**

1 How do you think the people are feeling?
2 How effective is public transport where you live?
3 Have you been on a journey in which you experienced a similar situation to this? Why were there so many people?

1 Urban cable car

The commute between the twin cities of El Alto and La Paz in Bolivia has always been a nightmare. The small white vans that serve as buses take over an hour to cover the winding 10 km route due to horrible traffic – which is why a new cable car system is being installed. Commuters can already use the first line, which carries them high above the houses from the shiny modern terminal at the top of the mountain to a similar one at the bottom. When all three lines are running – red, yellow and green to match the colours of the country's flag – the system will measure nearly 11 km, making it the longest urban cable car in the world.

2 Motorised canal boats

Formerly known as the 'Venice of the East', Bangkok has numerous waterways crossing the city. The Chao Phraya River runs through the centre, and there are also many canals carrying motorised canal boats. Commuters prefer these to the congested public transport on the roads because they are faster and often cheaper. One such route is the 18 km Saen Saep Canal, which is served by about 100 boats of 40 to 50 seats. The service operates from 5.30 a.m. to 8.30 p.m. on weekdays, closing at 7 p.m. at the weekend. The canal boats carry around 60,000 passengers each day, and fare collectors can often be seen jumping on and off the moving boats as they are arriving at or leaving a station.

3 Hanging train

Under normal circumstances, trains usually travel along tracks built into the ground. Not so the Wuppertal Suspension Train in Germany. This particular train is made up of carriages with wheels connected to the roof of the train so that it hangs from an elevated steel frame. The suspension railway runs along a route of 13.3 km at a height of between eight and twelve metres from the ground. The entire trip takes around 30 minutes. But the railway is not a recent addition to the city's transport system; the first track opened in 1901, making it the oldest electric elevated railway with hanging cars in the world. It is still in use today, moving around 25 million passengers each year.

4 Toboggan sled ride

To the east of Funchal on the island of Madeira lies a suburb called Monte. As the name suggests, the district looks over the city centre. In 1850, the residents created an innovative method of covering the few kilometres between the two sites more quickly: toboggans. These consisted of baskets with seats fixed onto wooden skis, which slid easily down the hill. The toboggan sled service began operating in the late nineteenth century, when uniformed pilots would guide the sleds from behind, using the rubber soles on their shoes as brakes. Today, the ride is merely a tourist attraction because of the cable car built at the turn of the millennium, which connects the two districts.

Reading

3 Match the texts with the questions below. Some questions match with more than one text.

Which form(s) of transport

A employ(s) workers who move between vehicles selling tickets? ☐ ☐
B hold(s) a world record? ☐ ☐
C is/are no longer used by commuters? ☐ ☐
D date(s) back to the start of the 20th century? ☐ ☐
E carry/carries passengers downhill? ☐ ☐
F is/are not finished yet? ☐ ☐

Grammar and vocabulary

4 Choose the correct answers.

TRAVELLING THE WORLD – THE HARD WAY

A Liverpool man has become the first person to visit all 201 countries in the world without ¹_____ a plane. Thirty-three-year-old Graham Hughes started his epic journey in Uruguay, South America. On his budget of $100 a week, he could not afford ²_____ many luxuries, and he often had to depend on the kindness of strangers. Not everything went smoothly on the trip. He was arrested when he was trying ³_____ Russia, and he was accused ⁴_____ a spy in the Democratic Republic of the Congo. Also, the boat that took him to Cape Verde was in very bad condition, so Hughes had a very worrying four days. If the boat had sunk, he ⁵_____ . Despite all of the setbacks, Hughes managed ⁶_____ the last country on his list after 1,426 days and 160,000 km. Journalists were waiting to greet him in Juba, the capital of South Sudan, a country which did not exist when he set out. When they asked Hughes why ⁷_____ the journey, he said it was because he loved travelling. He also ⁸_____ them that he wanted to show people the world was not a big scary place. Hughes went on ⁹_____ everyone he had met for helping him on his way. Now he plans to spend some more time ¹⁰_____ around Africa before he eventually flies home.

1	a boarding	b checking into	c hailing
2	a buy	b buying	c to buy
3	a enter	b entering	c to enter
4	a being	b of being	c to be
5	a would have died	b had died	c would die
6	a reach	b reaching	c to reach
7	a he had made	b did he make	c had he made
8	a said	b told	c told to
9	a thank	b thanking	c to thank
10	a travel	b travelling	c to travel

Writing

5 Imagine that you have recently returned from a holiday where you used one of the forms of transport mentioned in the Reading texts. Write an email to a friend in which you:

- describe the country that you visited.
- relate your experience travelling on the vehicle.
- mention something that went wrong during the holiday.
- invite your friend to go on holiday with you next year.

Writing Bank

A for and against essay

Many young adults choose to leave their parents' home in order to share a house with friends. Write an essay in which you present arguments for and against this course of action.

In the past, most people lived with their parents until they got married. But in the modern world, it's more common to leave home and share accommodation with friends. This choice has both positive and negative aspects.

- The first paragraph should be an introduction. Include a thesis statement, which summarises the main issue.

There are several advantages to sharing with friends. Firstly, it gives you the opportunity to spend time with your friends and to build strong relationships with them. Secondly, it allows you to develop some of the practical skills that you will need as an independent adult. For instance, you will learn how to manage household bills, how to shop and cook, and so on. And thirdly, it makes living in your own home more affordable, and the more people who share, the more cost-effective it is. For instance, a shared house for six people is far cheaper than two houses for three people.

- The second paragraph should focus on the advantages. If possible, include three.

- Give examples if possible, introduced by phrases like *For example*, ... or *For instance*, ...

On the other hand, sharing a home has its disadvantages. Sharing a house can often cause disagreements. For instance, housemates often argue about household chores. What is more, it can be difficult to have time alone when you need it. And finally, the houses which young people share are sometimes in poor condition and landlords are not always good at repairing appliances when they break.

- Begin the third paragraph with a phrase like *On the other hand*, ... or *However*, ... to express contrast with the previous paragraph.

- The third paragraph should focus on the disadvantages. If possible, include three.

Although sharing a house with other young adults is not always easy, the advantages definitely outweigh the problems. It is certainly something I would like to do in a few years' time.

- The fourth paragraph should be the conclusion. State your opinion and decide whether the pros outweigh the cons or vice versa.

Writing Bank

An article

Many people believe that animals living in zoos suffer. Write an article for your local newspaper in which you give your views. Present the advantages and the disadvantages.

- Choose a good title for your article.

- Start your article with an introduction which gets the reader's attention and introduces the topic.

- Include occasional rhetorical questions to make the style more engaging.

- Write in a simple, clear style appropriate to the publication (newspaper, magazine, etc. Avoid language that is too formal.

- Make sure you split your article into paragraphs with different arguments in each paragraph, in a logical order.

- Include a short conclusion. This can detail your personal opinion, or the most important point in the article.

ARE ZOOS CRUEL TO ANIMALS?

Most major cities in the world have zoos, with lots of weird and wonderful animals in them. Many people love to go and see amazing creatures from all over the world. But is it cruel to keep animals in places like zoos?

Personally, I think that zoos are a good idea for two reasons. First of all, they are educational and school children can visit zoos to learn about animals from different countries. Secondly, they can also help to keep endangered species alive by providing a safe place for the animals to breed.

However, some people believe that zoos are cruel and that it is wrong to keep wild animals in small cages. They think that animals should live in their natural habitats and be free to move around instead of being kept behind bars for humans to look at.

While I understand the arguments of people who oppose zoos, I believe that the benefits outweigh the disadvantages. If the animals are safe and looked after well, then there is no problem with zoos.

Writing Bank

An opinion essay

Many people believe that it is too late to reverse the harm which humans have done to the planet. Write an essay in which you present your opinion on this topic and suggest how people could limit further damage to the environment.

- The first paragraph should be an introduction. Include your thesis statement, which is a summary of your opinion on the issue.

- Write in an appropriately formal style, avoiding colloquial words and expressions.

For many decades, humans have been damaging the environment by polluting the atmosphere and the oceans. Global warming threatens to change the planet's climate forever and make large areas of it uninhabitable. In my opinion, it is impossible to reverse all of this damage, but we can certainly make a positive difference by changing our behaviour.

- The second paragraph should focus on the first element of the task.

- Use appropriate linking words like *Additionally, ...* and *However, ...* to connect your ideas in a logical way.

In recent years, there has been some progress in preventing pollution. For example, factories and car engines are far cleaner than they were fifty years ago. Additionally, some products that harm the atmosphere, such as aerosols that contain dangerous chemicals, are no longer available. However, some forms of pollution are more difficult to tackle. Plastic waste will remain in the environment for thousands of years. And although governments are attempting to limit carbon emissions, nobody is certain whether this will be enough to stop global warming. But it is important to remain positive and do everything we can to prevent further damage to our planet.

- Give examples, if possible, introduced by phrases like *For example, ...* , *For instance, ...* and *such as ... .*

- The third paragraph should focus on the second element of the task.

It is perfectly possible for individuals to limit their own impact on the environment. For example, they should save electricity by switching off lights, computers and other electrical appliances when they are not using them. As far as possible, they should avoid buying products with plastic packaging and drink water from a re-usable bottle.

- The fourth paragraph should be the conclusion. Restate your opinion from paragraph one, but do not repeat it word for word.

In conclusion, I would say that we should all do what we can to prevent more damage to our environment. However, only time will tell whether this is enough to reverse the harm that has already been done.

Writing Bank

A formal letter (complaint)

You and your family recently celebrated a special occasion in a small hotel but were unhappy with the experience. Write a letter of complaint to the hotel manager in which you describe what went wrong and suggest how the hotel could improve its service to customers.

Dear Sir or Madam,

I am writing to complain about a recent stay at the White Deer Hotel in Broadford between 8 and 10 May. The holiday had been arranged to celebrate my grandfather's 75th birthday and involved twelve family members. Unfortunately, the service we received from your hotel was completely inadequate and prevented us from enjoying what should have been a very special occasion.

Our problems began as soon as we arrived. The check-in process took more than an hour and it appeared the hotel was not expecting us, even though I had phoned the week before to confirm our reservation. After that, things went from bad to worse. For example, we had asked that my grandparents be given a superior double room. In fact, they were given a standard room overlooking the car park at the back of the hotel. When we complained, we were told that the hotel was full and a change of rooms was impossible.

May I suggest that in future the hotel makes better preparations for special events of this kind? You should make guests feel welcome from the moment they arrive. I also believe that your check-in procedure needs to be improved. For example, at busy times, more than one receptionist should be at the desk.

I expect to receive an explanation for our unsatisfactory treatment and would appreciate an offer of compensation. I look forward to your reply.

Yours faithfully,

M Wright

Mark Wright

- If you do not know the name of the person you are writing to, begin with *Dear Sir or Madam*.

- Begin your letter by saying why you are writing.

- Write in an appropriately formal style, avoiding colloquial words and expressions.

- The next paragraph should focus on the first element of the task. Remember to include details and examples.

- The following paragraph should focus on the second element of the task.

- End the main part of the letter by stating clearly what you expect to happen next.

- If the letter began *Dear Sir or Madam*, it should end *Yours faithfully*. (However, it should end *Yours sincerely* if you began by addressing the recipient by name.)

Functions Bank

Presenting your ideas

I agree that ... (1F)
I don't agree that ... (1F)
It's (not) true to say that ... (1F)
In my experience, ... (1F)
Personally, I believe that ... (1F)
I'm not sure about that. (1F)
For example, / For instance, ... (1F)

Polite requests

Would it be possible for you to ... ? (1H)
Could you please ... ? (1H)
Would you mind if ... ? (1H)
Would you mind (+ -ing form) ... ? (1H)
I wonder if ... (1H)

Explaining preference

I'd find it ... (2F)
It sounds really ... (2F)
It appeals / doesn't appeal to me because ... (2F)
I'm (not) really into ... (2F)
I'd rather ... (2F)
I can't stand ... (2F)
I don't mind ... , but ... (2F)

Expressing preferences

I quite fancy ... (2G)
I think ... would be (fun). (2G)
I'm quite keen on ... (2G)
I like the idea of ... (2G)
I think ... is a better option than ... (2G)

Raising objections

Sorry, but I don't really fancy ... (2G)
Don't you think it (would be expensive)? (2G)
The problem with ... is that ... (2G)
Sorry, but I don't think that's a very good idea. (2G)
I'm not keen on ... because ... (2G)
I don't think ... would be as (interesting) as ... (2G)
I'd rather (go climbing) than (karting). (2G)

Coming to an agreement

We need to make a decision. (2G)
Overall, ... would be better. (2G)
Can we agree on ... , then? (2G)
OK, I agree. (2G)
That's settled then. (2G)

Asking for a response / Offering a response

Do you agree? (3D)
What's your view / opinion? (3D)
What do you think? (3D)
I'm not sure I agree. (3D)
I think / don't think you're right. (3D)
That's what I think too. (3D)

Identifying people in photos

The man wearing (a yellow T-shirt) ... (3G)
The girl in (purple leggings) ... (3G)
The woman with (a ponytail) ... (3G)
The boy who is (on the ground) ... (3G)

Speculating

It looks like some kind of ... (3G)
I think it's a ... of some kind. (3G)
There's a sort of ... (3G)
It's most likely ... (3G)
... or something like that. (3G)
... I would say. / I'd say that ... (3G)
It looks to me / doesn't look to me as if they ... (5G)
They look / don't look (to me) as if / as though they're ... (5G)
They look / don't look like they're (+ -ing) ... (5G)
They seem quite (+ adj) (5G)
They don't look / don't seem very (+ adj) ... (5G)
I can't be sure, but I'd say that ... (8G)
It could be (that) ... (8G)
It's hard to say, but ... (8G)
It looks as if ... (8G)
I'm pretty certain that ... (8G)
It's clear that ... (8G)
Judging by (his expression), I'd say that ... (8G)

Introducing your opinions

I (strongly) believe that ... (3H)
In my opinion / view, ... (3H)
As I see it ... (3H)
It seems to me that ... (3H)

Making an additional point

Moreover, ... (3H)
Furthermore, ... (3H)
What is more, ... (3H)
Not only that, but ... (3H)

Functions Bank

Introducing other people's opinions
It is a widely held view that ... (3H)

It is often said that ... (3H)

It is a common belief that ... (3H)

Most people agree that ... (3H)

Introducing proposals and solutions
One solution might be to ... (3H)

What I propose is that ... (3H)

I would strongly recommend that ... (3H)

It is vital that ... (3H)

In order to tackle this problem, I suggest that ... (3H)

Concluding
To sum up, ... (3H)

In conclusion, ... (3H)

To conclude, ... (3H)

Describing where you live
It's a flat / detached house, etc. (4A)

It's in the town centre, etc. (4A)

There's a park / There are some shops nearby. (4A)

It's got ... (bedrooms). (4A)

There is ... (other rooms). (4A)

There's / There isn't a ... (4A)

It's a bit / very ... (adjective). (4A)

Phrases for gaining time
Let me see. I'd have to give that some thought. (4G)

Actually, now I come to think about it, ... (4G)

Well, thinking about it, ... (4G)

All things considered, I (don't) suppose ... (4G)

I suppose the thing is, ... (4G)

What else? Well ... (4G)

That's a good question. (4G)

Introducing opinions
It seems to me that ... (5G)

Personally, I think / don't think that ... (5G)

I believe that ... (5G)

The way I see it ... (5G)

For me, the important thing is (that) ... (5G)

Comparing photos
The common theme in the photos is ... . (5G)

Both photos show ... . (5G)

In the first photo, ... , whereas in the second photo ... . (5G)

Unlike the second photo, the first photo ... (5G)

Asking for information
Moving on to the question of ... (6G)

Another thing I wanted to ask / know is ... (6G)

Something else I'd like to talk about is ... (6G)

Could I ask you about ... ? (6G)

Speaking of ... (6G)

That reminds me, ... (6G)

Could you tell me ... (6G)

I was wondering ... (6G)

I'd like to know ... (6G)

May I ask ... ? (6G)

I'd be interested to know ... (6G)

Rhetorical questions
Who would want to live in a world where ... ? (6H)

How can it be right that ... ? (6H)

What could be better than ...   (6H)

Is it not just as important to ... ? (6H)

Is it not time we all ... (+ past tense)? (6H)

Why should / shouldn't we ... ? (6H)

Arguing your point
In my opinion, / As I see it ... (7F)

It could be argued that ... (7F)

I see your point, but ... (7F)

That may be true, but ... (7F)

Likes and dislikes
I'm a big fan of ... . (7G)

I'm quite into ... . (7G)

I'm really keen on ... . (7G)

I absolutely love ... . (7G)

I enjoy ... very much. (7G)

... is not really my thing. (7G)

I'm not really into ... . (7G)

I really can't stand ... . (7G)

I'm not a big fan of ... . (7G)

... doesn't do anything for me. (7G)

I've never been that keen on ... . (7G)

Describing stories
It's set in (place and / or time). (7H)

There are lots of twists and turns. (7H)

It tells the story of (character). (7H)

I would definitely recommend it. (7H)

It's a real page-turner. (7H)

Wordlist

Unit I

abseiling (n)	/ˈæbseɪlɪŋ/	
anxious (adj)	/ˈæŋkʃəs/	
ashamed (adj)	/əˈʃeɪmd/	
basketball (n)	/ˈbɑːskɪtbɔːl/	
beach (n)	/biːtʃ/	
beach volleyball (n)	/ˌbiːtʃ ˈvɒlibɔːl/	
believe (v)	/bɪˈliːv/	
belong (v)	/bɪˈlɒŋ/	
bike (n)	/baɪk/	
bike ride (n)	/ˈbaɪk raɪd/	
board games (n)	/ˈbɔːd ɡeɪmz/	
boat (n)	/bəʊt/	
boat trip (n)	/ˈbəʊt trɪp/	
bored (adj)	/bɔːd/	
café (n)	/ˈkæfeɪ/	
car (n)	/kɑː(r)/	
cards (n)	/kɑːdz/	
castle (n)	/ˈkɑːsl/	
cathedral (n)	/kəˈθiːdrəl/	
church (n)	/tʃɜːtʃ/	
confused (adj)	/kənˈfjuːzd/	
cross (adj)	/krɒs/	
cycling (n)	/ˈsaɪklɪŋ/	
delighted (adj)	/dɪˈlaɪtɪd/	
disappointed (adj)	/ˌdɪsəˈpɔɪntɪd/	
dishonest (adj)	/dɪsˈɒnɪst/	
disloyal (adj)	/dɪsˈlɔɪəl/	
disorganised (adj)	/dɪsˈɔːɡənaɪzd/	
eat out (v)	/iːt aʊt/	
embarrassed (adj)	/ɪmˈbærəst/	
envious (adj)	/ˈenviəs/	
excited (adj)	/ɪkˈsaɪtɪd/	
excursion (n)	/ɪkˈskɜːʃn/	
flexible (adj)	/ˈfleksəbl/	
forget (v)	/fəˈɡet/	
frightened (adj)	/ˈfraɪtnd/	
harbour (n)	/ˈhɑːbə(r)/	
hard-working (adj)	/ˌhɑːd ˈwɜːkɪŋ/	
hate (v)	/heɪt/	
hire (v)	/ˈhaɪə(r)/	
honest (adj)	/ˈɒnɪst/	
impatient (adj)	/ɪmˈpeɪʃnt/	
inflexible (adj)	/ɪnˈfleksəbl/	
insensitive (adj)	/ɪnˈsensətɪv/	
kayak (n)	/ˈkaɪæk/	
kayaking (n)	/ˈkaɪækɪŋ/	
kind (adj)	/kaɪnd/	
know (v)	/nəʊ/	
like (v)	/laɪk/	
love (v)	/lʌv/	
loyal (adj)	/ˈlɔɪəl/	
market (n)	/ˈmɑːkɪt/	

mean (v)	/miːn/	
mind (v)	/maɪnd/	
monument (n)	/ˈmɒnjumənt/	
mosque (n)	/mɒsk/	
mountain biking (n)	/ˈmaʊntən ˌbaɪkɪŋ/	
national park (n)	/ˌnæʃnəl ˈpɑːk/	
need (v)	/niːd/	
old town (n)	/ˈəʊld taʊn/	
opera house (n)	/ˈɒprə haʊs/	
organised (adj)	/ˈɔːɡənaɪzd/	
outgoing (adj)	/ˈaʊtɡəʊɪŋ/	
palace (n)	/ˈpæləs/	
patient (adj)	/ˈpeɪʃnt/	
prefer (v)	/prɪˈfɜː(r)/	
proud (adj)	/praʊd/	
reliable (adj)	/rɪˈlaɪəbl/	
relieved (adj)	/rɪˈliːvd/	
remember (v)	/rɪˈmembə(r)/	
restaurant (n)	/ˈrestrɒnt/	
ruins (n)	/ˈruːɪnz/	
sensitive (adj)	/ˈsensətɪv/	
shocked (adj)	/ʃɒkt/	
shopping (n)	/ˈʃɒpɪŋ/	
shopping district (n)	/ˈʃɒpɪŋ ˌdɪstrɪkt/	
shy (adj)	/ʃaɪ/	
skateboarding (n)	/ˈskeɪtbɔːdɪŋ/	
souvenir (n)	/ˌsuːvəˈnɪə(r)/	
square (n)	/skweə(r)/	
statue (n)	/ˈstætʃuː/	
sunbathe (v)	/ˈsʌnbeɪð/	
suspicious (adj)	/səˈspɪʃəs/	
swimming (n)	/ˈswɪmɪŋ/	
table tennis (n)	/ˈteɪbl tenɪs/	
terrified (adj)	/ˈterɪfaɪd/	
theatre (n)	/ˈθɪətə(r)/	
theme park (n)	/ˈθiːm pɑːk/	
tower (n)	/ˈtaʊə(r)/	
understand (v)	/ˌʌndəˈstænd/	
unkind (adj)	/ˌʌnˈkaɪnd/	
unreliable (adj)	/ˌʌnrɪˈlaɪəbl/	
upset (adj)	/ʌpˈset/	
video games (n)	/ˈvɪdiəʊ ɡeɪmz/	
visit (v)	/ˈvɪzɪt/	
walk (n)	/wɔːk/	
want (v)	/wɒnt/	
wildlife park (n)	/ˈwaɪldlaɪf ˌpɑːk/	

Unit 1

accusing (adj)	/əˈkjuːzɪŋ/	
adolescence (n)	/ˌædəˈlesns/	
adolescent (adj)	/ˌædəˈlesnt/	
adult (n)	/ˈædʌlt/	
aggressive (adj)	/əˈɡresɪv/	

Wordlist

arrogant (adj)	/ˈærəgənt/		
be born	/bi bɔːn/		
be brought up	/bi brɔːt ˈʌp/		
bitter (adj)	/ˈbɪtə(r)/		
calm (adj)	/kɑːm/		
career (n)	/kəˈrɪə(r)/		
catch up with (phr v)	/kætʃ ˈʌp wɪð/		
centenarian (n)	/ˌsentɪˈneəriən/		
complimentary (adj)	/ˌkɒmplɪˈmentri/		
concern (n)	/kənˈsɜːn/		
concerned (adj)	/kənˈsɜːnd/		
critical (adj)	/ˈkrɪtɪkl/		
criticism (n)	/ˈkrɪtɪsɪzəm/		
dependence (n)	/dɪˈpendəns/		
dependent (adj)	/dɪˈpendənt/		
distrust (n)	/dɪsˈtrʌst/		
distrustful (adj)	/dɪsˈtrʌstfl/		
divorced (adj)	/dɪˈvɔːst/		
drive (v)	/draɪv/		
elderly (adj)	/ˈeldəli/		
emigrate (v)	/ˈemɪgreɪt/		
emotion (n)	/ɪˈməʊʃn/		
emotional (adj)	/ɪˈməʊʃənl/		
engaged (adj)	/ɪnˈgeɪdʒd/		
enthusiastic (adj)	/ɪnˌθjuːziˈæstɪk/		
fall in love (phr v)	/ˌfɔːl ɪn ˈlʌv/		
family (n)	/ˈfæməli/		
fit in with (phr v)	/fɪt ˈɪn wɪð/		
free (adj)	/friː/		
freedom (n)	/ˈfriːdəm/		
get away (phr v)	/get ˈəweɪ/		
get away with (phr v)	/get əˈweɪ wɪð/		
get on with (phr v)	/get ˈɒn wɪð/		
get up (phr v)	/get ˈʌp/		
get up to (phr v)	/get ˈʌp tə/		
go back (phr v)	/gəʊ ˈbæk/		
go back on (phr v)	/gəʊ ˈbæk ɒn/		
go in (phr v)	/gəʊ ˈɪn/		
go in for (phr v)	/gəʊ ˈɪn fɔː(r)/		
go through with (phr v)	/gəʊ ˈθruː wɪð/		
grandparent (n)	/ˈgrænpeərənt/		
grateful (adj)	/ˈgreɪtfl/		
grow up (phr v)	/grəʊ ʌp/		
ideal (adj)	/aɪˈdiːəl/		
impatience (n)	/ɪmˈpeɪʃns/		
in your teens (adj)	/ɪn jɔː ˈtiːnz/		
in your twenties (adj)	/ɪn jɔː ˈtwentiz/		
infant (n)	/ˈɪnfənt/		
inherit (v)	/ɪnˈherɪt/		
irritated (adj)	/ˈɪrɪteɪtɪd/		
irritation (n)	/ˌɪrɪˈteɪʃn/		
job (n)	/dʒɒb/		
live up to (phr v)	/lɪv ʌp tə/		
look up (phr v)	/ˈlʊk ʌp/		
look up to (phr v)	/lʊk ʌp tə/		
make up (phr v)	/ˈmeɪk ʌp/		
make up for (phr v)	/meɪk ˈʌp fɔː(r)/		
married (adj)	/ˈmærid/		
middle-aged (adj)	/ˌmɪdl ˈeɪdʒd/		
miserable (adj)	/ˈmɪzrəbl/		
nostalgic (adj)	/nɒˈstældʒɪk/		
optimistic (adj)	/ˌɒptɪˈmɪstɪk/		
pass away (v)	/pɑːs əˈweɪ/		
pessimistic (adj)	/ˌpesɪˈmɪstɪk/		
privacy (n)	/ˈprɪvəsi/		
private (adj)	/ˈpraɪvət/		
put up with (phr v)	/pʊt ˈʌp wɪð/		
retire (v)	/rɪˈtaɪə(r)/		
run out of (phr v)	/rʌn ˈaʊt ɒv/		
safe (adj)	/seɪf/		
safety (n)	/ˈseɪfti/		
sarcastic (adj)	/sɑːˈkæstɪk/		
settle down (v)	/ˌsetl ˈdaʊn/		
sign up for (phr v)	/saɪn ˈʌp fɔː(r)/		
split up (phr v)	/splɪt ˈʌp/		
sympathetic (adj)	/ˌsɪmpəˈθetɪk/		
toddler (n)	/ˈtɒdlə(r)/		
university (n)	/ˌjuːnɪˈvɜːsəti/		
urgent (adj)	/ˈɜːdʒənt/		
walk out on (phr v)	/wɔːk ˈaʊt ɒn/		

Unit 2

25-metre (adj)	/ˌtwenti faɪv ˈmiːtə(r)/		
300-seat (adj)	/ˌθriː hʌndrəd ˈsiːt/		
across (prep)	/əˈkrɒs/		
air-conditioned (adj)	/ˈeə kənˌdɪʃnd/		
all along (prep)	/ɔːl əˈlɒŋ/		
all over (prep)	/ɔːl ˈəʊvə(r)/		
all-weather (adj)	/ɔːl ˈweðə(r)/		
art club (n)	/ˈɑːt klʌb/		
astronomy club (n)	/əˈstrɒnəmi ˌklʌb/		
athletics track (n)	/æθˈletɪks ˌtræk/		
bake (v)	/beɪk/		
baking club (n)	/ˈbeɪkɪŋ ˌklʌb/		
ballroom dancing (n)	/ˈbɔːlruːm ˌdɑːnsɪŋ/		
ballroom dancing club (n)	/ˈbɔːlrʊm ˌdɑːnsɪŋ ˌklʌb/		
basketball court (n)	/ˈbɑːskɪtbɔːl ˌkɔːt/		
below (prep)	/bɪˈləʊ/		
beside (prep)	/bɪˈsaɪd/		
BMXing (n)	/biːemˈeksɪŋ/		
bowling (n)	/ˈbəʊlɪŋ/		
bowling alley (n)	/ˈbəʊlɪŋ æli/		
boxing ring (n)	/ˈbɒksɪŋ ˌrɪŋ/		
brightly lit (adj)	/ˌbraɪtli ˈlɪt/		
by (prep)	/baɪ/		
camping (n)	/ˈkæmpɪŋ/		

Wordlist

chess (n) /tʃes/

climbing wall (n) /ˈklaɪmɪŋ wɔːl/

collect (v) /kəˈlekt/

computer club (n) /kəmˈpjuːtə ˌklʌb/

dance studio (n) /ˈdɑːns ˌstjuːdiəʊ/

debating society (n) /dɪˈbeɪtɪŋ səˌsaɪəti/

drama (n) /ˈdrɑːmə/

drama society (n) /ˈdrɑːmə səˌsaɪəti/

draw (v) /drɔː/

eighteen-hole (adj) /ˌeɪtiːn ˈhəʊl/

eight-lane (adj) /eɪt ˈleɪn/

film club (n) /ˈfɪlm klʌb/

fitness club (n) /ˈfɪtnəs ˌklʌb/

football pitch (n) /ˈfʊtbɔːl ˌpɪtʃ/

full-sized (adj) /fʊl ˈsaɪzd/

golf course (n) /ˈɡɒlf kɔːs/

gymnastics (n) /dʒɪmˈnæstɪks/

handball club (n) /ˈhændbɔːl ˌklʌb/

hang out (v) /hæŋ ˈaʊt/

high-speed (adj) /ˌhaɪ ˈspiːd/

horse riding (n) /ˈhɔːs ˌraɪdɪŋ/

ice hockey (n) /ˈaɪs hɒki/

ice rink (n) /ˈaɪs rɪŋk/

ice skating (n) /ˈaɪs skeɪtɪŋ/

martial arts (n) /ˌmɑːʃl ˈɑːts/

musical instrument (n) /ˌmjuːzɪkl ˈɪnstrəmənt/

open-air (adj) /ˌəʊpən ˈeə(r)/

photography club (n) /fəˈtɒɡrəfi ˌklʌb/

pie (n) /paɪ/

pudding (n) /ˈpʊdɪŋ/

rollerblading (n) /ˈrəʊləbleɪdɪŋ/

running (n) /ˈrʌnɪŋ/

salad (n) /ˈsæləd/

sandwich (n) /ˈsænwɪdʒ/

school choir (n) /skuːl ˈkwaɪə(r)/

school orchestra (n) /skuːl ˈɔːkɪstrə/

science club (n) /ˈsaɪəns ˌklʌb/

social media (n) /ˌsəʊʃl ˈmiːdiə/

solar-heated (adj) /ˌsəʊlə ˈhiːtɪd/

soundproof (adj) /ˈsaʊndpruːf/

soup (n) /suːp/

state-of-the-art (adj) /ˌsteɪt əv ði ˈɑːt/

stew (n) /stjuː/

stir-fry (n) /ˈstɜː fraɪ/

swimming pool (n) /ˈswɪmɪŋ ˌpuːl/

tennis court (n) /ˈtenɪs ˌkɔːt/

text (v) /tekst/

video blog (v) /ˈvɪdiəʊ ˌblɒɡ/

volleyball (n) /ˈvɒlibɔːl/

weights (n) /weɪts/

weights room (n) /ˈweɪts rʊm/

well-equipped (adj) /wel ɪˈkwɪpt/

Unit 3

afraid (adj) /əˈfreɪd/

anger (n) /ˈæŋɡə(r)/

angry (adj) /ˈæŋɡri/

ankle (n) /ˈæŋkl/

antibiotics (n) /ˌæntibaɪˈɒtɪks/

anxiety (n) /æŋˈzaɪəti/

bandage (n) /ˈbændɪdʒ/

bang your head /ˌbæŋ jɔː(r) ˈhed/

blood (n) /blʌd/

bottom (n) /ˈbɒtəm/

brain (n) /breɪn/

break a bone /ˌbreɪk ə ˈbəʊn/

bruise yourself (badly) /ˌbruːz jɔːself ˈbædli/

burn yourself /ˈbɜːn jɔːˌself/

calf (n) /kɑːf/

cheek (n) /tʃiːk/

chin (n) /tʃɪn/

cream (n) /kriːm/

cut yourself (badly) /ˌkʌt jɔːself ˈbædli/

depressed (adj) /dɪˈprest/

disgusted (adj) /dɪsˈɡʌstɪd/

dressing (n) /ˈdresɪŋ/

elbow (n) /ˈelbəʊ/

envy (n) /ˈenvi/

exercise (n) /ˈeksəsaɪz/

exercise (v) /ˈeksəsaɪz/

eyebrow (n) /ˈaɪbraʊ/

eyelid (n) /ˈaɪlɪd/

forehead (n) /ˈfɒrɪd/, /ˈfɔːhed/

happiness (n) /ˈhæpinəs/

happy (adj) /ˈhæpi/

hard (adv) /hɑːd/

hard (adj) /hɑːd/

have a (bad) nosebleed /ˌhæv ə bæd ˈnəʊzbliːd/

have a black eye /ˌhæv ə blæk ˈaɪ/

heart (n) /hɑːt/

heel (n) /hiːl/

hip (n) /hɪp/

intestine (n) /ɪnˈtestɪn/

jaw (n) /dʒɔː/

kidney (n) /ˈkɪdni/

level (n) /ˈlevl/

level (v) /ˈlevl/

light (adj) /laɪt/

light (n) /laɪt/

lip (n) /lɪp/

lung (n) /lʌŋ/

medicine (n) /ˈmedɪsn/

muscle (n) /ˈmʌsl/

nail (n) /neɪl/

painkillers (n) /ˈpeɪnkɪləz/

pride (n)	/praɪd/		cupboard (n)	/ˈkʌbəd/
record (v)	/rɪˈkɔːd/		curtains (n)	/ˈkɜːtnz/
record (n)	/ˈrekɔːd/		cushion (n)	/ˈkʊʃn/
rest (n)	/rest/		desk (n)	/desk/
rest (v)	/rest/		detached house (n)	/dɪˌtætʃt ˈhaʊs/
rib (n)	/rɪb/		dilapidated (adj)	/dɪˈlæpɪdeɪtɪd/
sad (adj)	/sæd/		dining table (n)	/ˈdaɪnɪŋ ˌteɪbl/
sadness (n)	/ˈsædnəs/		drive (n)	/draɪv/
scalp (n)	/skælp/		extension (n)	/ɪkˈstenʃn/
shame (n)	/ʃeɪm/		farmhouse (n)	/ˈfɑːmhaʊs/
shin (n)	/ʃɪn/		fence (n)	/fens/
shoulder (n)	/ˈʃəʊldə(r)/		fireplace (n)	/ˈfaɪəpleɪs/
show (v)	/ʃəʊ/		flat (n)	/flæt/
show (n)	/ʃəʊ/		flower bed (n)	/ˈflaʊə bed/
skin (n)	/skɪn/		front door (n)	/frʌnt ˈdɔː(r)/
skull (n)	/skʌl/		garage (n)	/ˈgærɑːʒ/
spine (n)	/spaɪn/		gate (n)	/geɪt/
sprain your wrist	/ˌspreɪn jɔː ˈrɪst/		hall (n)	/hɔːl/
stomach (n)	/ˈstʌmək/		hedge (n)	/hedʒ/
surprise (n)	/səˈpraɪz/		house plant (n)	/ˈhaʊs plɑːnt/
surprised (adj)	/səˈpraɪzd/		houseboat (n)	/ˈhaʊsbəʊt/
thigh (n)	/θaɪ/		housing estate (n)	/ˈhaʊzɪŋ ɪsˌteɪt/
throat (n)	/θrəʊt/		lamp (n)	/læmp/
thumb (n)	/θʌm/		landing (n)	/ˈlændɪŋ/
toe (n)	/təʊ/		lawn (n)	/lɔːn/
twist your ankle	/ˌtwɪst jɔː(r) ˈæŋkl/		lively area (n)	/ˈlaɪvli ˈeəriə/
waist (n)	/weɪst/		mansion (n)	/ˈmænʃn/
work (n)	/wɜːk/		microwave (n)	/ˈmaɪkrəweɪv/
work (v)	/wɜːk/		mirror (n)	/ˈmɪrə(r)/
wrist (n)	/rɪst/		mobile home (n)	/ˌməʊbaɪl ˈhəʊm/
X-ray (n)	/ˈeks reɪ/		path (n)	/pɑːθ/
			picture (n)	/ˈpɪktʃə(r)/
			pond (n)	/pɒnd/

Unit 4

armchair (n)	/ˈɑːmtʃeə(r)/		popular area (n)	/ˌpɒpjələ(r) ˈeəriə/
attic (n)	/ˈætɪk/		porch (n)	/pɔːtʃ/
balcony (n)	/ˈbælkəni/		rainwater (n)	/ˈreɪnwɔːtə(r)/
basement (n)	/ˈbeɪsmənt/		rubbish dump (n)	/ˈrʌbɪʃ dʌmp/
beautifully restored (adj)	/ˌbjuːtɪfli rɪˈstɔːd/		rug (n)	/rʌg/
blinds (n)	/blaɪndz/		semi-detached house (n)	/ˌsemi dɪˌtætʃt ˈhaʊs/
bookcase (n)	/ˈbʊkkeɪs/		shipping container (n)	/ˈʃɪpɪŋ kənˌteɪnə(r)/
bungalow (n)	/ˈbʌŋgələʊ/		shutters (n)	/ˈʃʌtəz/
carpet (n)	/ˈkɑːpɪt/		skyscraper (n)	/ˈskaɪskreɪpə(r)/
cellar (n)	/ˈselə(r)/		sliding doors (n)	/ˌslaɪdɪŋ ˈdɔːz/
charming (adj)	/ˈtʃɑːmɪŋ/		sofa (n)	/ˈsəʊfə/
chest of drawers (n)	/ˌtʃest əv ˈdrɔːz/		sofa bed (n)	/ˈsəʊfə bed/
coffee table (n)	/ˈkɒfi teɪbl/		solar panels (n)	/ˈsəʊlə(r) ˌpænlz/
conservatory (n)	/kənˈsɜːvətri/		spacious (adj)	/ˈspeɪʃəs/
contemporary (adj)	/kənˈtemprəri/		stairs (n)	/steəz/
conveniently located (adj)	/kənˌviːniəntli ləʊˈkeɪtɪd/		studio flat (n)	/ˈstjuːdiəʊ ˌflæt/
			substantial (adj)	/səbˈstænʃl/
cosy (adj)	/ˈkəʊzi/		terraced house (n)	/ˌterəst ˈhaʊs/
cramped (adj)	/kræmpt/		thatched cottage (n)	/θætʃt ˈkɒtɪdʒ/

tiny (adj)	/'taɪni/
villa (n)	/'vɪlə/
wardrobe (n)	/'wɔːdrəub/

Unit 5

a few (det, pron)	/ə 'fjuː/
a little (det, pron)	/ə 'lɪtl/
account (n)	/ə'kaunt/
all (det, pron)	/ɔːl/
any (det, pron)	/'eni/
app (n)	/æp/
art (n)	/ɑːt/
Bluetooth headset (n)	/ˌbluːtuːθ 'hedset/
Bluetooth speaker (n)	/ˌbluːtuːθ 'spiːkə(r)/
both (det, pron)	/bəuθ/
break a code	/ˌbreɪk ə 'kəud/
button (n)	/'bʌtn/
camcorder (n)	/'kæmkɔːdə(r)/
click on (v)	/'klɪk ɒn/
come up with an answer	/kʌm ˌʌp wɪð æn 'ɑːnsə(r)/
comment (v)	/'kɒment/
copy (v)	/'kɒpi/
create (v)	/kri'eɪt/
delete (v)	/dɪ'liːt/
design and technology (n)	/dɪˌzaɪn ænd tek'nɒlədʒi/
digital radio (n)	/ˌdɪdʒɪtl 'reɪdiəu/
double click on (phr v)	/ˌdʌbl 'klɪk ɒn/
each (det, pron)	/iːtʃ/
English (n)	/'ɪŋglɪʃ/
enter (v)	/'entə(r)/
enter a competition	/'entə(r) ə ˌkɒmpə'tɪʃn/
every (det, pron)	/'evri/
exchange messages	/ɪks'tʃeɪndʒ ˌmesɪdʒɪz/
few (det, pron)	/fjuː/
file (n)	/faɪl/
folder (n)	/'fəuldə(r)/
follow (v)	/'fɒləu/
forward (v)	/'fɔːwəd/
games console (n)	/'geɪmz kɒnsəul/
geography (n)	/dʒi'ɒgrəfi/
have a conversation	/ˌhæv ə kɒnvə'seɪʃn/
history (n)	/'hɪstri/
I.C.T. (computing) (n)	/ˌaɪ siː 'tiː/, /kəm'pjuːtɪŋ/
install (v)	/ɪn'stɔːl/
link (n)	/lɪŋk/
little (det, pron)	/'lɪtl/
log on (v)	/'lɒgɒn/
many (det, pron)	/'meni/
maths (n)	/mæθs/
memory stick (n)	/'meməri ˌstɪk/

MP3 player (n)	/ˌem piː 'θriː pleɪə(r)/
music (n)	/'mjuːzɪk/
no (det, pron)	/nəu/
page (n)	/peɪdʒ/
pass a test	/'pɑːs ə ˌtest/
password (n)	/'pɑːswɜːd/
paste (v)	/peɪst/
P.E. (physical education) (n)	/ˌpiː 'iː/, /ˌfɪzɪkl edʒu'keɪʃn/
print (v)	/prɪnt/
profile (n)	/'prəufaɪl/
program (v)	/'prəugræm/
rate (v)	/reɪt/
R.E. (religious education) (n)	/ɑːr'iː/, /rɪˌlɪdʒəs edʒu'keɪʃn/
recycle bin (n)	/riː'saɪkl bɪn/
reset (v)	/ˌriː'set/
satnav (n)	/'sætnæv/
save (v)	/seɪv/
science (n)	/'saɪəns/
scroll up / down (phr v)	/skrəul 'ʌp/, /skrəul 'daun/
search (v)	/sɜːtʃ/
search a website	/ˌsɜːtʃ ə 'websaɪt/
set up (v)	/set 'ʌp/
smartphone (n)	/'smɑːtfəun/
smartwatch (n)	/'smɑːtwɒtʃ/
social networking site (n)	/ˌsəuʃl 'netwɜːkɪŋ saɪt/
some (det, pron)	/sʌm/
subscribe (v)	/səb'skraɪb/
tablet (n)	/'tæblət/
trash (n)	/træʃ/
update (v)	/ˌʌp'deɪt/
upload (v)	/ˌʌp'ləud/
username (n)	/'juːzəneɪm/
video clip (n)	/'vɪdiəu klɪp/
win a prize	/wɪn ə praɪz/
word processor (n)	/ˌwɜːd 'prəusesə(r)/

Unit 6

ambition (n)	/æm'bɪʃn/
ambitious (adj)	/æm'bɪʃəs/
appeal to somebody (phr v)	/ə'piːl tə 'sʌmbədi/
arrest somebody (for something) (phr v)	/ə'rest fɔː(r)/
ask somebody out (phr v)	/ɑːsk 'sʌmbədi 'aut/
be good at communicating	/bi ˌgud æt kə'mjuːnɪkeɪtɪŋ/
bring something up (phr v)	/ˌbrɪŋ 'sʌmθɪŋ 'ʌp/
call something off (phr v)	/ˌkɔːl 'sʌmθɪŋ 'ɒf/
cheerful (adj)	/'tʃɪəfl/
cheerfulness (n)	/'tʃɪəfəlnəs/

Wordlist

come across something (phr v)	/kʌm əˈkrɒs/	
complain about something (phr v)	/kəmˈpleɪn əbaʊt/	
count on somebody (phr v)	/ˈkaʊnt ɒn/	
creative (adj)	/kriˈeɪtɪv/	
creativity (n)	/ˌkriːeɪˈtɪvəti/	
employ somebody as something (phr v)	/ɪmˈplɔɪ eɪz/	
enthusiasm (n)	/ɪnˈθjuːziæzəm/	
flexibility (n)	/ˌfleksəˈbɪləti/	
generosity (n)	/ˌdʒenəˈrɒsəti/	
generous (adj)	/ˈdʒenərəs/	
give something up (phr v)	/ɡɪv ˈʌp/	
good humour (n)	/ˌɡʊd ˈhjuːmə(r)/	
have a good sense of humour	/hæv ə ˌɡʊd sens ɒv ˈhjuːmə(r)/	
have lots of / no common sense	/hæv ˌlɒts ɒv / nəʊ ˌkɒmən ˈsens/	
have lots of energy	/hæv ˌlɒts ɒv ˈenədʒi/	
have organisational skills	/hæv ˌɔːɡənaɪˈzeɪʃənl ˌskɪlz/	
have physical courage	/hæv ˌfɪzɪkl ˈkʌrɪdʒ/	
hold somebody up (phr v)	/həʊld ˈʌp/	
honesty (n)	/ˈɒnəsti/	
idealism (n)	/aɪˈdiːəlɪzəm/	
idealistic (adj)	/ˌaɪdiəˈlɪstɪk/	
intelligence (n)	/ɪnˈtelɪdʒəns/	
intelligent (adj)	/ɪnˈtelɪdʒənt/	
lack self-confidence	/ˌlæk self ˈkɒnfɪdəns/	
loyalty (n)	/ˈlɔɪəlti/	
mature (adj)	/məˈtʃʊə(r)/	
maturity (n)	/məˈtʃʊərəti/	
modest (adj)	/ˈmɒdɪst/	
modesty (n)	/ˈmɒdəsti/	
optimism (n)	/ˈɒptɪmɪzəm/	
patience (n)	/ˈpeɪʃns/	
pessimism (n)	/ˈpesɪmɪzəm/	
punctual (adj)	/ˈpʌŋktʃuəl/	
punctuality (n)	/ˌpʌŋktʃuˈæləti/	
realism (n)	/ˈriːəlɪzəm/	
realistic (adj)	/ˌriːəˈlɪstɪk/	
respond to something / somebody (phr v)	/rɪˈspɒnd tə/	
search for something (phr v)	/ˈsɜːtʃ fɔː(r)/	
self-confidence (n)	/ˌself ˈkɒnfɪdəns/	
self-confident (adj)	/ˌself ˈkɒnfɪdənt/	
serious (adj)	/ˈsɪəriəs/	
seriousness (n)	/ˈsɪəriəsnəs/	
show lots of initiative	/ʃəʊ ˌlɒts ɒv ɪˈnɪʃətɪv/	

shyness (n)	/ˈʃaɪnəs/	
sit at something (phr v)	/ˈsɪt æt/	
sociability (n)	/ˌsəʊʃəˈbɪləti/	
sociable (adj)	/ˈsəʊʃəbl/	
stubborn (adj)	/ˈstʌbən/	
stubbornness (n)	/ˈstʌbənnəs/	
sympathy (n)	/ˈsɪmpəθi/	
take after somebody (phr v)	/ˌteɪk ˈɑːftə(r)/	
thoughtful (adj)	/ˈθɔːtfl/	
thoughtfulness (n)	/ˈθɔːtflnəs/	
turn into something (phr v)	/ˌtɜːn ˈɪntə/	
work for something / somebody (phr v)	/ˈwɜːk fɔː(r)/	
worry about something (phr v)	/ˈwʌri əˌbaʊt/	

Unit 7

act (v)	/ækt/	
actor (n)	/ˈæktə(r)/	
anybody / anyone (pron)	/ˈenibɒdi/, /ˈeniwʌn/	
anything (pron)	/ˈeniθɪŋ/	
anywhere (pron)	/ˈeniweə(r)/	
appear in (v)	/əˈpɪə(r) ɪn/	
art exhibition (n)	/ˈɑːt eksɪˌbɪʃn/	
beat (n)	/biːt/	
bench (n)	/bentʃ/	
bicycle rack (n)	/ˈbaɪsɪkl ˌræk/	
cartoon (n)	/kɑːˈtuːn/	
carve (v)	/kɑːv/	
choreographer (n)	/ˌkɒriˈɒɡrəfə(r)/	
chorus (n)	/ˈkɔːrəs/	
classical (n)	/ˈklæsɪkl/	
classical concert (n)	/ˌklæsɪkl ˈkɒnsət/	
classical music (n)	/ˌklæsɪkl ˈmjuːzɪk/	
compose (v)	/kəmˈpəʊz/	
composer (n)	/kəmˈpəʊzə(r)/	
conduct (v)	/ˈkɒndʌkt/	
conductor (n)	/kənˈdʌktə(r)/	
country and western (n)	/ˌkʌntri ənd ˈwestən/	
create (v)	/kriˈeɪt/	
dance (n)	/dɑːns/	
dance (v)	/dɑːns/	
dancer (n)	/ˈdɑːnsə(r)/	
direct (v)	/daɪˈrekt/	
director (n)	/daɪˈrektə(r)/	
drawing (n)	/ˈdrɔːɪŋ/	
everybody / everyone (pron)	/ˈevribɒdi/, /ˈevriwʌn/	
everything (pron)	/ˈevriθɪŋ/	
everywhere (pron)	/ˈevriweə(r)/	
flagpole (n)	/ˈflæɡpəʊl/	

folk (n)	/fəʊk/	
fountain (n)	/ˈfaʊntən/	
harmony (n)	/ˈhɑːməni/	
lamp post (n)	/ˈlæmp pəʊst/	
lyrics (n)	/ˈlɪrɪks/	
magic show (n)	/ˈmædʒɪk ˌʃəʊ/	
melody (n)	/ˈmelədi/	
mime (n)	/maɪm/	
no one / nobody (pron)	/ˈnəʊ wʌn/, /ˈnəʊbədi/	
nothing (pron)	/ˈnʌθɪŋ/	
novel (n)	/ˈnɒvl/	
novelist (n)	/ˈnɒvəlɪst/	
nowhere (pron)	/ˈnəʊweə(r)/	
open-air theatre (n)	/ˌəʊpən eə(r) ˈθɪətə(r)/	
opera singer (n)	/ˈɒpərə ˌsɪŋə(r)/	
paint (v)	/peɪnt/	
painter (n)	/ˈpeɪntə(r)/	
painting (n)	/ˈpeɪntɪŋ/	
pavement (n)	/ˈpeɪvmənt/	
perform (v)	/pəˈfɔːm/	
phone box (n)	/ˈfəʊn bɒks/	
piano recital (n)	/ˈpjɑːnəʊ rɪˌsaɪtl/	
play (n)	/pleɪ/	
play (v)	/pleɪ/	
playwright (n)	/ˈpleɪraɪt/	
poem (n)	/ˈpəʊɪm/	
poet (n)	/ˈpəʊɪt/	
pop singer (n)	/pɒp ˈsɪŋə(r)/	
rhythm (n)	/ˈrɪðəm/	
sculptor (n)	/ˈskʌlptə(r)/	
sculpture (n)	/ˈskʌlptʃə(r)/	
sing (v)	/sɪŋ/	
somebody / someone (pron)	/ˈsʌmbədi/, /ˈsʌmwʌn/	
something (pron)	/ˈsʌmθɪŋ/	
somewhere (pron)	/ˈsʌmweə(r)/	
speed (n)	/spiːd/	
stop sign (n)	/stɒp saɪn/	
tempo (n)	/ˈtempəʊ/	
tune (n)	/tjuːn/	
TV drama (n)	/ˌtiː viː ˈdrɑːmə/	
verse (n)	/vɜːs/	
write (v)	/raɪt/	

Unit 8

accuse (v)	/əˈkjuːz/	
admit (v)	/ədˈmɪt/	
advise (v)	/ədˈvaɪz/	
agree (v)	/əˈgriː/	
apologise (v)	/əˈpɒlədʒaɪz/	
ask (v)	/ɑːsk/	
beg (v)	/beg/	

bestseller list (n)	/ˌbestˈselə(r) lɪst/	
blame (v)	/bleɪm/	
book contract (n)	/ˈbʊk ˌkɒntrækt/	
break up (phr v)	/ˈbreɪk ʌp/	
call (v)	/kɔːl/	
call somebody back (phr v)	/kɔːl ˈbæk/	
cell phone (n)	/ˈselfəʊn/	
comic book (n)	/ˈkɒmɪk bʊk/	
contacts list (n)	/ˈkɒntækts lɪst/	
cut somebody off (phr v)	/kʌt ɒf/	
data roaming (n)	/ˈdɑːtə ˌrəʊmɪŋ/	
deny (v)	/dɪˈnaɪ/	
disable (v)	/dɪsˈeɪbl/	
enable (v)	/ɪˈneɪbl/	
encourage (v)	/ɪnˈkʌrɪdʒ/	
feedback (n)	/ˈfiːdbæk/	
get back to somebody (phr v)	/get ˈbæk tə/	
get through (to somebody) (phr v)	/get ˈθruː tə/	
hang up (phr v)	/hæŋ ˈʌp/	
high school (n)	/ˈhaɪ skuːl/	
insist (v)	/ɪnˈsɪst/	
leisure time (n)	/ˈleʒə(r) taɪm/	
loudspeaker (n)	/ˌlaʊdˈspiːkə(r)/	
love story (n)	/ˈlʌv ˌstɔːri/	
mention (v)	/ˈmenʃn/	
offer (v)	/ˈɒfə(r)/	
pen name (n)	/ˈpen neɪm/	
persuade (v)	/pəˈsweɪd/	
pick up (the phone) (phr v)	/ˌpɪk ʌp ðə ˈfəʊn/	
pop culture (n)	/ˌpɒp ˈkʌltʃə(r)/	
promise (v)	/ˈprɒmɪs/	
propose (v)	/prəˈpəʊz/	
refuse (v)	/rɪˈfjuːz/	
remind (v)	/rɪˈmaɪnd/	
run out of something (phr v)	/rʌn ˈaʊt ɒv/	
signal (n)	/ˈsɪgnəl/	
speak up (phr v)	/spiːk ˈʌp/	
suggest (v)	/səˈdʒest/	
switch something off (phr v)	/swɪtʃ ˈɒf/	
tell (v)	/tel/	
thank (v)	/θæŋk/	
top up (phr v)	/ˈtɒp ʌp/	
TV series (n)	/ˌtiː ˈviː ˌsɪəriːz/	
voicemail (n)	/ˈvɔɪsmeɪl/	
warn (v)	/wɔːn/	
wonder (v)	/ˈwʌndə(r)/	

Wordlist

Unit 9

aircraft (n)	/'eəkrɑːft/	_____
airport (n)	/'eəpɔːt/	_____
arrivals hall (n)	/ə'raɪvlz hɔːl/	_____
B&B (bed and breakfast) (n)	/biː n 'biː/, /,bed ænd 'brekfəst/	_____
break down (phr v)	/breɪk 'daʊn/	_____
buffet car (n)	/'bʊfeɪ kɑː(r)/	_____
bus stop (n)	/'bʌs stɒp/	_____
cabin (n)	/'kæbɪn/	_____
cable car (n)	/'keɪbl kɑː(r)/	_____
campsite (n)	/'kæmpsaɪt/	_____
car park (n)	/'kɑː pɑːk/	_____
caravan site (n)	/'kærəvæn ,saɪt/	_____
check-in desk (n)	/'tʃek ɪn ,desk/	_____
clubbing (n)	/'klʌbɪŋ/	_____
coach (n)	/kəʊtʃ/	_____
coach bay (n)	/'kəʊtʃ beɪ/	_____
coach station (n)	/'kəʊtʃ ,steɪʃn/	_____
cruise ship (n)	/'kruːz ʃɪp/	_____
deck (n)	/dek/	_____
departure gate (n)	/dɪ'pɑːtʃə(r) ,geɪt/	_____
ferry (n)	/'feri/	_____
filling station (n)	/'fɪlɪŋ ,steɪʃn/	_____
fishing (n)	/'fɪʃɪŋ/	_____
hiking (n)	/'haɪkɪŋ/	_____
holiday camp (n)	/'hɒlədeɪ ,kæmp/	_____
horse riding (n)	/'hɔːs ,raɪdɪŋ/	_____
hostel (n)	/'hɒstl/	_____
hot air balloon (n)	/hɒt 'eə bə,luːn/	_____
hovercraft (n)	/'hɒvəkrɑːft/	_____
level crossing (n)	/,levl 'krɒsɪŋ/	_____
lost property office (n)	/lɒst 'prɒpəti ,ɒfɪs/	_____
motorbike (n)	/'məʊtəbaɪk/	_____
platform (n)	/'plætfɔːm/	_____
port (n)	/pɔːt/	_____
scooter (n)	/'skuːtə(r)/	_____
scuba diving (n)	/'skuːbə ,daɪvɪŋ/	_____
self-catering apartment (n)	/self ,keɪtərɪŋ ə'pɑːtmənt/	_____
service station (n)	/'sɜːvɪs ,steɪʃn/	_____
sightseeing (n)	/'saɪtsiːɪŋ/	_____
skiing (n)	/'skiːɪŋ/	_____
sleeper (n)	/'sliːpə(r)/	_____
taxi rank (n)	/'tæksi ,ræŋk/	_____
ticket barrier (n)	/'tɪkɪt ,bæriə(r)/	_____
ticket office (n)	/'tɪkɪt ,ɒfɪs/	_____
train station (n)	/'treɪn ,steɪʃn/	_____
tram (n)	/træm/	_____
underground (n)	/'ʌndəgraʊnd/	_____
waiting room (n)	/'weɪtɪŋ ,rʊm/	_____
yacht (n)	/jɒt/	_____

I Irregular verbs

be	was / were	been
become	became	become
begin	began	begun
bend	bent	bent
bite	bit	bitten
blow	blew	blown
break	broke	broken
bring	brought	brought
build	built	built
burn	burned / burnt	burned / burnt
buy	bought	bought

can	could	been able to
catch	caught	caught
choose	chose	chosen
come	came	come
cost	cost	cost
cut	cut	cut

do	did	done
draw	drew	drawn
drink	drank	drunk
drive	drove	driven

eat	ate	eaten

fall	fell	fallen
feel	felt	felt
fight	fought	fought
find	found	found
fly	flew	flown
forget	forgot	forgotten

get	got	got
give	gave	given
go	went	gone
grow	grew	grown

hang	hung	hung
have	had	had
hear	heard	heard
hide	hid	hidden
hit	hit	hit

keep	kept	kept
know	knew	known

lay	laid	laid
lead	led	led
learn	learned / learnt	learned / learnt
leave	left	left

lend	lent	lent
lose	lost	lost

make	made	made
mean	meant	meant
meet	met	met

overcome	overcame	overcome

pay	paid	paid
put	put	put

read	read	read
ride	rode	ridden
ring	rang	rung
run	ran	run

say	said	said
see	saw	seen
sell	sold	sold
send	sent	sent
set	set	set
shake	shook	shaken
shine	shone	shone
shoot	shot	shot
show	showed	shown / showed
shut	shut	shut
sing	sang	sung
sink	sank	sunk
sit	sat	sat
sleep	slept	slept
smell	smelled / smelt	smelled / smelt
speak	spoke	spoken
spell	spelled / spelt	spelled / spelt
spend	spent	spent
spill	spilled / spilt	spilled / spilt
stand	stood	stood
steal	stole	stolen
swim	swam	swum

take	took	taken
teach	taught	taught
tell	told	told
think	thought	thought
throw	threw	thrown

understand	understood	understood

wake	woke	woken
wear	wore	worn
win	won	won
write	wrote	written